Chrysler's
MOTOWN MISSILE

CarTech®

CarTech®, Inc.
838 Lake Street South
Forest Lake, MN 55025
Phone: 651-277-1200 or 800-551-4754
Fax: 651-277-1203
www.cartechbooks.com

Edit by Wes Eisenschenk
Layout by Chris Fayers

ISBN 978-1-61325-475-2
Item No. CT655

Library of Congress Cataloging-in-Publication Data

Names: Stunkard, Geoff (Geoffrey F.), 1963- author.
Title: Chrysler's Motown Missile Mopar's secret engineering program in the dawn of pro stock / Geoff Stunkard.
Description: Forest Lake, MN : CarTech, Inc., 2020.
Identifiers: LCCN 2019043046 | ISBN 9781613254752 (paperback)
Subjects: LCSH: Chrysler automobile–Motors–Design and construction–History–20th century. | Stock cars (Automobiles)--United States–History–20th century. | Stock car racing–United States–History–20th century.
Classification: LCC TL215.C55 S78 2020 | DDC 629.228/5--dc23
LC record available at https://lccn.loc.gov/2019043046

Written, edited, and designed in the U.S.A.
Printed in China
10 9 8 7 6 5 4 3 2 1

CarTech books may be purchased at a discounted rate in bulk for resale, events, corporate gifts, or educational purposes. Special editions may also be created to specification. For details, contact Special Sales at 838 Lake Street S., Forest Lake, MN 55025 or by email at sales@cartechbooks.com.

Front Cover Photos
Top: The original 1971 *Motown Missile* is wheels-up at Dallas International Motor Speedway, a track that Don Carlton was undefeated at during its IHRA era. (Photo Courtesy Bob McClurg)
Bottom: Don Carlton and Dick Oldfield perform the scoop test. (Photo Courtesy Joe Pappas)

Back Cover Photos
Top: See page 74.
Center: See page 150.
Bottom: See page 6.

Frontispiece: *Missile* versus *Missile*—the former 1971 Dodge driven by John Livingston and Ted's 1972 Cuda driven by Don Carlton race each other at Dallas in 1972. (Photo Courtesy Steve Reyes)

Title Page: Joe Pappas holds it back while Donnie Carlton burns 'em up in the 1973 Duster built by Ron Butler. Seen at the IHRA Fall Nationals in Bristol, Tennessee, that year, the car was on the way to a 10th-consecutive IHRA final round. (Photo Courtesy Bob McClurg)

Table of Contents: The 1973 car is shown racing at speed during the IHRA World Championship quest. (Photo Courtesy Bob McClurg)

DISTRIBUTION BY:

Europe
PGUK
63 Hatton Garden
London EC1N 8LE, England
Phone: 020 7061 1980 • Fax: 020 7242 3725
www.pguk.co.uk

Australia
Renniks Publications Ltd.
3/37-39 Green Street
Banksmeadow, NSW 2109, Australia
Phone: 2 9695 7055 • Fax: 2 9695 7355
www.renniks.com

Canada
Login Canada
300 Saulteaux Crescent
Winnipeg, MB, R3J 3T2 Canada
Phone: 800 665 1148 • Fax: 800 665 0103
www.lb.ca

Mopar's SECRET Engineering Program at the Dawn of Pro Stock

THE LEE ELIMINATORS

Geoff Stunkard

Table of Contents

PUBLISHER'S NOTE:
In reporting history, the images required to tell the tale will vary greatly in quality, especially by modern photographic standards. While some images in this volume are not up to those digital standards, we have included them, as we feel they are an important element in telling the story.

Acknowledgments

Any project of this magnitude is a group effort. While I can take credit for the compilation of information, it would have been impossible without help from so many others. I am humbled that I was asked to do this by the very men responsible for what happened all those years ago and can only hope I have done justice to the effort they put forth in charting new territory. As my fourth Chrysler Hemi reference volume for CarTech, this book presents an honest understanding of why the Chrysler Corporation was so committed to American motorsports such as Pro Stock drag racing through the 1970s. While the individuals below are listed in order of their involvement, it is not necessarily the order of their importance. To everyone noted, and hopefully I have not missed anyone, thank you for making *Motown Missile* a reality, then and now.

Two of Don Carlton's victory trophies from 1976 and 1977 are pictured.

The last reunion of the Missile *men in 2014 is shown. From left to right: Don Carlton Jr., Ted Spehar, Joe Pappas, Mike Koran, Ron Killen, Dick Oldfield, Tom Hoover, Tom Coddington, Len Bartush, and Al Adam.*

The Team

Back in 2017, I was approached by members of the original team who asked if I would take on this project. To be honest, it was not a simple decision because I knew the amount of work it would entail. However, I agreed because we all wanted the story to be right. So, my sincerest thanks to Ted and Tina Spehar, Joe and Lynn Pappas, the Oldfield family (I was able to visit with Dick Oldfield just prior to his passing in 2018), and Donnie Carlton Jr. for the time they spent in interviews to get this process underway and to completion. Some sources even put up with me living in their homes on extended trips and gave me full access to all the paper-

work and photos I needed. Ted and Joe in particular were very patient to read the manuscript and clarify points of importance.

Al Adam, Tom Coddington, Ron Killen, John Wehrly, Len Bartush, and Mike Koran are also part of the group that assisted to make the *Missile* a legend. Once again, I called upon my friend Thomas M. Hoover, the late godfather of the 426 Hemi, via our previously recorded interviews to flesh out the tale. My past interviews with Dave Koffel were added to the narrative, and insider Tom Cunningham provided insight into the Woodward Avenue street scene from his recollections as well. So, whether we actually talked during this process or not, to all of you, my sincerest thanks.

The Experts

While this project was in its early stages, a resource I learned about was Gene Yetter of New York. Gene had moderated, recorded, and transcribed several critical roundtable discussions with the team during reunions before Mr. Hoover's passing, and he gave me permission to quote extensively from those discussions, invaluably adding to the texture of this book. Thank you, Gene. You were basically my coauthor and researcher on the *Missile* project.

In that same vein, veteran NHRA and former IHRA announcer Bob Frey selflessly read through and fact-checked performance references for both Don and Dick as well as other competitors, verifying racing performance numbers from his extensive library. Also supplying data in that regard were archivists Dick Gerwer and Mike Goyda, who assisted in some of the NHRA rules references I needed. *Mopar Action*'s editor Cliff Gromer was instrumental in providing some of the material on the 1971 car's recent history as well.

The Shooters

In addition to the materials provided by the team itself, I called upon valued friends from my years of racing photography to help with the excitement of illustrating this era. Professional photographers Bob McClurg and Steve Reyes came through with amazing photos of both the *Missiles* and their competitors, as did photographer Dan Williams. Tom S. Hoover, son of Tom M. Hoover, supplied a number of Tom's original transparencies, an effort also assisted by Ramcharger team historian Dr. Dave Rockwell. Dan Gallo Jr. and Paul's Body Shop also provided images of the cars in modern times. Coupled with material from my own photo library, if you end up appreciating this book for the pictures, thank them. They put in the sweat equity almost 50 years ago.

The Car Owners and Friends

To Arnie Klann, Ben Donhoff/Larry Mayes, and others who became the caretakers of these immensely important artifacts over the years, I appreciate being able to see these cars and take photographs of them during the times they were on display (and Ben, for the unintentional but great wheelie shot at Columbus at the beginning of chapter 8). Mark Williams, long-time owner of the 1972 'Cuda, was a subscriber to the original *Quarter Milestones* magazine I published in the 1990s, and we are glad that he was able to find a way to get that car formally preserved and subsequently cosmetically restored. The late Stewart Pomeroy, who helped me when I did a history of the Dodge Colts years ago, also gets credit for his past *Missile* ownership, once again with special thanks to Gene Yetter's team interviews. To David Hakim and Dale Mathews, who were my road trip associates on some of these jaunts; again, your friendship is always appreciated. Finally, editor Wes Eisenschenk of CarTech kept me out of trouble when I failed to show up for round one on time. I appreciate it, pal!

Greatest thanks and true love to my wife, Linda, for dealing with the emotional and lifestyle upheaval that any book creation brings to life. By God's grace, we go forward—and soon go on vacation!

Dedication

Of course, this book is dedicated to driver Don Carlton, coolest of cool science guys, a loving father and husband, and one the who gave it all for drag racing. We remember . . .

Race driver Don Carlton is shown.
(Photo Courtesy Joe Pappas)

Don Carlton Jr. (left) and Ted Spehar are honored at the 2014 East Coast Drag Times Hall of Fame induction ceremony. (Photo Courtesy Tina Spehar/Spehar Family)

The truth is, I thought my dad was just like all the other racers. During the time he drove and owned the *Missile*, I considered it to be normal life. It wasn't until later that I understood what he accomplished in his career and how special the whole *Missile* thing really was. To be honest, what my dad's work accomplished and demonstrated is what led to the work ethic I still have today.

My earliest memories were of the Southern-style match races my dad did before then in the best-of-three format. Right near here in Lenoir, North Carolina, we had the Hudson and Wilkesboro drag strips within a half-hour drive of our home; then, there were places such as Piedmont, Farmington, and others. He would work all week, go out and run on Friday night, Saturday afternoon, Saturday night, and Sunday. Then, he'd go back to work again. When Pro Stock began to get popular, he could win $500 or so at each of those tracks on the weekends, which was more than he made during a week in the factory. He would often come back home between the races to sleep and would also pull the pan down and put fresh bearings in the Hemi. He worked in the furniture industry back then, and he also did mechanical work on other hot rods, helping people get ready for the races that weekend. I just thought that was the way every racer lived.

When he began doing the *Motown Missile* program in Detroit, Michigan, I didn't travel much yet, but our family eventually moved up there. I wanted to be part of it and came over to the shop sometimes. They would let me help clean up, wash parts, and sweep the floor. Joe Pappas and Dick Oldfield were always kind to me, and I was in awe of the factory guys who would come by and talk. When I was a little older, I was more involved and could help take a Lenco transmission out, handle some tools, and sometimes mix our special gas. Back then, we had our own blend of Sunoco and AV gas, and I would take the proportions from each barrel and mix a batch up. That was a pretty important job.

At the same time, Clyde Hodges ran the shop that was in our old house. My dad grew up right on this property, and it had been in the family a long time. Clyde was a real country backwoods sort of guy, but he could weld and knew how to build engines. People said the engines

Young Don and his dad are pictured at a 1974 match race at Milan Dragway. (Photo Courtesy Joe Pappas)

he built were as good as Ted Spehar's stuff. I admit right now, that was a matter of opinion, but it was his reputation. Anyhow, my dad had already started building the new concrete-block 100 x 40-foot building here even before the factory backing went away. When it was over, he and Clyde did it all and even built whole cars here, including the Colt that Dad was killed in. When the operation moved back here, we received a huge amount of parts and lots of titanium stuff, plus cylinder heads, blocks—you name it. We had a warehouse full of parts.

I was about 15 when he was killed in 1977. Of course, it was very hard on all of us. At my age, I was busy being interested in girls and school, and the shop eventually closed. In the late 1970s, I tried a little drag racing, but since my name is Don Carlton as well, there was a lot of pressure on me at the local tracks to measure up to his reputation. Still, I enjoyed racing, and after I tried circle-track driving once and liked it. I actually did a bunch of Sportsman circle track racing locally. I was never a professional, but I did pretty well with that for some years. By then, however, we no longer had any affiliation with Chrysler, and it eventually became expensive enough that I decided to quit.

You know, my dad was never a *top-hatter*. He was cool, but he didn't have airs, fancy clothes, or flashy stuff. I would probably look like a showboater compared to him, but that was just the way he was. I think that for him, driving a race car was just the thing he did. It was natural. He could work on them too, and that whole *Missile* team fit together very naturally. Plus, the guys were all friends. Richard Oldfield, Dick's son, and I were about the same age, and we spent time together. Our parents would get together and play cards sometimes, and we also went on the road with the team to a few of the events in the summer.

The car my dad was killed in was buried in the landfill on Lick Mountain, right above where Hudson Dragway used to be. The guy who ran the bulldozer there was an old high school drag racing buddy of dad's, and he told me years ago it would get uncovered every once in a while. He understood what it meant to us, and even with some of the parts left on it, it was never stripped apart. Just buried. I think a few guys might have taken souvenirs from it, but the landfill has been closed due to some of the other nasty stuff people sent there. I think that is just as well.

I still have the old shop, but it has expanded. I run several businesses out of it, making materials for the local furniture industry and packing business. The old motor room is used as an office by my plant manager, and some of my dad's trophies are still in his display case, even though that area is used for storage now. Some of the family still lives on the property too, just like always.

As for me, I often play a round of golf with Stuart McDade, who is still in the area. He doesn't talk much about those days now. Still, it was really good to see the whole *Missile* team back together at Henderson for that reunion event a couple of years ago. Looking back, we really did have an amazing time when we raced. The reunion recalled a time that is still very special to all of them, and I think my dad would have loved it.

Introduction

The sport of drag racing, once the bane of local law enforcement and the subject of teen exploitation flicks of the 1950s, grew alongside the performance vehicle era of the early 1960s. While running a pair of anything side by side to determine a victor is certainly older than the automobile, it was drag racing that made it possible for anyone to compete, whether his or her vehicle was a bone-stock car fresh off the showroom floor or a contraption of cubic inches, steel tubing, and bravado.

As the sport segued into more specialized compartmentalization, those promoting it as a spectator sport constantly looked for ways to make certain that there were cars appearing to be stock but were actually modified. They tried Factory Experimental, and things got out of hand with Funny Cars. They tried Super Stock versus pure Stock but found that the need to equalize performances between various designs created racing challenges.

In 1968, the American Hot Rod Association (AHRA) created a specific heads-up Super Stock class with rules carefully governing appearance but also allowing powerful enhancements. In late 1969, the bellwether organization, the National Hot Rod Association (NHRA) did likewise. The result was Pro Stock, and the book you are reading focuses on a group of Chrysler engineers and associates who deter-

Dick Oldfield and one of the Spar brothers from B&M get ready for work on the transmission in the pits at Indy in 1970. Tom "The Ghost" Coddington is in the background. (Photo Courtesy Tom Hoover Family)

mined early on that using science was the way to win.

Let's begin by introducing three of the main partici-pants: Chrysler engineer Tom Hoover, engine builder Ted Spehar, and driver Don Carlton. Each of them established a reputation as an expert in his respective field. All three had a certain drive not often found in any discipline, the type of drive that can only lead to success over the long run if everything is on a level playing field. And the three of them functioning in harmony was a beautiful thing.

That stated, not a single one of them would have taken sole credit for what happened in the era that the *Motown* (and later *Mopar*) *Missile* program began. The team was surrounded by people who valued hard work and had a passion to win.

For Hoover, leading the factory development pro-gram, it was his fellow engineering cabal, many of them former members of a drag racing team called the Ram-chargers. By the late 1960s at the height of the Detroit performance era, they remained strategically placed in Chrysler Corporation management, marketing, and development. Dave Koffel, liaison for the racers who began working for the firm in mid-1968, once noted they

worked for a number of bosses over the years, but the focus never wavered. Whatever was needed to succeed was done. You will meet many of them on these pages.

For Spehar, it was the crew of guys who worked with him at his engine shop. Car builder and driver Dick Old-field, engine-building associate Leonard Bartush, and shop manager Mike Koran shared in that effort. Ted himself was always in close association with factory boss Tom, who is reverently referred to as "Mr. Hoover" to this day. In his role of developing pieces for the racing envi-ronment, Spehar did relentless and thorough testing, finding solutions to problems that had never been seen before. Sometimes shown in the periodicals of the day working on an engine-based challenge during a long race weekend, Ted was typical of the mechanical geniuses the sport attracted, and the machine spoke for his effort.

Carlton, also bespeckled in black rims like the other two, was perhaps the person least expected to be the image of a drag racer. In an age of Aquarius and tough-guy drivers, Don was not someone normally showing up in beefcake photos. However, put him in a 4-speed race car, and he was quickly a hero to the fans. Indeed, his competency as a driver quickly proved itself in his native North Carolina, and he came into focus for the team in 1971 after driving stints with other teams. Once the factory turned the team over to Carlton full-time, Dick Oldfield would come to work for him, as would another die-hard wrench named Joe Pappas, and Don would continue maintaining his own race operation on his family property in the South, assisted by Clyde Hodges and fellow driver Stu McDade.

Together, this collective was to change the focus of the sport from its sometimes shade-tree roots into something that could be quantified by computer science, applied practically for answers, and then used to dominate the sport. The data generated for this program helped all Chrysler factory-associated Pro Stock teams, not just their own, and some advances were also applied to further benefit all racing of this type.

In every good story there is a nemesis, and in this case it would end up being those in charge of parity. You see, this volume is about a single Chrysler team but encompasses everyone who raced these products. Early on, they won. They won a lot. As the other popular (and frankly better-selling) Detroit products were beaten on a regular basis, those enthusiasts complained to listening ears in the sanctioning bodies who ran organized racing. These so-called "high sheriffs" of the rule book in turn steadily applied conditions that would eventually make all Chryslers in Pro Stock uncompetitive, regardless of how much effort and money these men and their associates put forth. If it is said that life is unfair, this would certainly be the case for these teams that put so much focus into this era to no avail.

But this is no place to whine about all of that. As you progress through this book, you will get a real sense of the time when this effort happened, the people who made it possible, and the drama of the sport of drag racing in the upper echelon of the factory hot rods. In later

This photo was sent to Don Carlton (standing, center) from Wally Parks following the 1972 win at Gainesville and is in Don Carlton Jr.'s business office.

years, when a much greater amount of money was spent on research into competition engineering (coupled with an almost boring level of product conformity), development would allow for performance levels undreamed of in the age of the *Motown Missile.*

But these guys did it first. For many fans of this era, they also did it best . . .

Noted artist David Snyder created this symbolic view of the legendary Woodward Sunoco garage during the era of the Silver Bullet *Plymouth*, seen parked outside. The passion for performance is what spearheaded the work that led to the Motown Missile *on a more national scale. Jimmy Addison owned the service center at this time. (Photo Courtesy www.davidsnydercarart.com)

Chapter One

Preflight Check in Autumn 1969: Origins of the Motown Missile

*D*usk began to fall as Jimmy Addison worked to get the nondescript Dodge ready for the night, his work-worn hands up underneath it inside the lit garage bay. Outside the Sunoco station, automobiles in bright shades of paint cruised by, some drivers looking over briefly at the car hoisted up on the lift, others more intent on getting to Ted's drive-in restaurant, to the next stoplight, or beside the next wise guy. There was a rumble outside and the ring of the service station bell as a rich green Corvette roadster with factory side-pipes rolled up to the pumps. Any 435-hp L71 Tri-Power out on Woodward wanted what was needed, and what was needed was gallons of Sunoco 260. After a quick glance from Jimmy, one of the young guys in the garage bay wiped off his hands and walked out to see a young executive (maybe right from GM) and his lady friend sitting inside the brand-new car. He saw the $20 bill hanging out the window, heard him say "Fill 'er up!," and started the pump. Jimmy went back to work underneath the rough-looking 1962, getting the Max Wedge Mopar ready to win some Saturday chump change.

* * *

Addison became one of the legends of Woodward Avenue in its heyday. Muscle cars and marketing were the going thing in the bedroom-community suburbs of Detroit, and this long stretch of four-lane pavement running northwest from the center of the city to the town of Pontiac was considered by many to be ground zero for the cause. Indeed, so much so that Pontiac, the car brand, originator of the GTO, had run a national advertisement showing a new version of its *tiger* with a Woodward Avenue street sign prominently displayed that was clearly intended to show everyone which way was up.

For the cruisers and the crazies, *up* was someplace close to 19 Mile Road (near where the popular local eatery Ted's drive-in was located), and then it began a circuit southeast toward Ferndale or to 9 Mile Road. Each of these east-west numbered "Mile" streets was named for the number of miles from the center of the city of Detroit. On a busy night, most participants would turn around and make the circuit a few times, perhaps stopping at Addison's Woodward Sunoco fuel depot for a tank of hi-test fuel if the ride required it. The respectable ones all did.

Addison was a short, stocky guy noted for a somewhat gruff demeanor and a fearless driving style. A former line mechanic for an Oldsmobile dealership, he had been at the Sunoco station at 14 Mile since 1968 and would soon own it himself.

Thanks to Ted Spehar's meticulous engine building skills and the car's unkempt outward appearance, the stroked Max Wedge 1962 Dodge was something of an unknown terror on the street—which was good for business if your business was street racing and dudes such as that guy in the 'Vette were looking to impress a member of the other sex. They had money. You wanted to take it. Let the best man win.

At any rate, while the Woodward Dream Cruise has now become a part of yearly American automotive culture, in 1969 it was simply a thrill for the participants, a pain for the police, and a legend across the nation. This was a place where you might see something new from the factory before everyone else, show off the latest mods to your street machine, meet friends and friendly foes, and maybe find out who the king of the hill was for the night. If a stoplight-to-stoplight joust wasn't enough, you could chase more serious competitors to top-end honors into the triple digits (MPH) on the under-construction I-696 (basically the former location of 10 Mile Road) or on a temporarily measured quarter-mile on a more deserted side street after midnight. When that happened, there was a deal, there was money, and there was the danger of arrest or worse. It was a unique moment, perhaps a semi-requiem from the madness of Vietnam, politics, labor unrest, and the like. "Papa's got a brand-new bag, and it was street racing," as one magazine scribe explained it. The machine spoke, and it had a reputation to uphold. Perhaps this passion is where the *Motown Missile* truly had its roots.

* * *

Mr. Hoover looked over his glasses at the needle on the dyno as the roar increased and the RPM level climbed again. Built into the basement of the company research building in Highland Park, the dynamometer cells were normally tasked with more pedestrian projects these days, but Tom could get special dyno use for his projects when needed, especially since he had friends who were the actual operators. Today, it was another potential idea—this time just a simple change to a new race camshaft that might show some improvement to airflow and a little more horsepower. It wasn't much, but it had already proven to be worthwhile in real-world conditions over at Detroit Dragway the previous week in a test car.

With the right carb adjusting complete, the needle showed there had been about a 7-hp improvement over the previous-best version of that cam. The numbers were denoted by a slightly higher bump on the top of the hand-drawn arch when plotted on a subsequent graph. Now proven to be truly beneficial, a notice was forwarded to the chosen Chrysler racers across the nation, announcing the exact part number to order from the manufacturer. Tom Hoover smiled to himself.

* * *

In the teardown barn at Pomona in 1963, engineer Tom Hoover casts a warning glance over his shoulder. The Ramchargers played a vital role in how Chrysler Race Engineering was accomplished in the early days of development. (Photo Courtesy Tom Hoover Archive)

Even as the Race Engineering guys became involved in engine development, the Ramchargers team was winning races. Shown after a victory at the 1963 NHRA Nationals are Herman Mozer and Jim Thornton (standing, left to right); Gary Congdon, Tom Hoover, and Dale Reeker (front row); Dan Mancini and Tom Coddington (middle row); and Mike Buckel and Dick Maxwell (back row). All were smart guys, hard workers, and passionate racers. (Photo Courtesy Spehar Family Archive)

Engine science. For Thomas Meridith Hoover, this subject was his life's focus for more than a decade, working diligently in the depths of Chrysler Engineering's buildings in the Motor City. He had been a hot-rodder since high school, and after training as a graduate physicist at Penn State, he landed at the company in 1955, just as performance began to get more serious. Following training at the Chrysler Institute, he worked on various projects as an engine developer until new company President Lynn Townsend called on him in late 1961 to head a new Race Engineering project with the explicit goal to put a Chrysler vehicle into the winner's circle at "Big Bill" France's huge superspeedway in Daytona Beach. The Daytona 500 was now important enough to sink real money into. After all, the motto was "Win on Sunday, sell on Monday," right?

With that as the plan, Tom lost no time surrounding himself with similar-minded gentlemen who he knew within the firm. In fact, he was even somewhat recog-

nized outside of the corporate world, as he and other young members of the Chrysler Engineering team had formed a drag race club in the late 1950s, calling themselves the Ramchargers. This was named after a closely guarded secret about fuel-related intake tuning that the company's engineers had discovered, scientifically verified, and put into practice while testing the original 1950s-era Chrysler Hemi engine for an Indy Car program.

During the NHRA Nationals drag races held at Detroit Dragway in 1959 and 1960, the 'Chargers had frustrated the tech inspectors with a prewar Plymouth featuring many hair-raising ideas. Mission accomplished. Tom and his band of slide-rule renegades had next jumped into what was known as Stock Eliminator for 1961, where they could measure their technology and prowess against other factory-designed equipment. While NASCAR success may have been a more visible focus on the corporate front, Tom's own passion was fueled by the quarter-mile bursts (events in which anyone could participate), and the company was soon developing special cars just for this. The first of them used a 413-ci engine using the ram-tuning intake technology, the same 1962 engine package that Jimmy Addison was later street racing. Formally called the Maximum Performance package, it was better known simply as the Max Wedge.

Meanwhile, with the Ramchargers team busy winning races on the weekends, Tom Hoover was hard at work during 1963 getting a reconfigured Hemi cylinder head prepared for future Daytona and drag racing use alike. Working with specialists, including legendary airflow engineer Sir Harry Weslake of England, Hoover determined a way to mount a revised version of the head onto the latest wedge-head 426-ci RB-series engine block. Everyone involved then went to work on a very tight schedule to get the new powerplant to live for a full 500 hard miles—with the dyno cells in Highland Park screaming for hours on end during the winter months of early 1964. The effort was highlighted by near-unreal background drama and a movie-type happy ending—with young star Richard Petty thundering his Hemi Plymouth Belvedere to victory in the final act at the 1964 Daytona 500, leading several other new 426 Hemi Chryslers across the finish line. The world was never the same after that February afternoon. At least not in the automotive world, and certainly not in places such as Woodward Avenue.

Compared to most other engines, the Hemi engine was huge in its overall dimensions, nicknamed by some as as "the elephant motor." It had big ports and large valves positioned opposite each other at a 53.5-degree axial difference inside a hemispherical (or half dome) combustion chamber. This was a perfection discovered by long-since-retired Chrysler engineers during extensive testing on a wartime airplane engine in the 1940s. It had forged aluminum pistons that were the heaviest design created for a passenger car engine at the time, and a race-specific reciprocating design and hardware that was created for durability. Ultimately, the Hemi created an icon for Chrysler as a company and a lasting legacy for its "godfather," Tom Hoover.

It also created a lot more headaches for the tech guys and rule makers in all sorts of racing because it could win—which it did, a lot. In fact, NASCAR actually banned the Hemi for 1965 as a non-production engine, allowing Mr. Hoover and company a little spare time to figure out how well it might run on nitromethane fuel in the supercharged Top Fuel dragster environment with a new Ramchargers team dragster. The Ramchargers also raced and won with it that season after installing a fuel-injected variation of the engine into a series of radical creations they had recently dreamed up as an "unlimited stock" idea in late 1964.

These so-called altered-wheelbase machines, featuring the front and rear wheels both pushed far forward beneath the body, quickly became known as Funny Cars. Meanwhile, the factory released a group of 200 1965 all-steel 426 Hemi race cars for the NHRA's Super Stock

The ban of the Hemi by NASCAR for 1965 freed up resources to experiment in drag racing, which resulted in cars such as the altered-wheelbase Dodge the Ramchargers campaigned that year, which was both fuel-injected and running nitromethane when this photo was taken. (Photo Courtesy Tom Hoover Archive)

class. One of those was a Plymouth Belvedere being successfully campaigned by local racers Dick Housey and Ted Spehar that year. Against this backdrop, work was ongoing throughout 1965 to address the NASCAR problem directly. This was done by creating a more pedestrian version (as if such terms ever applied to a Hemi) of the engine that could be sold in a street "stock production" model.

In fact, Mr. Hoover bought one of these cars as soon as they arrived for 1966—a green Dodge Coronet. He once recalled that the car had a brand-new Hemi installed that had been built incorrectly from day one at Chrysler Marine & Engineering, which was where all the code A102 street Hemi engines came together for the street models. Once sorted out, he did some drag tests with it and drove it for fun on the street, sometimes turning it over to Spehar, a man he trusted, for tune-up care and feeding.

Starting in 1965, several factory-associated cars were often under the care of Spehar, who owned a Texaco service center and later a Gulf gas station franchise in the area. On that note, on some occasions, Mr. Hoover made sure he was attending a company or social function in the evening, because Spehar's mechanic Jimmy Addison was covertly taking the Hoover green meanie out near Woodward to uphold company honor against the other guys. He usually did, too.

Tom Hoover's factory crew was not huge. His first guys in the Race group were Dante "Dan" Mancini and Jim "B.B." Thornton, both trusted associates from the Ramchargers team. Indeed, other Race Engineering guys would include fuel systems specialist Tom Coddington, nicknamed "The Ghost," Ramchargers driver and engine specialist Hartford "Mike" Buckel, and several others, all of whom understood the passion that drove the projects.

Members of the Ramchargers worked throughout other areas of the Chrysler Corporation, where they were called on to do special race-focused projects when their production-associated work was completed. Not commonly recalled is that the Ramchargers (and a sister factory-member team named the Golden Commandos that raced Plymouths) were nearly independent from the corporate offices. Other than what little money could be had from dealership sponsorship and professional access to the factory development tools, it was pretty much an out-of-pocket proposition for both groups, and neither team ever had big factory dollars to live lavishly. The teams relied on member dues and winning real races to stay viable financially. It was ingenuity and dedication that would often spell the difference in that regard.

Science Class

Though professional cars often made racing news headlines, it was the everyman's stock-class drag racing divisions that remained more important to the factory for promoting new car sales, and the Race Engineering group stayed busy with projects and research related to that during the 1960s. Indeed, many in the team's cadre of engineers formally dropped out of actual competition in late 1967, retiring their ever-evolving Funny Car and turning the Top Fuel car over to a mostly outside crew. After all, the exploding muscle car business had grown into a big part of vehicle marketing, which was further spurred on in 1967 when the NHRA divided its raced stock cars between a Junior Stock–style lower division simply named "Stock" and a new standalone Super Stock division to showcase the best factory cars and drivers.

Ever scientific in approach, Hoover knew testing was paramount to this division's success. As a result, select factory-associated cars and drivers began showing up one day a week at Motor City Dragway near Mt. Clemons, Detroit Dragway at Sibley, Dix south of downtown, Milan Dragway west of the city, or even a faraway location such as a track in California when the racing season started. Rented by the company for private use to experiment with new ideas such as hood scoop shapes, special tires, or promising cam designs, these test sessions became part of the legend of Chrysler Engineering "doing so much with so little." By 1969, Al Adam, yet another Ramcharger alumni, was managing that aspect of real-world testing with Spehar doing the engine prep; both men were meticulous at record-keeping. Edited notes on successful experiments were forwarded to Chrysler racers across the nation.

Some tests were done with cars recently prototyped in an offsite-from-Engineering location simply known as the Woodward Garage. Located in a former Pontiac dealership at the corner of Woodward and Buena Vista in Highland Park, this small private shop served as the skunkworks for ideas that Hoover or his compatriots dreamed up for racing under factory authorization or for special projects done on existing cars. UAW shop steward and top mechanic Larry Knowlton was the unofficial manager at the garage.

During late 1967 and early 1968, at Mr. Hoover's request, Knowlton and a brilliant, somewhat flamboyant young engineer named Robert "Turk" Tarozzi reworked a Race Hemi into the small Plymouth Barracuda. Once they

Development in the 1967–1968 era resulted in what many still consider the ultimate Chrysler race package: the Hurst Hemi package cars. This is the first Sox & Martin 1968 Barracuda, seen here at its initial drag test session at Cecil County Dragway in Maryland in April 1968. (Photo Courtesy Tom Hoover Archive)

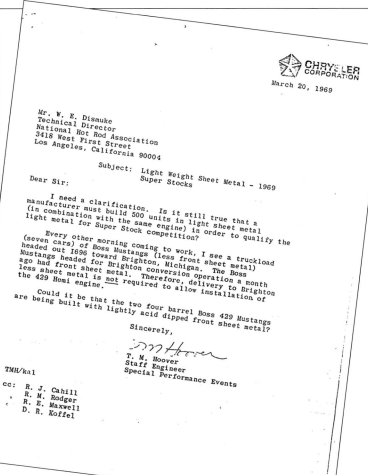

CHRYSLER CORPORATION

March 20, 1969

Mr. W. E. Dismuke
Technical Director
National Hot Rod Association
3418 West First Street
Los Angeles, California 90004

Subject: Light Weight Sheet Metal - 1969
Super Stocks

Dear Sir:

I need a clarification. Is it still true that a manufacturer must build 500 units in light sheet metal (in combination with the same engine) in order to qualify the light metal for Super Stock competition?

Every other morning coming to work, I see a truckload (seven cars) of Boss Mustangs (less front sheet metal) headed out I696 toward Brighton, Michigan. The Boss Mustangs headed for Brighton conversion operation a month ago had front sheet metal. Therefore, delivery to Brighton less sheet metal is not required to allow installation of the 429 Hemi engine.

Could it be that the two four barrel Boss 429 Mustangs are being built with lightly acid dipped front sheet metal?

Sincerely,

T. M. Hoover
Staff Engineer
Special Performance Events

TMH/kal

cc: R. J. Cahill
    R. M. Rodger
    R. E. Maxwell
    D. R. Koffel

This signed letter to the NHRA was among many that went back and forth between the factories and the NHRA in those days. Tom Hoover was always looking for an advantage, although he later admitted that the NHRA never forgave Chrysler for some of the things it did, such as the 1969 Mini-Nationals. (Photo Courtesy QMP Research Files)

put it all together, the result was one of the most notorious drag racing combinations ever authorized by Detroit. That spring under contract for Chrysler, shifter-company-turned-vehicle-constructor Hurst Industries converted approximately 160 of these A-Body models (both Barracudas and Dodge Darts) into Hemi-powered drag-race-only machines in a Detroit-area facility. They came to conquer under the tutelage of factory-favored drivers, such as Ronnie Sox, Arlen Vanke, Don Grotheer, and Dick Landy. By then, Dave Koffel, a trained metallurgist who had been racing himself for many years, handled the deals with the racers.

Again, the rule makers were stymied. Reams of correspondence from Hoover, Koffel, Product Planning's Dick Maxwell (yet another former Ramcharger), and others were sent out to NHRA officials in California, asking pointed questions about the factored horsepower the NHRA had placed on Chrysler engines, why Ford was allowed to run a combination no one in Detroit had seen except in the hands of that company's best-known drivers, or why the new Six Pack Road Runners and Super Bees had no owner lists because they were actually sold as "street cars."

Though perhaps frustrating, Mr. Hoover was always all-in on this game, figuring out the rule book, finding scarce racing combinations that had an advantage, and pushing the envelope. At times, those creative solutions likely had NHRA president Wally Parks cursing quietly at the sheer genius of it. At the same time, one of his angry division directors called NHRA tech boss Bill "Farmer" Dismuke at the organization's North Hollywood offices to complain about what "them Chryslers" had done to the record book the past weekend. Hoover would laugh for a moment, then go right back to work to "crush them like ants," as he was prone to state in private company.

It all came to head at the 1969 NHRA Nationals held in Indianapolis over Labor Day weekend. The NHRA

Super Stock:
Racing on the Brakes

Each Super Stock car had a set elapsed time index. This was derived from the possible performance of that combination based on an NHRA-factored horsepower-to-weight ratio. Each engine was rated for horsepower as estimated by the NHRA's Technical Committee, which in turn was coupled to the manufacturer's stated overall weight for each car as released off the assembly line. Weighed without driver, the engine/car package would then fall into a select letter category. For example, "A class" was the highest horsepower/lightest car combination, followed by B, C, D, etc. Automatic and manual transmissions were further broken into their own subgroups in each class to provide additional equality; automatic-equipped models had an A after the class letter.

At big events, each group of identically classed cars raced each other for a class victory among peers, and winners then advanced to final eliminations. At smaller races, the driver would simply be timed against the index. Once racing among all those classes was underway, the slower-classed car was given a head start by whatever the calculated index difference was.

During the 1969 season, entries in the Super Stock classes ranged from SS/B (solely the Hurst Hemi cars

because no one had built a car in a weight legal in SS/A at that time) through SS/J. A like number of cars were classified in the automatic transmission classes that were identified with an additional A at the end of the classification. So that year, the 10 class letters and 2 transmission choices meant 20 possible classes.

Originally stated as an NHRA-set minimum elapsed time, the index for each class in 1969 was based on the current class record for that class. No one wanted to beat that record if possible because it left no room for error. In other words, resetting a soft index record might make winning less possible by requiring the maximum effort on every single run. Furthermore, changing the record would affect every driver racing that combination, not just the cars capable of running to that level. As a result, and sometimes at factory direction, the fastest cars were often braking at over 100 mph to prevent this from happening.

Hemi race car drivers, such as Dick Oldfield in New York and Don Carlton in North Carolina, were familiar with this technique. It was dangerous, and the racers frankly hated it. Pro Stock would eventually solve this problem for many of them.

knew that the best drivers in Super Stock (a very popular class by that time with factory attention) were hitting the brakes well before the finish line to keep from showing their top performances. At that time, if your car went too fast, you lost. Basically, any performance made during eliminations that exceeded the current NHRA elapsed time index broke out, going beyond its established performance. When that happened, the car was disqualified from advancing to the next round.

So, going into their biggest event of the year, the NHRA decided to catch the racers at their own game. This was when the NHRA stated that at Indy every run down the track could become the index for Monday's finals. Since only the class winner and runner-up from Saturday afternoon's class runoffs were allowed to advance to race in Monday's final eliminations, these new racing indexes would obviously be derived from the fastest runs made during that weekend. This was because the NHRA

assumed every driver would have to run flat out to win a class crown. Still, to make it fair, they also agreed that the index would not change again on Monday. For the first time, drivers could run flat out all day and the record rule would not apply until the final. In the final round, the drivers could run as fast as necessary, but that fast time was the new index heading into the following event.

On Friday morning, the Chrysler racers slowly left town, heading for a little track just over the Ohio state line a couple of hours east. Dave Koffel rented the track with his American Express card, and now each of the three-dozen-plus drivers arriving there would make three passes to see who was truly fastest. The two best in each class would then return to Indy to run for the class win and runner-up slots. Once Chrysler had determined who the fastest guys were fair and square (away from the oversight of NHRA officials), the three chosen duos in SS/B, SS/BA, and SS/CA (all Hemi cars exclusively)

The staging lanes at Indy in 1969 did not host a lot of Hemi SS entries after the runoffs were done at Tri-City Dragway in Hamilton, Ohio, early in the weekend. Ted Spehar still calls the so-called "Mopar Mini-Nationals" the greatest race in which he was ever involved, as there had never been a true no-holds-barred NHRA Super Stock runoff to the last man standing before that. (Photo Courtesy Dick Landy Family)

This photo in the Spehar family archive from November 1970 shows the Silver Bullet when it was first completed. This car would be as legendary on the street as the Motown Missile was on the track, which was something Mr. Hoover took pride in. (Photo Courtesy Spehar Family Archive)

returned to Indianapolis and basically cruised downtrack on Saturday for the class battle and "new" records. The predetermined faster car from the so-called "Mini-Nationals" also deliberately ran slower to be the class runner-up, all of which kept the old indexes used before the Nationals completely intact. Meanwhile, the other guys fought each other hard, and most had *killed* or reset their indexes when clocking their best possible number

round after round in taking class victories. For their part, Hoover, Maxwell, and factory race boss Bob Cahill wandered around the Indy pits on Friday morning, shrugging off questions about where all the absent racers had gone.

When Monday's big event arrived, the only thing the Mopar racers from those classes needed to do was make sure they did not redlight at the start. When the smoke cleared from five rounds, Ronnie Sox won, beating a 1964 Hemi Plymouth driven by Dave Wren to basically close out the professional Super Stock era. On that Tuesday morning, NHRA officials, the movers and shakers in

Imitating a popular sanctioning body design, this is a North Woodward Timing Association decal.

Super Stock, and their factory bosses all got together and agreed to formulate new rules that would create a heads-up class for 1970, which they would call Pro Stock. Finalized after the NHRA World Finals in Dallas that October, this was a new challenge, one Mr. Hoover would relish even as factory street performance was increasingly choked by emissions, insurance costs, and other factors.

By 1969, Hoover's terrible Coronet was now sitting at home more often than not, as Jimmy Addison and Ted Spehar kept the 1962 Dodge with its Max Wedge powerplant busy making money. They would soon begin converting a former factory-tested 1967 440-ci GTX into perhaps Woodward's most notorious competitor, the *Silver Bullet*. That project would come together for the street as the *Motown Missile* would soon do for the dragstrip. "Crush them like ants," Mr. Hoover said and smiled.

*   *   *

Ted Spehar was quietly contemplating what would come next in his future as he looked over the empty 1,500-square-foot building on Fernlee Avenue near where it intersected West 14 Mile Road in Royal Oak. Perhaps it was a big jump to go into this business of special car fabrication and maintenance, but he had the confidence, the connections, and the work ethic to be successful. He needed room for cars such as The Iron Butterfly and the factory test cars, for this new Pro Stock thing for spare parts, a clean room for engine construction, space for machine tools, and whatever else the new contract from Chrysler required. Most important for everyone involved, it was a secure, quiet place almost invisible to the outside world. After all, ideas that matter could be kept quiet until they were needed, which they certainly were. The commercial space realtor talked softly with Jack Watson, better known as the "Hurst Shifty Doctor" and the person who had arranged the meeting. Giving Ted some personal space to figure it all out, the realtor was expectant, hoping this day spent with the unassuming gentleman who was supposed to be some kind of engine genius would indeed become a successful sale.

*   *   *

Ted Spehar, who would play the most primary role as the *Motown Missile*'s builder and owner, traveled a special road to get to where he was that afternoon. From service station owner to engine builder, the past dozen years laid the groundwork for what would become Spehar's most visible position in motorsports, though such efforts characterized his entire career. With Chrysler's

Ted Spehar stands next to a dragster he owned in the early 1960s, driven by racing buddy Deowen "De" Nichols. This was the third chassis ever built by the Logghe Brothers and used a flathead Ford for power. (Photo Courtesy Spehar Family Archive)

A snapshot from December 1963 shows the Texaco station where Ted did his early work. The dragster is parked outside on a cold but snowless Michigan day. (Photo Courtesy Spehar Family Archive)

out of the Texaco station located at 15 Mile Road and Adams Street that he purchased when he was 22 years old. He called the engine business Spehar's Performance Automotive and began working almost exclusively on Chrysler products.

In 1967, he sold the Texaco franchise and bought a Gulf station located at 14 Mile Road (one block from Woodward) and continued to grow his corporate portfolio by working with Dale Reeker and Dick Maxwell from Chrysler's Product Planning arm on media test car prep and building engines for specific Chrysler racers. The following year, Ted purchased the legendary Sunoco franchise right on 1775 Woodward that he subsequently turned over to his top mechanic, Jimmy Addison, for doing *regular* car work. Note that the sale of petroleum was not always a big money generator at these outlets because Ted was often so focused on whatever horsepower task was at hand that actual fuel customers would drive off in disgust, waiting for a pump jockey who never arrived. Ted noted wryly that this was a likely factor in the Gulf franchise eventually changing hands.

Meanwhile, that Gulf station served his more immediate purpose of being the place Product Planning sent new cars to be super tuned for the automotive media. Ted would blueprint the distributor and cam, dial in the carburation as needed, and (when called on) would perhaps add a little more to the as-released vehicle. This was very

business getting more tied down with government and industry volatility, executive Cahill and Mr. Hoover had concluded that Ted was the right guy to help manage the firm's drag race development work as an outside contractor. The unionized Woodward Garage would likely be shuttered regardless, so from here on out, the things Mr. Hoover wanted to change from dream to reality were done in a comprehensive manner under Spehar's tutelage.

Ted was a Detroit-area native (having grown up in Birmingham) and a hot rodder from the late 1950s, following in the footsteps of his older brother Peter. He and street racing partner Deowen "De" Nichols got serious and bought the third dragster chassis ever built by the legendary Logghe Brothers firm, but Ted's true penchant was engine building. It was through his prowess in this arena that he made initial introductions to Chrysler's corporate office and the Ramchargers team during the mid-1960s, which was thanks in part to a working relationship with Dick Branstner, who was a larger-than-life figure in Detroit's car-building scene at the time. Ted's wife, Tina, a young beautician, ironically did hair styling with some of the other wives of Detroit's performance set, which is how the Branstners and Spehars met.

While Tom Hoover handled the Ramchargers racing engine builds personally, Ted was often given the recommendation when others came asking for services. His real interaction started in 1965, when he was still working

When Dick Housey drove a 1965 Plymouth for which Ted had built an engine, they went to the runner-up spot at 1965 NHRA Winternationals and reset several records, running in Modified Production on occasion. (Photo Courtesy Spehar Family Archive)

The Iron Butterfly, *built in two weeks from a 6-cylinder car that Ted Spehar's wife Tina had been driving, was created to fit into SS/CA by using an aluminum front end and a circa-1964 Hemi race engine. Seen here under the tutelage of driver Dick Oldfield, on this day the car posted runner-up honors to Ronnie Sox at the 1969 NHRA World Finals. (Photo Courtesy quartermilestones.com, Ray Mann Archive)*

This is an early decal from Ted's business, which for several years was based out of the service stations he owned. (Photo Courtesy Spehar Family Archive)

rare, and the most visible occurrence happened when he was told to put a just-released 1969 M-code 440 Six Pack Road Runner together for Ronnie Sox to drive for *Super Stock & Drag Illustrated* magazine. Sox made several quarter-mile runs in the 12-second range, which was faster than the large car could have been expected to accomplish, even with Hemi power!

The now-recognized Detroit engine builder had a very busy year in 1969. In addition to the factory magazine demonstrators and at the behest of Mr. Hoover and company, that late summer found Ted converting his wife Tina's street-driven Slant Six 1964 Dodge Polara into an SS/CA-class Hemi car he called *The Iron Butterfly*. Accomplished in a few weeks leading up to the Indy Nationals by working mainly outside behind the Woodward Sunoco station because garage space in all of the buildings was at a premium, the fresh vehicle was driven first by noted Detroit racer Wally Booth at the Nationals. Then, it was turned over to a new mechanic with a college engineering background from New York named Dick Oldfield.

Oldfield's deployment as the driver came about from Dave Koffel's recommendation and the shop contract Spehar recently signed with Chrysler. Oldfield was a dominant figure in NHRA Division 1 racing, and he already had the driver points from racing his *Good Guys* Dodge Dart

that were needed to be able to compete with the *Butterfly* at the NHRA World Finals. This he did well, going to the event's final round before falling to Ronnie Sox, who won his first NHRA World Championship in the other lane.

Moreover, that Chrysler contract was the reason for the new location Ted found on Fernlee with friend and Hurst employee Jack "Doc" Watson. The Gulf station was being sold, and Jimmy Addison bought the Sunoco station from Ted at the same time. As winter approached, the 1960s came to an end and Ted and his new group of employees got to work. None of them ever looked back as the revolution of Pro Stock dawned on the horizon for 1970.

* * *

Ahead stretched a measured eighth-mile of pavement as Don Carlton squinted through his black-rimmed glasses at the Christmas tree. He was oblivious to the girls on the fence, their guys leaning forward for a better view. The top bulb turned on, and the staging bulb below it flickered on in the evening haze and remaining tire smoke as he carefully rolled the Hurst-built Hemi Barracuda that he named Lil' Thumper into the starting beams. His opponent, in a Ford Mustang, did likewise. Now came the countdown of five lights.

Yellow . . . Yellow . . . Yellow . . . Yellow . . .

Don knew that if he saw the green light come on, he was

too late. With the pedal to the metal and the Hemi engine screaming for mercy, he sidestepped the clutch and the Plymouth leapt forward with its front wheels hanging a half-foot off the pavement, aided in part by gold-dust rosin sprinkled on the starting line. The next throw was down into second, and the Mustang could no longer be heard as the Hemi engine's RPM climbed the second time against the steep 5.13 rear gear. With a quick read of the tachometer and the ball-knob shifter in his hand, he flashed across the shift pattern up into third, and the finish line loomed immediately ahead. Fourth gear in the eighth-mile was almost anticlimactic, but he took it down through the final gate anyway with the Mustang behind by a car length. Round one down; two more to go.

* * *

"Run whatcha brung" Southern-style match racing in the Carolinas was a way of life for many amateur racers by this time in 1969. They ran against each other on grass-aproned strips of asphalt barely wide enough for two race cars to fit side by side. Indeed, some of the cow pasture emporiums ended in shut-down areas that required the drivers to quickly lift up from the gas and brake hard because the track actually narrowed to a single lane.

Lenoir, North Carolina, is a quiet town located north of US Route 70 and Interstate 40 in the hill country known as the Piedmont region of the Tar Heel state, and Don Carlton was one of several talented drivers from the area. NASCAR star Bobby Isaac was from nearby Hickory, while the Petty clan was over in Randleman, and Junior Johnson led his crew of circle-track merry men from up North Wilkesboro way. Drag racers included Ronnie Sox in Burlington, young upstart Roy Hill from Randleman, and Stuart McDade, who was also right from Lenoir.

To be honest, Southern-style racing of all forms was its own breed. The NASCAR guys had been the forerunners in competition, earning their stripes at the track in Darlington since 1950 and occasionally in prison garb when caught running or making high-grade moonshine. Drag racing was a simple contest of getting to the end first, and if you didn't buy enough right from the factory, you innovated to make sure you had more: a little weight removal, sticky retreaded tires, California-type speed parts, or nitromethane blended into gasoline on some occasions for a concoction known locally as cherry mash. Promotors (such as Bobby Starr at Piedmont near Burlington) paid cash to the winners, and the rules were sometimes as simple as "four wheels, 3,000 pounds, and doors."

Don Carlton posed for these publicity photos when a sponsor package came to the Motown Missile team. (Photo Courtesy Spehar Family Archive)

Don was not the son of some scion of Southern gentility. He funded his racing through long hours of work at one of a myriad of furniture factories that then dotted the countryside of the Piedmont. After a stint in a 4-speed Chevrolet, he bought an RO-code 1967 Plymouth Belvedere that was somewhat similar to the 1966 car Mr. Hoover owned but with some race-lightened parts right from the factory. He then waited in line to buy one of the Hurst-built Barracudas in 1968.

He raced it locally, but the car was badly damaged late that year in a towing accident. He called Buddy Martin over in Burlington, who not only agreed to buy the carcass but offered Don the job of driving one of the team's many cars: first, a Modified Production Road Runner;

In 1969, Don spent considerable time driving for the Sox & Martin team in this match-race Barracuda set up to run in heads-up AHRA races. It is seen here at the 1969 Super Stock Nationals in York, Pennsylvania, running a special SS/X division at that solitary race. However, Ronnie Sox himself drove it on that weekend. (Photo Courtesy quartermilestones .com, Pit Slides Archive)

The Missile tests were both frequent and effective, and for those involved, it really was rocket science. Seen at Gainesville, the new A-Body for 1973 was the most successful of all of them all. (Photo Courtesy Joe Pappas)

then, *Lil' Thumper*, a 1968 Barracuda set up as a match racer. This car was created to run Southern-style events and in the AHRA's new heads-up Super/Stock Experimental class, where Ronnie Sox himself sometimes took over the driving. Still, Buddy could book the car Don drove when he and Mr. Sox were out on tour with the monstrous Chrysler clinic responsibilities that Sox & Martin operation then performed. Carlton had already established himself as a fearsome driver when that 4-speed was in his hand.

At this point, Don was likely unaware that he would soon become one of the most notorious drivers in the formative years of Pro Stock, a class that was similar in theory to what the AHRA was already running as S/SE or Super Stock Experimental. Humble and well-versed in what a hard day's work entailed, he and the Sox & Martin operation soon parted ways. After a stint with colorful car owner Billy Stepp, Don had a chat with Mr. Hoover and agreed to take over driving the *Motown Missile* test mule from Dick Oldfield in early 1971.

His black-rimmed glasses actually made him the perfect complement to what Chrysler by then was calling the Special Vehicle Engineering group. They had computers and a weather station, brilliant ideas, and a tireless calling via testing to make it all work. On the 4-speed, Don Carlton was considered the equivalent of a cyborg, half man and half machine, repeating test after test after test. It would yield impressive results until a fateful 1977 day when he proved to be all too human.

* * *

The *Motown Missile* legend emerged from this soup of people and backgrounds. The world of drag racing was about to see what was possible when you pushed the envelope of technology. The silo was now ready for a weapon.

The Motown Missile began its charge into the 1970s with a wild paint job, engineering excellence, and an effort to make the former Super Stock drivers of the 1960s' 7-inch-tire/TorqueFlite-automatic era willing to forgo the use of the more temperamental 4-speeds. It is seen in its optimum form using this configuration at the NHRA World Finals in Dallas. (Photo Courtesy Steve Reyes)

Chapter Two

1970 Challenger: The First Spark

Pro Stock. Those two words impacted the sport of NHRA drag racing for the next 50-plus years. Though the racing politics of 1960s competition did not disappear, the rules package solidified the NHRA's excellent refocusing of the factory hot rods and drivers from Super Stock to a higher level. An innovation in what the NHRA deemed its "Super Season" for 1970, this introduction of a heads-up class for production-appearing vehicles had been on a long and winding road to that point, one that stretched back a number of seasons in other forms of drag racing.

En Route to Pro Stock

The NHRA's 1970 Pro Stock debut had some forerunners. For the 1968 season, the rival American Hot Rod Association (AHRA) organization announced a class called Super Stock Experimental. As noted in the previous chapter, the NHRA divided the Stock and Super Stock (S/S) groups into separate classifications in 1967. While S/S allowed some changes, the NHRA Super Stocks still had fairly restrictive rules and, more importantly, still required handicap starts like the former Top Stock/Junior Stock breakdowns. This maintained the "You go too fast, you lose, pal!" policy because established indexes were still required for each body/engine combination. The lower-class combination had a head start off the line, and performances that dipped under that index by a certain margin meant disqualification. These indexes were now based on an NHRA-evaluated horsepower rating rather than the one released by the factory, leaving the door open for no small amount of politicking by both the factories and the racers themselves as well as occasional input from biased sanctioning body officials. For the most part, the drivers hated it.

In contrast to this, the AHRA, a group from Kansas City that was originally organized and operated by promoter Jim Tice, took a page from the heads-up "run whatcha brung" Southern-style outlaw tracks and created a class for stock-bodied cars that used a flat weight break, maximum engine displacement and carburation quantity, and gasoline for fuel. In this S/S Experimental class, the car and manufacturer needed to be by the same American company with minimal exterior changes to keep the wheelbase and overall appearances correct. However, there was little restriction on tire width (something NHRA Super Stockers had to deal with), and acid dipping of parts was already being practiced by this time.

It should be noted that the ongoing evolution of the nitromethane-burning Funny Cars at this point also created a desirability to go back to a category with more OEM-based vehicle architecture and technology, especially with the growing popularity of the muscle car business from Detroit. Beyond their ever-increasing safety risks, the Funny Car designs were ever more radicalized in appearance, so the limitations to stock body shapes, carburetors, and gasoline in AHRA's SS/E category were an important component in this regard.

Free from the dreaded break-out rules, this class attracted efforts by many of the biggest drivers in NHRA Super Stock for the simple reason that it was a "first one to the finish wins" class. Meanwhile, since some of those same stars already had national name recognition due to magazines and weekly racing newspapers, special cars were modified and built just for this S/SE category. Some drivers were actually booked by Tice for a guaranteed attendance fee to run in the AHRA's racing series, an understanding he already had with a few of his fuel-powered stars. These same drivers, if factory associated, still retained other cars for NHRA racing as well with versions of their standard Super Stock packages kept in an NHRA-legal configuration when racing in that series.

Creating an additional vehicle capable for the AHRA also had the secondary benefit of keeping a turnkey match-race car for any independent racing dates where NHRA Super Stock rules enforcement was not being followed. As can be imagined, the heads-up idea of leaving the line side by side with the first car across the finish line winning was very popular with fans. To this end, several regional organizations sprung up to promote these types of events in circuit form around the nation.

One major proponent of such a heads-up category was the popular magazine *Super Stock & Drag Illustrated*, which hosted a yearly East Coast racing event that had a new SS/X (also for Experimental) classification for these cars in 1969. Beyond this, if a driver still wanted to run an AHRA-type vehicle in the NHRA, he or she could do so by competing in the Modified Production classes. However, this was still handicap-type racing, and a breakout rule was still in effect. In summary, although the NHRA did not announce the formal introduction of Pro Stock until the 1969 World Finals held in Dallas that October, all of these factors played into having a sizeable group of cars already built for the new class when initial rules were printed in the NHRA's *National Dragster* newspaper.

Pro Stock's First Rules

The initial Pro Stock rules did not make a long list. First and foremost, cars needed to be from an American manufacturer and equipped with an engine from that same manufacturer. However, it did not require a production engine, allowing the use of the competition-only single overhead cam (SOHC) Cammer Ford release and Chevrolet's race-exclusive aluminum Can-Am blocks, the latter being rare enough that basically only Bill Jenkins had the connections to obtain one. Chrysler, of course, had an iron race-designed production engine in the 426 Hemi, and development for this new purpose was already fairly advanced because of the continued factory testing.

Second, Pro Stock vehicles could not have a wheelbase less than 97 inches, the wheelbase was required to be stock to the vehicle being used, and the vehicle needed to be from a 1968 or later model. This allowed first-generation Camaros, Ford's previously released Boss Mustangs, and the 1968 Hurst-built 426 Hemi Darts and Barracuda Super Stockers to run in 1970. This rule was part of a three-year limit on Pro Stock body types, so the 1968 vehicles would only be legal this single season. Nonetheless, a majority of the better-heeled and factory-associated teams were quick to build current-year models for the new category. In turn, those same cars solely built for Pro Stock quickly rose to the top of the qualifying charts once any initial problems were sorted out. Meanwhile, AHRA Super Stock Experimental rules remained similar to the NHRA's, allowing the same vehicle to compete in both sanctioning bodies. Incidentally, AHRA retained the title Super Stock for its heads-up stockers in 1970.

To prevent revisiting the "ultra stock" experiments that created the Funny Car revolution, limits were imposed on body, engine, fuel, driveline, and chassis alterations. Unlike the flat weight break employed in some cases, NHRA Pro Stock legal weight was determined by dividing the total weight by cubic-inch displacement on a 7-pound margin with a minimum weight of 2,700 pounds and maximum cubic-inch displacement of 430 inches. This meant that at 426 inches, the car weight would be 2,982 pounds. The only fiberglass components allowed were hoods, front fenders, and decklids, and a 100-pound maximum of ballast allowed. The engine could not be set back, and the stock firewall location was required to be retained. The maximum hood scoop height for 1970 was 7 inches above the surface, which was a number deliberately given to be just enough to allow Jenkins's notable *Grump Lump* air box to remain legal in the category. Rear tires could protrude no more than 2 inches from the wheel well, and the radius on the wheelhouse needed to retain its stock design. Drivers brought high-test gasolines only because fuel was subject to checking via a hydrometer.

Finally, glass windows were required, and cars needed two seats with upholstery, stock front suspension, and headlights. No street exhaust was necessary. Let's go racing!

Express Travel to Dodge City

The NHRA was not the only organization announcing changes for 1970. The Dodge Division of Chrysler just released a new model named the Challenger. Designed to compete with the similarly priced Mercury Cougar and Pontiac Firebird, the Challenger was the company's first real entry into what was known as the *pony car* marketplace, which was named after the Mustang because it initiated the niche back in 1964. The Dodge Challenger was the final new model to enter this field. By that time, Ford was refocusing on the new Maverick and the even smaller Pinto, and Chevrolet was laying plans to supersede the discontinued Corvair with a model called the Vega.

The Challenger was a perfect fit for Pro Stock as a hot two-door vehicle featuring aggressive styling, 11 engine options that ranged from the small 198-ci Slant Six to the fearsome 440 Six Pack, and a plethora of body trim possibilities and optional equipment. The company quickly committed to making a special edition for running in the SCCA Trans Am road race series. A fiberglass

The Dodge Challenger was the last of Detroit's pony car releases and was targeted toward an upscale market; the R/T was the performance design. This highly optioned factory demonstrator convertible is in the Wellborn Musclecar Museum's collection.

replica owned by Charlie Allen debuted in the Funny Car ranks at the same time the street models were released in late 1969, and one of Ted Spehar's first assignments from Chrysler was to begin making one a testbed for Super Stock because the Pro Stock category had not been announced yet at the time.

Performance Automotive

When the sanctioning body announced the new Pro Stock class, Spehar was already tooling up his new contract business for Chrysler, which was called Performance Automotive. Ted immediately brought Leonard Bartush on board.

"Our families were close friends," Ted said at a team reunion in 2014. "His older brother and I went to school together in Detroit. Len started with me in the mid-60s working in the engine shop as a fabricator. In those days, that meant you did everything. You weren't a master of anything. You were self-taught. Eventually, Leonard did most of our engine work."

Lenny went to work at Ted's gas stations as a helper and parts washer during the mid-1960s when he was 16. With an interest in hot cars thanks to his older brothers (just as Ted's interest had been piqued by his sibling), Len

Ted Spehar (left) and Dick Oldfield are shown during one of the car's early outings. Once on the track, the car rarely left without being Top Qualifier. (Photo Courtesy Dick Oldfield Archive)

Tom Hoover, the legendary Chrysler engineer responsible for the 426 Hemi, was always a part of the effort. Mr. Hoover enjoyed the idea that Pro Stock presented but quickly understood that there was just one Ronnie Sox. From its inception, a primary role for the Missile *was automatic transmission development for former Chrysler TorqueFlite pilots. Leonard Bartush and Mike Koran are in the foreground. (Photo Courtesy Dick Oldfield Archive)*

quickly progressed in skill and ability to become second only to Ted when it came to building engines. He eventually became the primary Performance Automotive motor man regardless of project, unless Ted or Tom Hoover were planning to do the work themselves.

Also on board full-time now was Dick Oldfield.

"[The] NHRA was discussing Pro Stock, and the rumors were going around about that," Ted recalled. "When we came back from Indy, I moved into the new shop. It was only about 1,500 square feet because at that time I really just needed a place to build engines and keep the car. Now, [Dave] Koffel and Tom Hoover were getting cars together for the NHRA World Finals, and Koffel told me that he had a guy in New York who had just blown up his engine but had the points in his division to drive *The Iron Butterfly* at the World Finals. That was Dick Oldfield. So, I called Dick up, and he did not know me and I did not know him. We brought the car to the last points meet in York, Pennsylvania, and met him there."

Dick drove Tina's converted 1964 Dodge street car first at that event. As noted earlier, he then drove it to the final round in Dallas a few weeks later and was the runner-up to Ronnie Sox in what was the final-ever round of professional-level drivers in the handicap Super Stock division.

Dick's college background was part of his hiring, but so was his work ethic. For him, this employment represented a transition from campaigning the *Good Guys* Hemi Dart for the Dodge dealers' association in upstate New York. That deal supplied him with a car but

required him to do all the maintenance as well as travel, making him the perfect fit for what Ted needed at the moment. Like Len, Dick was on the Performance Automotive payroll and was paid by Ted, but now his efforts turned toward three facets in the work that Chrysler needed: race car construction, transmission maintenance, and (based on his prior experience) driving the new car. All pieces would play very heavily into the early history of the new Pro Stocker called the *Motown Missile*.

That name itself was coined by "Akron Arlen" Vanke, who saw the new Challenger in black paint rolling into one of the Chrysler early 1970 test sessions and declared, "Well, here comes that *Motown Missile*!" The name stuck and became a logical way to define the car's hometown and factory association.

"I inked the contract with Chrysler sometime in September or October, as they could see the need to have somebody running the program for package development for the racers," Ted noted. "The [factory] Performance Parts stuff under Brian Schram was coming together, and they were not going to do it at the Woodward Garage. Once that was settled, I moved from that first shop to one about a block over, which was probably 3,500 square feet, and I sold the Sunoco to Jimmy Addison soon after-

ward. That was when I hired Dick and also brought Len Bartush over and hired a good friend of his, Mike Koran."

Meanwhile, Ted noted that he never had an engine dyno in those early years. After all, the team wanted real-world data for performance, and that meant track time.

"The Ramchargers never had a dyno; the first one in Detroit was Wally Booth's that AMC got him," Ted said. "Keith Black had one; some of the West Coast shops did, but for most of us, it was drag strip testing."

So, just as when the legendary Woodward Garage was operating, the regular factory test programs continued to be very important. With the news from the NHRA that there was a heads-up program quickly coming for 1970, the construction of a new test Challenger for SS class racing became a test car for Pro Stock instead.

Before the *Motown Missile*

The NHRA's Super Season was partway finished before the world got a look at the new car. The Pro Stock class started in 1970 and was frankly spectacular in its popularity, especially when coupled to changes in Detroit production models for the 1970 year, and many of the biggest stars of the Super Stock division were fully committed to racing in the category.

Because of that, the big issue for Tom Hoover as Chrysler's Race Program coordinator was figuring out how best to maintain some sort of parity between stick-car aces, such as Sox, versus the other Chrysler factory drivers who had formerly been in Super Stock cars with TorqueFlite automatics. The first two fresh Pro Stockers built were used in testing at the brand-new Gainesville Raceway in Florida over five days in December 1969 to evaluate those differences.

Sox was in his first 1970 'Cuda as was competitor Don Grotheer with Grotheer running a Hemi-type Torque-Flite. After a series of tests on tires and cams, coupled with the good Florida winter air, Grotheer ran as quick as 9.96 at 136.94. Meanwhile, Sox, evaluating the latest clutch technology, ran several passes in the 9.70-second range, including a 9.75 best at over 141 mph. Driving the 1969 Modified Production SS/X car pictured in the last chapter at 2,680 pounds (20 pounds under NHRA-legal Pro Stock weight), Sox also clocked an incredible 9.54 using the just-released Holley 4500-series Dominator carburetors on a new inline intake manifold.

Al Adam, the engineer who wrote up this test, thought that going with a 3- or even 4-speed clutch-type automatic may help make up for the variance seen in the action. So, here was where Mr. Hoover and company began to really turn their attention in the opening days of Pro Stock racing.

"The company thought they could help them out with an automatic, a clutch-type automatic," Spehar recalled during a reunion seminar in 2012. "So, the major reason that the Challenger existed was first to be

Here is the Missile *going together in early 1970. Mike Koran sits behind the cowl, Dick Oldfield is figuring out the new rules, and Ted Spehar is thinking about that Hemi. (Photo Courtesy Tom Hoover Family)*

a development car, and then somehow it turned into a race car. But, it's job was to be a development car for the Chrysler race group."

This whole thing was actually much more "brave new world" than it is often credited for. The Challenger used for the *Missile* program was initially among the earliest of the body-in-white shells that Chrysler authorized for the new class. The same company that had done the 1965's notorious altered wheelbase cars, Aero-chem, now took 1970-model shells shipped from the plant (likely Los Angeles, which did some E-Body construction) and dropped them into the acid-dipping tank normally used for airplane components. These bodies were stored in a nearby California warehouse for distribution to Chrysler-authorized racers. It reportedly included Challengers, Dusters, Barracudas, and Dart Swingers in 1970 with the Demon design coming in for 1971 to replace the Swinger. Incidentally, most of the Swingers were component separated with pieces reworked onto existing 1968 Hurst Dart chassis.

Though the Challenger was the latest new release from the company, it was not chosen for the *Missile* because Spehar made that choice. The factory selected the brand and body, and Dodge and Plymouth both were used for *Missile* vehicles during the coming years. Ted recalled how that first car went together.

"They sent us a body in white, and Warren Tiehart, who was doing all the parts for the factory cars, was to get all the parts for us," he said. "We probably started in January and finished it in May. That word 'stock' was really still part of Pro Stock at that point, meaning they needed to be VIN tagged. The factory simply sent over a 1970 Hemi Challenger to us, and we stripped that car of whatever parts we wanted on the Pro Stock. I took the Hemi out of that car and put it in a box; today, that motor is installed in my 1964 street car. Once we took the dash out of the donor car, that put a VIN number on the body in white. I think the shell went to Vanke, but it was just a carcass."

The rules were fairly simple, and one thing that the group wanted to make sure of was that the car was legal. Though the NHRA made a lame effort at disallowing acid dipping, it was impossible to detect it thoroughly, and the truth was that every serious team (regardless of manufacturer) was playing with the process. The real issue for most teams was getting the weight moved to either the center or the back, where it could play the best role in traction and off-the-line launch transfer. It was to Chrysler's credit that the OEM-style leaf-spring rear suspension design was capable of withstanding the ever-increasing amount of power that Pro Stock engines generated.

Racing development coordinator Tom Hoover concured. "The first E-Body car was a Super Stocker suspension, basically," he noted at the 2012 meeting. "To my recollection, it went through its whole two years of service, the fundamental thrust of which was to do a clutch-operated automatic just standard. So, it's amazing how well that initial set of biased rear springs and shock absorbers could do the job of launching the car straight without excessive spin on the right rear wheel—and keep it straight, through the successive shifts and so forth, even up to exaggerated power at the weight levels, compared to what it was intended for in the beginning.

"In fact, that basic suspension even survived up through all the stock-bodied Ramcharger Funny Cars. This was at 1,300 hp on nitromethane! So that's my little thrust in favor of keeping in mind how good that [factory] rear suspension is, [even] fundamentally unaltered!"

The front suspension on the first *Missile* also retained the torsion-bar design. In fact, it was critical that the car remained as close to what others were racing so that the development work was applicable across the board. There were no precedents for what they were doing, so they stuck with tried-and-true Super Stock conversion plans, removing weight as much as possible and gathering up the special parts that Mr. Hoover desired to try out.

Another view of the 1970 car is shown a little later in the process. Even now, Dick (seen behind) was figuring out ways to make things lighter. (Photo Courtesy Tom Hoover Family)

The reworked floor in the first car shows the extensive changes to the floor pan. The 3-speed ClutchFlite was used at first, but the floor was already modified to use the 6-speed once development got further along. (Photo Courtesy Tom Hoover Family)

Front and foremost was the ClutchFlite, a package that was developed first by B&M for the so-called gassers, which were usually supercharged modified production bodies running on gasoline. For Pro Stock's narrower engine band from the start, a simple 3-speed model would probably not work.

"In 1969, [the] NHRA let it be known that there would be a Pro Stock class for the 1970 season," Hoover noted in response to a question I asked at the 2012 event. "[Product Planning manager] Dick Maxwell looked at me, and I looked at Maxwell, and we said, 'We're in big trouble!' The reason, we thought, was that over the whole progression (1962 to 1968), we had one 4-speed manual team: Sox & Martin. The rest of our well-known racers grew up on automatics with 7-inch tires. You can't take those guys and put them into a 140-mph 4-speed manual car with tires like that. So, we knew we had to do something. That's when we contracted Ted [for the Pro Stock project]. That was the purpose of the whole *Missile* program in the beginning: What are we going to give these guys who had been raised on automatics and 7-inch tires to be competitive with the Fords and Chevys with 4-speed manuals?"

The competition had good stick drivers, the best at the time being Jenkins, Dave Strickler, and a handful of others for Chevrolet, and "Dyno Don" Nicholson led an equally small contingent of Ford racers. Sox & Martin, for their part, hired noted southeastern racer Herb McCandless as a second team driver by the time the *Missile* was actually done. McCandless's nickname was "Mr. 4-Speed" because of his prowess on the shifter. Dodge's main man was Dick Landy, who won races but was not noted like Sox for clutch-shift coordination; frankly, no other driver was known to be as accomplished as Sox, whose lengthy win record showed. To that end, the choice for the Dodge as the initial *Missile* might have been in hopes of getting "Dandy" Dick to use the automatic. The bottom line was that Chrysler had every intention of continuing to win in 1970 in Pro Stock as it had done in Super Stock most of the prior decade.

Pro Stock Racing Through May 1970

The first race of the 1970 NHRA season was the Winternationals in Pomona, California. Testing, as noted, happened in Florida in December, and a second session was completed at Irwindale during the week leading up to the race. Meanwhile, the AHRA decided to open its 1970 season at Beeline Dragway near Phoenix the weekend before. By this time, the Sox & Martin team had its new 1970 Hemi 'Cuda up and running, and although the team was not among the booked-in racers at the AHRA event, Sox qualified well and took home the AHRA win.

Bill Jenkins and his long-running 1968 Camaro, however, proved to be more formidable for the next month; he consecutively won the NHRA Winternationals, an all-open Pro Stock match race at Orange County International Raceway (OCIR) a week later, and the new

Don Carlton drove for Sox & Martin in the early 1970 events and is seen here at the wheel of the 1969 Barracuda that had originally been used in AHRA S/S-E and NHRA Modified Production. In this photo, it is in NHRA Pro Stock and AHRA Super Stock–legal trim. (Photo Courtesy Steve Reyes)

NHRA Gatornationals in Gainesville, Florida, beating Sox at both NHRA events and Nicholson for OCIR's title.

However, as testing continued, that success ebbed. Jake King, the engine builder at S&M, worked tirelessly to figure out what it would take to go ever quicker. Indeed, Sox's loss to Jenkins at the Gators had been on a hole-shot: 9.90 to a quicker 9.86. When the AHRA held the third of its 1970 Grand American races at Rockingham, North Carolina, in mid-April, Sox tromped Grotheer, Jenkins, and finally Nicholson to win that title. He followed that effort by winning an enduro-style multiday eliminator at the *Super Stock* magazine event in York, Pennsylvania, then won the AHRA's big Spring Nationals in Bristol, Tennessee, and the NHRA Springnationals title in Dallas, Texas, a weekend later. All proved that Mr. Hoover and Mr. Maxwell had been correct; everyone else was in big trouble.

It should be noted that Don Carlton was working for the Sox & Martin team during this half of the year. He had driven the 1969 Barracuda early on at the big winter races out West, as well as the first of the new S&M Plymouth Dusters, which made its debut at Rockingham. However, as he would take on some outside responsibilities late in the spring, Herb McCandless was hired to be the full-time team driver by Buddy Martin.

On and Off the Drawing Board

While all of this was going on, Ted, Lenny, Mike, and Dick were busy getting the *Missile* ready for its dual role of racing development and transmission testing. All having prior experience in building competitive Chrysler Super Stockers, the trio was in its element, and now it was possible to work careful interpretation of what the rules allowed. A humorous image shows Ted, Dick, and Mike working on the base shell of the 1970 model as the car went together, rule book and level in hand.

As noted, the Street Hemi car's pieces were adopted to the body in white as needed. The team used the production variance in wheelbase that had been part of factory-backed racing since the Ramchargers' early days. In appearance, the car's OEM sport hood configuration changed first to the Six Pack version from 1969, and then to a ramp-front hood scoop design that had recently been evaluated by Chrysler fuel systems specialist John Bauman. Also on the new car, safety equipment consisted of a roll bar, driveshaft loop, and (perhaps most importantly) a shield to be used in the event of a transmission explosion. Aerodynamic testing performed with Arlen Vanke on an earlier project showed that a 3-percent overall body rake was the best position for airflow over the car, and that amount was also adopted to this project.

In conclusion, once the *Missile* team finished the car, it was a pretty straightforward package. The biggest change from every other entry, of course, was the transmission. B&M, a long-noted West Coast automatic transmission specialty firm, supplied the first of the TorqueFlite-based ClutchFlites for the car. B&M adapted a special clutch assembly in place of the torque converter.

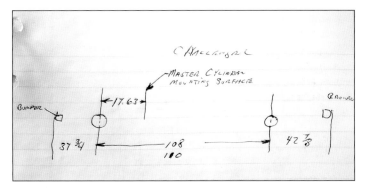

This drawing in Dick Oldfield's extensive notebook shows the measuring points that the NHRA used to determine the legality of the wheelbase and engine placement. Tom Hoover humorously recalled that they sent the car to its first NHRA tech inspection with Dick by himself. The biggest change from stock was the maximum allowable production variation of the wheelbase from 110 inches to 108 inches, while the amount of front and rear overhang was substantial. (Photo Courtesy Dick Oldfield Archive)

This image was likely from an early test in Detroit before the car was taken to Tri-Cities Dragway in Saginaw. The car had a cross-ram intake and a standard TorqueFlite at this time. (Photo Courtesy Dick Oldfield Archive)

However, Ted Spehar recalled there were even some converter tests made in the earliest rendering of the *Missile*.

"Right after the car was done, Oldfield and I took it up to Tri-City Dragway on a Sunday," he noted. "It was still all black then with a cross-ram intake and a Six Pack hood scoop. At the time, the factory was testing with all of these little torque converters from Cortinas and cars like that. Because the plan already called for us to run the ClutchFlite, which wasn't ready yet, we put an automatic in it and threw a couple of extra converters into it so we could at least evaluate them."

Spehar continued, "They were running a UDRA [United Drag Racing Association] match race that day,

which we did not know about. We had figured that nobody would be there. Well, those guys were running 10.40s and we were running 10.20s right off the trailer. The next day, [Chrysler racer and then-current UDRA champion] Larry Griffith, who I did not personally know yet and who was part of that series, phoned Dick Maxwell and said, 'Man, we were running yesterday and a couple of guys were there with a black Challenger and an automatic and they were running faster than us!' Maxwell just laughed; he knew what was going on."

Ted noted it was this sort of performance that led to the idea the *Missile* would be raced in the real world, not just a testbed. "We went out there and saw it was quicker not only than the competition, it was quicker than the other Chryslers too," he said. "That was when it went from being just this test car to becoming a race car. It would give the company one more chance to win events."

Beginning in black, the *Motown Missile* was painted into its first scheme by Shadowoods Auto Service, a well-known shop in the Detroit area, and lettered by Jim Stadinski of Indiana. The paint scheme consisted of black and orange colors with reflective lettering in Mylar with the major sponsor noted as Fernwood Dodge on the rear quarter panels. Chrysler performed the initial renderings for the paint, using a custom font across the sides for the "*Motown Missile*" title that Vanke recently christened.

Once it was realized that the car was used in actual races, a few product decals on the lower rocker areas that could pay possible contingency money were added in the event that the car went to the final round at an NHRA event. The now-colorful *Missile* made its formal NHRA debut at a Division 3 points race at Indianapolis Raceway Park in early July following some more testing and a fresh motor from Ted's engine stand.

Ted's meticulous records have survived, and here are his details on that engine: "Engine number 24 was used the first time in competition at the Indy points meet July 1970, where it set an NHRA ET and speed record 9.94 at 138.47. This was a 1965 Hemi block, lightened, 426-ci +0.030 overbore, Chrysler Grand National crankshaft, Chrysler Grand National Rods (7.06 inches center-to-center) with 1/2-inch bolts, TRW pistons with 1.09 pins. The Chrysler aluminum heads ported at Mullen & Co. used standard Chrysler Hemi rockers. A fabricated steel independent runner (IR) intake manifold with two Holley 4500 carbs, the Isky 0.590 flat-tappet cam and 0.030 oversize lifters, Chrysler electronic ignition with 8 plugs, a fabricated steel oil pan, made deeper and wider with a

Fresh out of the paint shop at Shadowoods Automotive operated by Tom and Jim Tignanelli, the first Missile was lettered by a well-known Indiana man named Jim Stadinski, who would letter up each Missile during Ted's ownership. (Photo Courtesy Ted Spehar Archive)

This photo shows the rear quarter/trunk. Another shot from the front shows the hood pins and standard Mopar Six Pack scoop that John Bauman designed in 1969. It would very shortly give way to a new narrow-open version with a ramp toward the entrance. (Photo Courtesy Ted Spehar Archive)

swinging pickup, and the Chrysler Hemi hi-volume oil pump. With a final 12.8:1 compression ratio, this engine was not very flashy, mostly all Chrysler components, such as rings, bearings, gaskets, timing chain, valve springs, etc., Smith Brothers pushrods." He added, "The first two drag test engines were similar—just with a different manifold and cam."

Dick recorded several problems with the normally brutal Dana 60 SureGrip rear, especially the ring or pinion cracking under stress. The solution was using very tight tolerances on the 5.13 gearset in 1970 and then getting more durable pieces that became available in 1971. (Photo Courtesy Tom Hoover Family)

A final touch was the driver's name above the door. As Oldfield was the pilot, the team harkened back to a half-century earlier by putting the name of the famous barnstorming, fairgrounds-charging, cigar-chomping Barney Oldfield over the driver's side of the roof. Interestingly, the original Mr. Oldfield, no relation, was a spokesperson for Chrysler in the 1930s. It was something that certainly gave Tom Hoover, who was an ardent student of history in general, a reason to smile.

Of course, even if Ted had a factory deal with the project, it did not mean deluxe accommodations all the way. Indeed, the budget was spread across all the projects Chrysler gave to Performance Automotive, and the use of those dollars did not mean steak and caviar meals.

"In the early days with the first car, I think we flat towed with a station wagon and an open trailer," Ted later remembered. "Then, I finally got some sponsorship money and I was able to buy a van-type truck. That's pretty much what we did. We didn't have tractor-trailers like they have nowadays. We were still on a budget, believe me! And a very small budget."

Tom Hoover added, "Oldfield showed up with a huge aircraft carrier–sized Dodge station wagon. It was known as the *Queen Mary*."

First to the IR

"After we did the deal at Tri-City, we put the first ClutchFlite in and also an IR [independent runner] intake," said Ted. "That was on and off the car several times until we went to the plenum intake. If it has a high hood scoop on it, the plenum was on it. Meanwhile, the problem with the original IR is that it would go about 30 feet and run out of fuel; the plenum model made it much more driveable. John Bauman struggled with that for a while but finally sorted it out."

Intake development was an ongoing point of concern for all of Pro Stock in that early time. As noted, the NHRA had allowed the 7-inch height in part because Bill Jenkins already adopted a tall tunnel-ram design with a large plenum (the open area between the bottom of the carburetors and the beginning of the intake manifold runners to the cylinder heads and valves) to his Chevrolet big-block canted-valve engines. Chrysler's Edelbrock-cast "rat roaster" design was somewhat similar but in flattened format. A major theory at that moment was the independent runner design. This basically required a single barrel of a 4-barrel carb to function from the demands of one cylinder of the engine. During the 2012 discussion, Mr. Hoover recalled there was a well-known non-Chrysler Detroit engineer who received credit for this.

"Holley [Carburetors] had done a lot of work on that [idea], and they had brought into their team Zora Arkus-Duntov, a world-famous European guy!" he said.

Of course, the Belgian-born Duntov's development work for Chevrolet on the Corvette is very well-known.

"But Zora had a sports car background," Hoover said. "Cars had to go around corners; they had to stop. Who cares! [laughs] You know?"

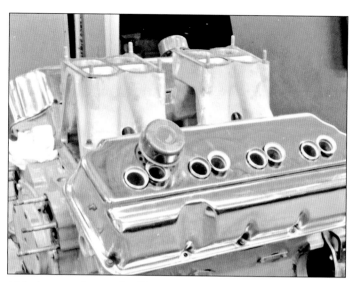

This image shows the IR-type intake, to which a plate supporting two Holley 4500 Dominators would have been mounted, allowing each cylinder to be fed by a single barrel of the carburetor. (Photo Courtesy Tom Hoover Family)

The statement was somewhat in jest, as Mr. Hoover had real respect for the well-known GM engineer.

"I'd say his two fundamental contributions to thinking at that time were: number one, you had to have a valve gear that would run at very high speeds because if you were running a sports car and you'd be heel and toeing it, you'd overspeed the engine," Hoover said. "So, the famous Duntov cam for the small-block Chevy followed up. Zora was also in favor of the Weber carburetor approach, essentially of a single carburetor for each cylinder.

"So Holley then put some time and effort into developing a so-called (as Ted suggests) IR approach, or individual runner. The Japanese motorcycles all had one carburetor; that's the same kind of thinking."

The work on the IR continued from Holley's initial design to the dyno rooms in Highland Park.

"Another reason for the *Missile* program was that late in the 60s [the] engineering division was kept busy by the Federal Emission Compliance Regulations, which was an enormous amount of work," Hoover noted in 2014. "So, the pressure was on in terms of the division's time available to do things. Believe me, the Grand Nationals got the bulk of engineering time available for racing. So, we got squeezed in a corner and almost out the door, and we had to go outside for that component."

"But the IR manifold program was successful, partly owing to the fact that John Wehrly, the engineer in charge of development, snuck us in, so to speak," Ted said. "He facilitated development and refinement of the IR manifold on a NASCAR engine, so it was ready to try on the drag cars. It was an improvement over the A990 setup that was the basic initial cross-ram with two little Holly 4-barrels."

The result on the track was mentioned earlier in this chapter: Sox's huge 4500-series Holley Dominator setup ran a 9.54 in early testing. Reportedly developed for Ford's new Boss 429 NASCAR engine, this carb was never intended for a street application, and since Pro Stock allowed for two 4-barrels, why not double a pair of them up?

"It is a different 4500 that's required to do that [use in the drag racing environment]," noted Hoover. "Those carburetors were always really rich in the mid-speed range because the pulsing would cause the air to pass the boosters more than once."

This was something Mr. Hoover was intimately aware of because runner length and pulse from the intake events had been so crucial to the benefit of Chrysler's ram-tuning principles in the prior decade. Essentially, although the engine had access to more fuel with the 4500 design, on the IR manifold, the air confusion at the booster area was a major issue. This happened primarily because there was no plenum area to clean up that demand between cylinder events, and during the constantly changing fuel demand transitions that a drag racing motor goes through, the result was inefficiencies. Nonetheless, it would still take much testing throughout the entire 1970 season with the assistance of John Bauman and his boss Tom Coddington to realize this was a non-reconcilable issue in terms of engine performance.

"The way to notice the [IR version] on a Holley 4500 is that the boosters stick up about an inch and a half above the plane of the air cleaner gasket," Hoover concluded. "You look at any of the plenum manifolds, and they don't look anything like that."

Then a Clutch Play

Of course, the biggest thing about the *Missile* program overall was that it would remain the single automatic transmission entry competing in the Pro Stock class.

"The idea there was to get our big-name people who had been born and raised on 3-speed TorqueFlite automatics and 7-inch tires interested," Tom Hoover noted. "But in the long run, maybe we gave them too much time.

"Certainly, the *Missile* ran well. But we were a little disappointed because as Pro Stock got running, the guys didn't accept the ClutchFlite. Everybody's got an ego; their attitude was something like 'If Ronnie Sox can do it with 4-speed, so can I.' Well, some of the guys could do it: Don Carlton, Herb McCandless, maybe Butch Leal. But the rest of them, including some big names, really didn't get it. They'd just look bad."

So beyond using the *Missile* to make the ClutchFlite into something that worked in Pro Stock, the hope was that this in turn would become something other Chrysler racers might be willing to adopt. Hoover noted wryly that Dodge driver Dick Landy was a real concern, simply because he had not been known as a big 4-speed driver in events past, and Hoover personally felt that Mr. Landy often declutched the engine longer than needed. Dick and his crew in California experimented more than other factory-associated teams, modifying parts that Chrysler already modified scientifically.

So, because Dodge had so much riding on Dick Landy's visibility, this concern was real but may have been biased. Based on the struggles that Landy was challenged with during the 1965 program, he had become one of the only manual-transmission Chrysler drivers to switch back to the TorqueFlite. However, by 1970, his Pro Stock wins at places such as Bakersfield, the Modified victory at the 1970 NHRA Winternationals, and a close runner-up finish to Sox at the aforementioned AHRA Spring Nationals in Bristol showed that he was just as at home with a clutch pedal as anyone else. Sox was better, but Sox was probably better than just about everybody.

The real benefit of the ClutchFlite was gear shifts without declutching during a run (it was used only to launch the car), but this was still an OEM 3-speed configuration. There is always an inherent advantage of keeping an engine as close as possible to its optimum RPM level, and an additional gear was hard to overcome. The reality was that guys such as Tom Hoover were already thinking ahead not only to have a clutch to allow instant launch control but also to have additional gears within the confines of a fluid-driven automatic transmission. Meanwhile, the *Missile* (in its IR-intake/3-speed automatic configuration) needed some track time, first for testing, then for its first NHRA appearance.

"I can't remember, but Oldfield and I, and somebody—Leonard Bartush maybe—we took the car to Indianapolis to a points meet," Hoover said.

The Queen Mary was the first tow vehicle, seen here in front of the Motown Missile at the NHRA Summernationals at York US Dragway in July 1970. Dick looks on while one of B&M's technicians, likely Don Spar, takes a look at what's going on underneath it all. (Photo Courtesy Ted Spehar Archive)

Tom Hoover was known as the godfather of the 426 Hemi engine, and the *Motown Missile* was truly his baby. Unhindered by the sort of rules that frustrated his engineering prowess in the factory-stock class divisions, he was free to play with new ideas on the *Missile*. While Ted Spehar was technically the owner of the car, Mr. Hoover always dictated the specifics on how it was raced.

As both a hired gun and wrench, Dick Oldfield remembered his role in this process as well.

"My job was working on everything from the flywheel back, and the first car was fairly easy to work on," Oldfield said. "The ClutchFlite had a terrible low gear: 2.45; you had to really launch at a high RPM. Sometimes it would take off and sometimes it would just spin the tires. The most common thing that broke was the overriding clutch; it was always a problem with that thing."

Therefore, Dick then had the wonderful job of figuring out what might have broken, having a front row seat to whatever was going to happen behind the power in the engine Ted Spehar had built.

"With the ClutchFlite, I had to service it," Oldfield recalled in 2018. "Since I was in the car, I knew what was happening or going to happen. There were problems with both the transmission and the clutch."

Still, that did not mean it was always a failure.

"The 3-speed ClutchFlite—we had the thing working pretty well," Hoover fondly recalled about its first NHRA appearance. "Dick was familiar with it. We set the first

new national [ET] record that weekend! It wasn't by a little bit either; it was by a real mouthful."

Into the Record Books and First Time Out

At a time when the NHRA's professional records were set only at these regional points races, for a fresh car to go out and set a record was a big deal. This was recorded as a 9.94 (for the record) at 138.47 mph, which was not enough to top the then-current 139.10 mph held by Dodge driver Bill Bagshaw. Although some racers had been even faster at some of the larger national events, the *Missile* did this with an automatic transmission, which was huge news at the time. Garnering Low ET, Top Speed, and Top Qualifier honors, the media and the competition both took notice of this on the weekend after the Fourth of July holiday of 1970.

"The first time we raced the car, we set the record," Ted noted in 2012. "And this is better than the manual-shift cars, which are supposed to be the dominant cars. But as racers figured out the manual-shift thing too, the manuals started to excel. For the ClutchFlite to be competitive, it had to be at the top of its game every time it went out."

That itself was a problem that first weekend.

"We didn't get to race!" Hoover exclaimed. "Something happened to the starter. The ClutchFlite being fundamentally an A727 automatic, it had no rear pump in

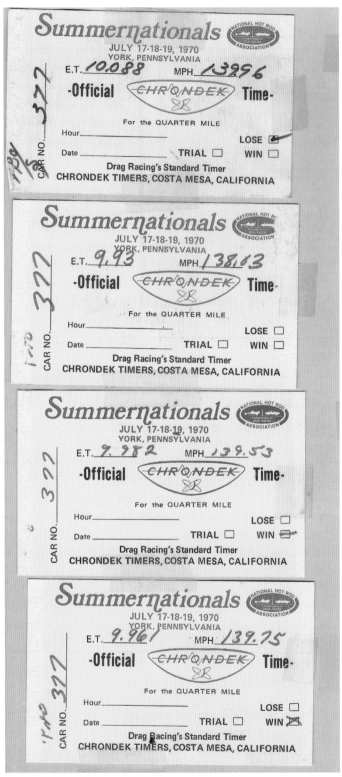

Time slips from York show the 9.93 best that topped qualifying, the two 9-second runs on Sunday, and the 10.08 that allowed Dick Landy to advance and win his only NHRA national event in Pro Stock. (Photo Courtesy Ted Spehar Archive)

it. That means you can't push it, drop the clutch, and get the engine started. The starter's got to work! We set the record, but we didn't get to race that day because the starter didn't work, and we couldn't fix it in the time that was available."

Ted recalled that at that early point, the team probably did not have a spare starter on hand with the minimal parts they had brought with them in the *Queen Mary* wagon.

However, it was fixed in the next few days because the car made its first NHRA national event appearance the following weekend at the first-ever NHRA Summernationals July 17–19 at York US30 Dragway in central Pennsylvania. York was actually an airport that hosted racing events on the weekends and had been the site of very significant drag events in prior years. A good number of racers were there only weeks earlier for the race hosted by *Super Stock* magazine that Sox won. Now, over 60 Pro Stocks from around the nation converged on the track in addition to a huge field of other Pro and Sportsman entries. Indeed, the facility was quite overwhelmed by the volume, leading the NHRA to never again attempt to host this event at York US30 Dragway.

Being mid-July, the peak of the eastern seaboard's summertime, this was the opportunity that Mr. Hoover hoped would show his troops that the ClutchFlite could be competitive. For his part, Dick "Barney" Oldfield did not disappoint. When qualifying concluded for the 16-car program, Ronnie Sox had been 1 of 2 drivers to break into the 9-second zone with a 9.99. Oldfield was leading the whole pack and going faster than his new record to a 9.93 at 139.96 during an evening session that stood as both Low ET and Top Speed of the entire event.

On Sunday, the car began to show that it was possible to go rounds as well. To open things up, Dick beat fellow Michigan driver Mike Fons, and Dick became the only driver to go back into the 9s when he took down Arlen Vanke in round 2 with a 9.98. Against Dick Landy in the semifinals, the car fell off to a 10.08 time with a huge 139.96-mph top speed, allowing Landy's solid 10.01 to advance to the finals. There, Dandy Dick shifted to victory and beat Sox & Martin driver Herb McCandless in the S&M Duster (who lit an uncharacteristic red light) to score his only NHRA Pro Stock win.

Despite the early exit for Barney, the result was a bit of solid advertising on the car from B&M and other manufacturers and left both Spehar and Hoover with grins. However, the reality with the ClutchFlite was that

Back at Detroit for an evening race, Ted watches carefully as the car leaves the starting line. The ideas for testing were being proven in the real world as well, and the car was a winner at enough points events that it finished second in NHRA Division 3, right behind "Akron Arlen" Vanke. (Photo Courtesy Ted Spehar Archive)

it would require maintenance on a regular basis. Dick found that his front-row seat to the carnage was not always pleasant, especially as the experimentation continued during test days in the summer and fall.

"When it blew up, it tore up everything," Dick said. "I got to the point where I was moving closer to the door as I went downtrack if I thought it might be going. "Usually, it was inside the case, but sometimes it was parts and fire. You have to consider that, in testing, I had to make it to the end to get a recording. You didn't lift. It would get in its own oil; I spun it around once during a test at Milan.

"I remember one run where I had someone in the car with me. It was Tom Coddington, 'The Ghost.' He wanted to see how the transmission worked. Well, it started coming apart. I know I didn't even have the car stopped yet, but he jumped out and ran away! [laughs]"

Ted also remembers those days.

"It took us months to get the ClutchFlite going," he said. "I remember seeing all the gasser guys like K. S. Pittman with three or four transmissions on their trailer and thinking, 'Man, these guys are really bucks-up!' Little did we know that you had to have that many to get through the day.

"We would only get two runs out of it. When it went away, it ruined everything. Once you fixed one part, you immediately found the next weakest link. If it wasn't the transmission, it was the clutch. Other people had been

running it, but we really wanted it to last and be durable. In the end, we got to the point where it ran 30 passes.

"I got sick of ATF," Ted continued. "We always had the pan off of it. It had to be serviced, and if we qualified one day with it, we would put in another for the next day. Then we went from the 3-speed to the 6-speed, which was a huge amount of development time. B&M did them initially, then Dick [Oldfield] learned it and he did it. He and Mike [Koran] took that on themselves so we were not sending them across the country all the time."

Three to Six–The Big 'Flite

Tom Hoover knew that part of the issue was keeping the car within its optimum power band. To that end, he and B&M went to work on creating a single transmission that used a pair of TorqueFlites. This project was already underway when the first *Missile* was put together in the spring of 1970; the installation required major surgery to the floorpan for the 6-speed model to fit.

"[The standard ClutchFlite] was followed up by a big contraption that Oldfield is very familiar with, generated with the support of B&M on the West Coast," Hoover recalled. "It was just half of a 727 transmission tacked onto the back of a standard 727, so it really had six ratios forward. It had two shifters. It was up to Dick to figure out which one needed to be pulled at the right time!

The 6-speed B&M transmission was basically a standard A727 TorqueFlite transmission with a 2-speed version bolted behind it. The hope was that the use of additional gears would help keep the engine in its optimal power band, but the cost was both added weight and greater reciprocating inertia inside the cases. (Photo Courtesy Tom Hoover Family)

The shifters in the car were parallel and required skill to master. Even Mr. Hoover was still giving Dick credit for his effort in 2014 in knowing which one to grab when. The transmission used the manual valve body design Chrysler developed in the Super Stock days, so it required active gear changes. (Photo Courtesy Tom Hoover Family)

This is another view of the driveline outside of the car. Note the use of a Lakewood bellhousing for safety. The external lines between the oil pump and pan sump are for the swinging pickup, which was innovated due to wheelstands that could leave the fixed version of the pickup starved for oil. (Photo Courtesy Tom Hoover Family)

The prototype 6-speed was already being considered when the Missile was coming together in the spring of 1970. Though it never found a home in drag racing, it turned out to be an excellent choice for school buses! (Photo Courtesy Tom Hoover Family)

"The whole first year, the major thrust of the 1970 Missile car was to come up with something that the 7-inch tire, automatic-transmission driver could be competitive with against 4-speed manuals in the new Pro Stock. It's that simple. It evolved later into this multispeed, which was not really successful. It functioned fine. But, number one, it made the car heavier; number two, it vastly increased the rotating inertia of everything. Although, we could have (we think) gained some performance for having more ratios available and more abrupt shifts and so forth, the overall bottom line is [that] it wasn't really an improvement over the regular 3-speed ClutchFlite."

With two pans, two shifters, and whatever had happened inside, there was nothing easy about the 6-speed.

In the January 1971 issue of *Hot Rod* magazine, a lengthy article on the B&M multispeed 6-speed product was written up. In that latest version, however, the transmission's factory-style tailshaft housing was basically converted to an overdrive/underdrive unit.

Feel the Light

So, even before the 6-speed was in, the added weight of anything on the stock 3,800-pound car was already part of what Ted was dealing with, and he began to really expand on the ideas of lighter components even as the first car went together. This related to a number of areas; one was the engine itself.

"You know, we've got aluminum blocks now. Back then, we had the *wonder metal*: cast iron!" Ted said. "And Chrysler blocks, because they were deep skirted, were notoriously heavy. So, we got into lightening the blocks and we were probably taking over 25 pounds out of the block. Which was a lot of material. But it's risk versus reward when you do things like that because you make them thin and you lose rigidity, which is not what you want to do if you are trying to keep the bores straight at wide-open throttle. We found ways to get around that. It's just an ongoing development thing. It's not something that you just do once and say 'Oh, it worked, we'll go on.' It's not that easy."

Mike Koran also remembered the adventures of their early days. Though only in his early 20s, Koran had a good sense of management, and Ted was giving him those types of responsibilities, but he was still hands-on with the tools and parts.

"I remember Len and I were supposed to acid dip a bellhousing," Koran recalled during the 2014 roundtable discussion. "We didn't know anything about nitric acid and what the ratio of acid to water should be. So, we buy a plastic garbage can, fill it with dilute nitric acid, and lower in the Lakewood bellhousing. The next thing you know, the plastic garbage can heats up and starts to melt, and the bottom opens up. Dilute nitric acid is going all over the place, and there's not a whole lot of bellhousing left! We learned such things as we went along."

Dick Oldfield was also involved in this.

"To lighten things up, we were acid dipping stuff. I remember we would pull the wires up out of the acid sometimes and there would be nothing left on it. Then you had to start over.

"I learned fabrication on the job," Oldfield continued.

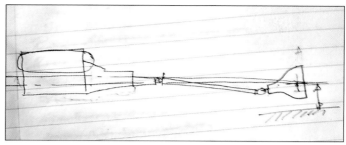

This quick drawing by Dick Oldfield shows the critical nature of the pinion angle. Ted recalled that this situation was almost as frustrating as the ClutchFlite maintenance, and the ring and pinion required very regular examination by either Dick or Mike Koran. (Photo Courtesy Dick Oldfield Archive)

"I knew how to use tools, but I had to figure out how to make pieces for all the cars I worked on during that time. Once we started getting the titanium, I loved it."

Oldfield's college background came in handy here as well. He began taking careful measurements and weights on every individual component to determine (down to the ounce) what had been done in the acid tank, with a die grinder, or being made of the expensive titanium. These amounts he kept in a handwritten notebook with each part identified once it had been completed. This data could then be aggregated into a total, and if weight needed to be put back in, he or someone could figure out where its return might work best and how much could be used.

An area that proved to be an issue was something that Chrysler muscle car buyers swore by: the 9.75-inch Dana 60 SureGrip rear end. In Dick's notes are a string of reports on the ring and/or pinion cracking after only a handful of runs in 1970. The resolution was to optimize the clearances for both endplay and contact as the testing continued and use stronger hardened equipment from Spicer when the 5.38 ratios replaced the 5.13 versions in early 1971.

The titanium was its own thing, and Ted remembered that its use came about in a unique way.

"This car needed to represent the professional testing program; it would be as good as any of the cars the [professional] teams built," he said. "Moreover, it gave us the data on how to build the car. I had never built a car like that before. Earlier, I built the Super Stocks with standard stuff—a few lightweight tricks on the front end but nothing more. This was like building an A/Gasser or something. It was at this time that I met the guys from Apollo Welding, who were just a couple of doors down from us. They were certified welders and they put the roll cage in for us. Regis Gulley, who owned the company, was doing a lot of military work for the government and Dow Chemical. So he started telling us about this miracle metal, titanium. I thought, 'Wow, this stuff is really cool,' and we started to make a lot of parts out of it.

"A lot of stuff that was not titanium we made out of aluminum," Ted continued. "Things like the front strut bushings, which were steel, we did in aluminum; you are not driving the car down the freeway. The strut bars were hollow; the drag link was hollow. We modified that ourselves. When we made the original wet sump pan, we dropped the drag link under it. Then, [engineer Tom] Coddington redid that once we knew the car would have a low attitude. Then we went through a bunch of adjustments to change the caster as the car's nose rose up, bending bars. I remember we spent days with Al Adam at the shop jacking the car up and down trying to figure out what was going on. Then, they did the spindles and the parts, and the whole thing was aligned at a front-end shop located behind the Woodward Garage that was used by a lot of the Detroit-area racers. Remember, we needed to do something that could be put down in writing that we could send out to Sox & Martin, Landy, and those guys about what we had figured out."

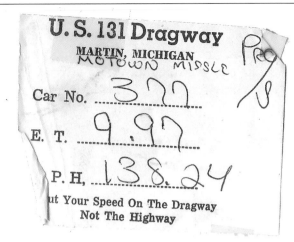

With this time of 9.97, Dick was again at the top of the charts when many of the nation's best racers showed up at US 131 Dragway in Martin, Michigan, for the Popular Hot Rodding *magazine meet that doubled as an NHRA points race. (Photo Courtesy Ted Spehar Archive)*

Success at First, But the Show Goes On

In a letter to B&M on August 18, Tom Hoover proudly recorded the accomplishments of the team those first weeks of summer. Ted noted the car was out for testing every week, using the typical methodologies that helped keep Chrysler up in front during the Super Stock era.

Here is the Missile at Martin, going forward on Sunday before falling to Mike Fons in the final round. This was a big deal, as it was one of the nearest races to all of the Detroit manufacturers. (Photo Courtesy quartermilestones .com, Pit Slides Archive)

"That first year, we only ran about five big events with the *Missile*," Ted said. "We were testing two days a week, and we were testing some of the other stuff on other cars as well. I was at the tests because I was doing the cams. Everyone from the shop would be there, and then Lenny would work late getting stuff ready."

Ted developed ways to make things, such as cam swaps, easier. There were also related measurements being taken, one being via the weather station factors developed by Chrysler engineer George Wallace, who was associated with the NASCAR program. A chart allowed the tests to be standardized by using a careful calculation from a baseline of barometric and atmospheric readings. By doing this, testing could eliminate variables from changes in the weather during the course of a day or week. (We'll look more extensively into this aspect of the *Missile's* program in the next chapter.)

The other dates mentioned in Mr. Hoover's list were two NHRA points races the team had won: one at Donnybrooke, Minnesota, and the other a national open in Windsor, Ontario, as well as its performance at the *Popular Hot Rodding* magazine race at Martin 131 in Martin, Michigan. There, like at the two other NHRA events, Dick set both Low ET and Top Speed and was first in qualifying.

In front of the big crowd of both Detroit-area fans and factory reps, the *Missile* began its march to the front, downing Larry Griffith in round two and getting around Dandy Dick Landy to head to the final. There, the *Missile* was up against the Chevrolet of Mike Fons, a local independent driver who was very talented. Everybody loves a Chevy-versus-Mopar final, and at the green, Fons pulled a classic gate job to run a fast 10.16. In the other lane, the original Barney Oldfield would have swallowed his cigar because Dick Oldfield ran a 10.08 but could not make up the difference lost at the starting line.

It was a bitter moment but was the reality of racing; Oldfield had seen both Landy and upstart Bobby Yowell in a new S&M-built Duster redlight in the semifinals earlier and did not want to lose the race at the start. Fons, as the underdog who was racing the top qualified car and favored-to-win package, had nothing to lose and made the most of it.

Then came the biggest event of the season: the NHRA Nationals in Indianapolis over Labor Day. This event featured perhaps the largest field of Pro Stocks that the NHRA would ever assemble: 90 cars from around North America showing up for an expanded 32-car program.

The decal was a big deal because Indy was a big deal.

This is a rare picture of Tom "The Ghost" Coddington. He was named this because he was often quietly involved in various projects. An engineer from the Ramchargers club, Coddington's specialty was fuel systems, and he and associate John Bauman were regularly involved in projects in that regard. That is Ted sitting on the hitch of the Queen Mary, *and this is the typical thrash by every race team in a hotel parking lot at Indianapolis in 1970. (Photo Courtesy Tom Hoover Family)*

The competitors were indeed catching up. Don Nicholson had the best qualifying time in his Ford at 9.90 and was followed by Jenkins (9.91), Sox (9.93), and Oldfield (9.97)—the final car to break the sub-10 second barrier. Against yet another independent Chevrolet racer, Paul Longenecker, Dick again saw taillights as he hit the traps, running a terrific 10.00 to Longenecker's winning 10.19. Herb McCandless won the final round over Arlen Vanke that afternoon. The trip home from Indy was probably longer and quieter than the one from Martin. Losing sucked. Losing on a holeshot sucked more.

Seen here during Saturday or Sunday qualifying, a huge crowd at Indy watches as Dick and Hubert Platt in a Maverick make timed runs. Over 90 Pro Stocks were on hand that weekend. (Photo Courtesy Tom Hoover Family)

These three 9-second slips are from the 1970 Nationals; the 9.97 was quick enough to qualify fourth. (Photo Courtesy Ted Spehar Archive)

"With Dick, they [the racing media] were making statements like, 'Somebody needs to go kick the quarter panel to get the car going,'" Ted grimly recounted later. "It was very high-pressure for him, and he did not want to make the mistake of redlighting. In hindsight, I probably should have gotten him out of there sooner. It was rough on all of us."

Testing Continues

Ted remembered some of the other things that occurred in 1970 as the team ran near-constant weekly testing as long as the weather held out.

"Of everything we did that year, I would have to say it was the camshaft stuff that made the biggest differences," he said. "Valve springs have always been a problem; Isky made pure titanium retainers back then, but they were like semi-hard butter because the metal was CP, commercially pure. The retainer always wanted to pull through.

"As we got to know Regis [at Apollo] and his partner Joe, who was a great machinist, they did all kinds of stuff for us. They thought the race car stuff was cool, and it gave them a break from doing things like machine guns for the Israeli army. Anyhow, we were going from the flat-tappet to the roller cams, and engine speed was going

The Dual-Plug Hemi

Before turning away from the 1970 racing season, there was one other advance to cover in a year of advances. Air, fuel, and spark make horsepower. Air was coming through the scoop and fuel flowed through the 4500s, but one area that was tested starting in 1970 was spark—using dual distributors.

The effort had actually begun as an exercise conducted by BRM, the British firm that did occasional horsepower subcontracting projects for Chrysler. By using two distributors, they saw a horsepower gain at higher RPM levels, so work began to create a design that would allow this to function in the real world. A second spark plug opening was machined into the head opposite the present "A" location, and two distributors would now fire a pair of spark plugs in each cylinder instead of a single one. One benefit was that the units did not need to spark in exact tandem, meaning that one of the distributors could be advanced or retarded as needed.

Quite interestingly, it appears that in the interest of time, the company gave this prototyping job to Dick Landy to figure out. According to *Hot Rod* magazine, in late 1969 and early 1970, Landy worked with Stu Hilborn and Mallory to develop a pair of 90-degree offset distributor heads both driven by the conventional slotted camshaft-driven distributor gear though a modified Hilborn injector drive. This drive was already available for the Hemi engine in supercharged applications.

Later, ignition supplier Accel offered a commercial version. However, it offered marginal performance benefits after years of testing, and the advent of multi-spark discharge designs would be the final factor in its discontinuance. It was noted that Ronnie Sox liked it due to the multiple dry-hop launches he would do before making a run as the two spark events helped clean up the resultant wet cylinders. (Photo Courtesy Joe Pappas Archive)

Changed internally, the two ports in the drive were designed so that a stub-shaft distributor head could be added to each one. The unit first showed up on Landy's Pro Stock Challenger in March 1970, and the idea was later adopted by a number of Chrysler teams.

"We tried the twin distributors, which was essentially a Hilborn fuel injector drive," said Ted, "and where you would run a distributor and a fuel pump for your Hilborn fuel injection, we adapted another distributor with the twin-plug cylinder heads. We tried it for a long time. In the end, it made the engines run smoother, idle better, but there was no real performance gain there."

Tom Hoover concurred.

"When the dust settled, for absolute power, the B [plug] position at 37 degrees advance was the equal of the twin plugs at 33. That was the bottom line. But the twin plugs kept it idling and clean a lot better that way."

The early dual distributors used a Hilborn drive as a splitter. By replacing the normal fuel pump drive with a second gear retrofitted for mounting another distributor, both units could be driven off the standard cam gear inside the block, yet each distributor could be set to a specific advance. (Photo Courtesy Ted Spehar Archive)

Ironically, the real benefit with twin plugs was to be in the supercharged nitromethane categories, where huge compressed fuel volumes could easily put a single plug out of operation. Using a parallel twin-head magneto and set of 16-plug heads, the Ramchargers team adopted this layout to their Challenger Funny Car in early 1970. It resulted in the first six-second runs in that class in June. Though far more advanced and powerful now, dual magnetos are still in use on those cars. Incidentally, dual-plug ignition systems are also on the Gen III Hemi engines built by FCA for street use today (in part to meet emissions standards).

up. So I had an Optitron, which is a lot cruder than a Spintronic, and we used a Polaroid camera to try and get an image of the oscillation on the scope as the valvetrain began to go into false motion. [This means it is no longer stably following the camshaft due to engine speed]. This was using a single-cylinder/single-spring test fixture with an electric motor on it I had here in my shop. The camera was focused through a valve cover and you are spraying air to keep the oil away while watching the tach to see when it fluttered. Like, that was really accurate, right? [laughs]

"Of course, once it goes . . . *breeepp* . . . it was done, junk," Ted continued. "So you would put it back together and try to creep up on it again. We knew the manual-trans guys had it bad, but they were not going to pull off a valve cover for us to look at what had failed when it did; they didn't want anyone to see what things they had figured out. Anyhow, Al Nichols and Ron Killen knew a lot about all that stuff, and they came up with the idea that we could probably put that information on a tape and record it. Now we could play it back, and that was a major breakthrough to seeing what the point of failure was.

"Then Regis said, 'Hey, I can make those things out of an alloy.' He made us a set of alloy retainers and they never pulled through. In fact, we were at the track and somebody noticed we were not pulling off the valve covers. People watch, so we had to put that advancement out there after a couple of races. Meanwhile, we were still evaluating springs. You would get them from General Kinetics, Isky, Crower, and frankly a lot were junk; but once in a while we found ones that were consistently good. The Crower orange stripe and red stripe were good. You got a couple hundred more RPM out of them. By mid-1971, Carlton was shifting at 8,600–8,800, so we had some real improvement in that area. Once the retainers were no longer moving and doing things that effected RPM, we could begin looking at other areas of improvement."

Ted added that it was not always just his ideas or even things dreamed up by Tom Hoover or his crew.

"We did pick up stuff in the valvetrain from the NASCAR side," Ted said. "We got a higher valve layout. The cam designs from Crane, Heffington, and Tullius—they were light-years ahead of some of the West Coast shops. Our job was evaluating stuff like that, and Tom [Hoover] was very methodical about it. We might test something two or three times to make sure it was right. It needed to be for the factory to put their approval on it. We fought the racer mentality; if it went quicker this run, it will be quicker every run. Mr. Hoover was like, 'Yeah, so why did it go quicker? Did the weather change? Rosin on the track? Tire pressure? Lighter-weight oil? Why?' We learned that you can only change one thing at a time, and that could be hard because you wanted to make it work and change other things to make it better.

"So, it was always A-B-A testing—two runs on the first one, two on the replacement, and then two again on the original. Al Adam worked up the correction factors so we could monitor the weather and calculate what was really happening even if the weather changed. A degree or two of air temp or humidity could make a big difference. We came to rely on that good data, and it was very important to know if you were at a race when somebody was quicker than you. You could use the weather data to calculate a corrected number, and you might find out that they were simply better that day; you knew from the past testing that you were already going as quick as you could. This was 1970. Nobody was thinking about that stuff yet."

Grand Finales

The last two events for the team were the NHRA World Finals in Dallas, Texas, in October and a brand-new race at a brand-new track: the NHRA Hot Wheels Supernationals at Ontario Motor Speedway in Southern California. In Texas, once again the *Missile* was Top

Absurd Rumors

Latest improvement out of Detroit is an alarm clock, designed to wake up sleepy Pro Stock drivers from that city.

Though not mentioned by name, this little tidbit was typical of the comments the media made following Dick's holeshot losses at Martin and Indy. As usual, the reporters were not the ones driving the car. (Photo Courtesy Ted Spehar Archive)

Ronnie Sox and Dick Oldfield prepare for racing at the final event for 1970, the Hot Wheels–sponsored NHRA Supernationals at the brand-new Ontario Motor Speedway. Sox is benefitting from the intake manifold that had been installed on the engine the day before. (Photo Courtesy Steve Reyes)

Ted, with a cigarette in his mouth waiting out a rainy day in the pits at Dallas, and Mike Koran clean up the car during the World Finals. No job was beneath anyone on the team. (Photo Courtesy Tom Hoover Family)

Qualifier at 9.95, and Dick advanced to the second round before he was topped by Arlen Vanke. Sox beat Vanke for the event title and the 1970 NHRA Pro Stock crown.

At Ontario, Dick made what was his last start as a Pro Stock driver that season. Advancing over Paul Longenecker in round one was sweet revenge for Indy. It was the noted Ford pilot Dick Brannen who fell in round two, and Oldfield won his round-three battle over the Challenger of Billy Stepp driven by Dick Humbert. He lined up against Ronnie Sox in the all-Chrysler semifinal runs. After all the abuse about being late off the line, Dick let the clutch fly for the last time and sparked a red light! In that final, Sox again won a match over Arlen Vanke to complete a sweep of the final two events of the year. Ted noted that one other thing happened at this event: with approval from factory higher-ups, Buddy Martin asked

for and received the physical intake manifold off of the *Missile's* engine at the end of qualifying to use on Ronnie's just-updated 1971 Plymouth 'Cuda on Sunday. At that time, it was crucial from the factory standpoint that Sox be the big winner at the highly visible special race, but that situation did not do anything to endear the two teams.

In the issue of *Super Stock* magazine covering this final event of the 1970 NHRA Super Season, the editors added a special awards category article, and its engineering award in the Pro Stock category was given to Ted, primarily for the work the team had done using the transmission to be Low Qualifier so often and the effort expended by the entire Chrysler group in building the factory car. They concluded, "[The] *Motown Missile* started off to be the ultimate trick car, and if Ted Spehar has anything to say about it, it will see the winner's circle very soon in spite of the fact it is not supposed to work at all."

Pro Stock was transitioning out of its infancy year both healthy and happy. There were some true adjustments for the team in early 1971, and that "not supposed to work at all" adage gave way to a more conventional approach. Although, it was still pushing the technological envelope. Because there was no longer a need to continue testing this particular technology, they pulled the plug on the 6-speed in early 1971.

"The automatic deal was ending," Ted noted. "We found out that nobody else wanted it; they might not be

A magnetic pickup on the front spindle measures wheel speed on another run at Detroit. Testing became more and more serious as 1970 continued, and data collection was now done by Ron Killen, formerly of Chrysler's missile program in Alabama. (Photo Courtesy Ted Spehar Archive)

Ronnie Sox, but they all still wanted to manually shift. The car wasn't any quicker because of it, and Dick was in there working two shifters."

When the first season ended, Dick Oldfield noted that the automatic was a frustrating project and he was frankly glad to see when it was over with as well. His work with the unit was intimate enough that he knew where the real problems were.

"I think the biggest problem we had was that the case wouldn't hold up," he noted in the 2014 roundtable discussion hosted by Gene Yetter at the *Drag Times* racing reunion in Henderson, North Carolina. "It would distort and then we'd start losing pressure. We tried several vari-

Once the work was over, it was time to sit and have a cold beer as Dick and Lenny joke with Mike during the construction of one of the early cars. Hard work and hard play would be part and parcel of the **Missile** *base for as long as it lasted. (Photo Courtesy Dick Oldfield Archive)*

eties. A high-pressure transmission, low-pressure . . . a few clutches, a lot of clutches.

"If you went with a couple of clutches and low pressure, you could definitely get some good speed out of the car. But only for one run! And if you ran a reliable transmission you could get maybe five or six runs, but then it wouldn't go quite as fast. We probably went through about 35 transmission cases that year just to run one season.

"The engine was ready to go," recalled Dick. "So, in the early days, I was getting the car ready, driving to the track, driving the car at the race, and servicing the transmission. I did not do every single thing, but I was responsible for a lot of it."

Driving the car was one thing he would not take far into 1971. Unhappy being so visible as the driver of perhaps the most notorious Pro Stock with a factory association out on the racetrack, the snide comments in the racing media about his lack of aggression off the starting line were painful. Redlighting in front of the factory bosses who wrote Ted's checks was as unacceptable as losing, which the transmission could achieve on its own. Losing while still going quicker than the other guy was the worst.

In early 1971, Tom Hoover made the decision to put the car under the tutelage of a good manual-shift driver. In the end, that was Don Carlton, who became the next big thing launched from the silos of the *Motown Missile* base.

The **Motown Missile** *is seen at Dallas, where Bob McClurg was on hand with color film. The newly repainted car would become a major winner in 1971. Though a victory on the NHRA circuit proved to be elusive, records were reset and the car took home victories in AHRA, IHRA, and independent competition. (Photo Courtesy Bob McClurg)*

Chapter Three

1971: A Real Race Car and the Mad Scientists

The year 1971 dawned with some truly radical changes. The Nixon administration, dealing with economic malaise and the ongoing Vietnam conflict, hunkered down with the Democrat-led Congress to enact major legislative changes, including the formation of the Occupational Safety and Health Administration (OSHA), United States Department of Housing and Urban Development (HUD), and Amtrak, forever altering the framework and purpose of the federal government. The entire automobile industry was now trying to meet upcoming federal emissions standards that were recently established as well.

Furthermore, the impact of reworked insurance premiums on all performance cars was ending that era of automotive production with Chrysler curtailing its development of possible replacements to the 426 Hemi engine architecture. This included the "ball-stud" engine design that Tom Hoover had been spearheading. The sport of drag racing itself was far from static as well.

Perhaps the most dramatic change for this year was the formation of Larry Carrier's new International Hot Rod Association (IHRA). The founder and owner of the multipurpose race facilities in Bristol, Tennessee, Carrier was a larger-than-life force in motorsports who vowed to change the status quo for both racers and track operators. Into his fold went tracks in Bristol and Rockingham, North Carolina, that were formerly associated with the AHRA organization. In addition to picking up a number of other tracks throughout the Mid-Atlantic, Midwest, and Southeast regions before the year was over, Carrier took sanction over a recently opened multipurpose facility in Lakeland, Florida, as well as the NHRA's well-established use of Dallas International Motor Speedway in Texas, forcing the NHRA World Finals to a new home in Amarillo, Texas. Overall, this was the introduction of a third major drag racing sanctioning body. The IHRA had financial backing from Carrier's associates and the support of the independent racing media.

That said, from Detroit's perspective, all racing was already taking a back seat. The advancement of Lee Iacocca to the head of Ford had put most of that company's involvement in motorsports on hold, immediately canceled, or finished at the conclusion of existing contracts. Whatever involvement remained from them would be the way Chevrolet had operated; independent racers with research budgets. Even from its undercover place, General Motors pulled further away as well, especially now that emissions and insurance issues were making the company a frequent target of the political factions in Washington. Before the end of that year, Chrysler curtailed the long-running clinic programs of Sox & Martin and Dick Landy; made Petty Enterprises the primary conduit for all NASCAR associations; canceled all their involvement in the SCCA series; and subcontractors, such as Ted Spehar, were to become the way that the company continued any of its development efforts.

Of course, one thing those other manufacturers did not have was Tom Hoover and his former Ramchargers team of engineers who had always made the most with fewer resources. Chrysler's Lynn Townsend, now chairman of the board, still saw racing as a viable way to sell automobiles; and while budgets were cut, there was still money for what mattered, which was winning. To that end, Petty would earn his keep on the newly enjoined Winston-sponsored NASCAR Cup Series during the next half-decade, while variations of the 426 Hemi engine continued to maintain a dominant position in the NHRA, AHRA, and IHRA forms of drag racing.

The 1970 season came and went with big wins for Chrysler. Thanks to the aero-styled Daytona and Superbird packages, the firm won all the stock car world championships in NASCAR, the American Racing Club of America (ARCA), and the United States Auto Club (USAC). Gene Snow drove a replica of the new Dodge Challenger to a championship in the Funny Car classes in both AHRA and NHRA, which is what Ronnie Sox did in Pro Stock for Plymouth as well.

For the *Missile* team, 1970 had been a half-year of testing and development adopted to the racing series when convenient. Before beginning the recollection of 1971, which was to be the program's second year and

first full season in Pro Stock, a number of related circumstances played into its functionality.

Working for a Living

As a subcontractor, Performance Automotive was always busy because Ted was doing more than just the *Missile* program with other developmental vehicles under his association. Len Bartush's friend Mike Koran was moving more into the role of shop management, Len and Ted were building and tuning the engines, and Dick Oldfield handled not only the maintenance for the evolving automatics and suspension with Mike but also driving of the Pro Stock car whenever it hit the track. He handled most of the over-the-road towing duties as well. In addition to this was near-constant input from Chrysler's engineering brain trust led by Tom Hoover. Beyond Mr. Hoover, that included Al Adam, who managed the

This is the young crew that guided the Missile: *Len Bartush, Dick Oldfield, and Mike Koran. Seen during a West Coast event, the three had already been involved in the sport for many years. Len had been with Ted since the gas station days. (Photo Courtesy Ted Spehar Archive)*

The Whale, *a 1971 Charger used for testing B-motor parts, was one of the cars maintained at Ted's shop for doing evaluations that would be turned into the technical bulletins. There was an A-Body and an E-Body as well, plus the* Missile. *(Photo Courtesy Joe Pappas)*

drag testing program; Dave Koffel, who interfaced with the racers; former Ramcharger member Tom Coddington, whose background in fuel systems and chassis science was pivotal; his assistant John Bauman's ongoing carburetor work; and others. Dick Maxwell, another Ramcharger alumni, was now in management of the overall racing program via the product planning department, and he worked directly under Bob Cahill, who was the big boss over all Chrysler racing efforts.

"Not only were we building the *Missile*, but we had an A-Body and a B-Body and were going to have an E-Body for Super Stock work," Ted remembered. "Big-block, small-block, and Hemi combinations. We had a bunch of cars to be used for development work, and the guys from Product Planning were always coming around here too. I still did my normal stuff for them [preparing press cars].

"Soon after that, as the new program [Chrysler Performance Parts] that became Direct Connection got underway, I became the main guy to evaluate parts. If they had a cam they thought might be useful, I would take whichever car was needed for that test down to the drag strip, they would meet us, and we would do the testing to see if it really worked. Al Adam would be there, and the driver was usually somebody from Chrysler like Bauman or Larry Shepard. Bauman had a brown E-Body with a shaker, and that car was used for Super Stock D [Hemi] development. I didn't drive for any of that, though I did get a new 340 Duster for my regular driver and made a

couple of passes with it on the track. Whatever Direct Connection wanted, we did. Then, Shep [Larry Shepard] would write all of the tune-up tips using that information and would talk to me about cylinder prep or how a procedure was done."

These programs were never simply done for the sake of internal information because Chrysler used the resultant data for the greater good. The program was funded by Chrysler in part to get fresh information out to the racers, something that had been part of the original Max Wedge and Hemi releases of the 1960s. The need was to document by demonstration which parts the factory could recommend as well as give Chrysler racers (all the way up through Pro Stock) answers to their questions. Though the dealer clinic program was discontinued in this era, a major reason that Pro Stock development fell to Ted was because factory associates, such as Sox, Landy, Grotheer, and Bill Tanner (the four bigger clinic promoters), did not have time to do any major testing themselves because of their already-full travel schedules.

"Everything we did always went to the teams; our information always went to the racers," said Ted. "Now, in the end, when we actually started racing, I felt it was unfair. Even though I told those teams everything I knew, I never got reciprocating information from them. Sox and Martin were not calling me saying, 'Hey, Ted, we just found this extra power!' So, there were a couple of times when we switched out parts and did not tell them. Of course, once they heard about it, they complained. But with testing, it was always being up front about the data and information. Racing was more of a one-way street, and they sort of understood that once Donnie [Carlton] came on; we were serious about winning."

There was always work enough to go around at Ted's shop. While certain people had certain roles, there was no sense that any person was above a task no matter how dirty that job might be. This was in part out of necessity but also out of pride of ownership, an "everyone pulls together" mindset quite unique in any corporate setting.

"We made a real effort to make the group such that everybody could contribute, and everybody have ownership in the results," Tom Hoover noted in a Yetter-transcribed roundtable discussion. "That everyone felt like they were part of the reason why things were happening. We operated in a horizontal manner. That is to say, in those days all American corporations were organized vertically, as many as 13 to 15 layers, between the guys that turned the wrenches or operated the pencils and the main boss. It was very cumbersome, stiff, and things didn't always go smoothly. Many people at the lowest levels didn't have ownership of what they were doing, nor were they able to contribute any of their ideas. With the *Missile* program, it was different.

"I think one of the main cornerstones of all that is what we laughingly called the *cabal meeting*," Hoover continued. "It was usually on Thursday afternoon. The purpose was to get everybody to stop everything and sit around the table and talk. Where are we? Where are we going? Why are we going there? What ideas do you have? I want to hear them as long as they aren't contrary to the fundamental laws of physics. We'll take a good look at them. That contributes over time to a feeling of ownership. Not, 'I'm a robot. Push my button and I'll do something for you.'"

Mike Koran probably summed it up best in 2014 when he made this statement: "One thing about this group, everybody to a person would work after hours without either worry or pay. And it was for a simple equation summed up as, 'We win; they lose!'"

The efforts in testing had also taken on a new angle during the era of the ClutchFlite that would play a vital role in the collection of data. Tom Hoover was well aware of some of the work being done with data recording and made a call to the Chrysler military offices in Huntsville, Alabama, when it was shown that there had been some data work done in this regard on the NASCAR program. The result was Ron Killen joining into the mix.

Rocket Science

"It came in with the double-stack TorqueFlite at Cecil County, Maryland," Hoover recalled in 2012. "[Ron] Killen came up in a little white pickup from Huntsville. It was a real simple deal—eight-channel, reel-to-reel recorder, tape. The frustration with that was, in order to understand it, the tape doesn't do you any good after you've made the run. Killen had to go back to the van and transcribe what was on the tape onto a little needle printer. He would stretch it out. I remember at Cecil County, we had paper stretching out 30 or 40 feet!"

In that era's computing sophistication, computer mainframes took up entire floors of buildings for even rudimentary tasks, so this simple recording effort was a big deal. Though a first for Chrysler's drag racing program, there was a very primitive on-board recording effort attempted by Ford during the 1965 season in

The original data recorder in the car required long print-outs of each run, which could then be extrapolated to determine the results. At the time, this was truly cutting edge in the field of drag racing. (Photo Tom Hoover, Courtesy Dave Rockwell)

A/FX, but that test was a one-time shot on a prototype 427 Mustang and did not result in any serious adjustments in actually developing a package. Ron Killen, who the team nicknamed "Electro-cat," found his stay was a little longer than even he expected, which he relayed during the 2014 gathering of former team members.

"I was working at Huntsville, Alabama, at the time, [which was] Chrysler's facility at the Marshall Space Flight Center," Killen recalled. "My boss at Aerospace got a phone call to come up to Cecil County and put a bunch of instruments in the car because they were looking for increments that were pretty small. With the variation from run to run, there were things you just couldn't follow. With the instrumentation, we could measure distinct results. In the evenings, we could sit back and look

While at the Cecil County test, Ron Killen found out that he had been laid off at the Huntsville missile facility. Tom Hoover found the money to hire him, and he worked out of an area in Ted's shop. (Photo Courtesy Dick Oldfield Family Archives)

DRAG TEST DATA

TAPE NO. 2 LOCATION: IRWINDALE CAR: NEW MISSILE TEST NO. 1/2

5.38

CH	MEASUREMENT	XDUCER	SIG. COND.	SCALE	N_s	N'	ZERO	FILTER
1	ENG. RPM	N_1	TG6 3:1	0-10,000	3.00_{10}	2.91		25
2	LONG. ACC.	LONG	LONG	±2.5₇	0.40_{10}	0.31		75
3	P.S. RPM	TG7	TG5 2.5:1	0-10,000	1.75_{10}	3.18		75
4	FT. WH. RPM	TG8	TG2 2.5:1	0-2000	2.48_{10}	2.93		100
5	OIL PRESS	1-3420B	P1	0-200	2.83_{10}	2.74		25
6	FUEL PRESS	2-51448	P2	0-20	0.18_{10}	0.31		75
7	TANK LEVEL	STATHAM	SG3	4→14	0.56_{10}	2.72		150

DATE	RUN	GO FT. TIME	E.T.	M.P.H.	TIME	REMARKS
1/26	10	1.437|1.443|1.447	9.721	142.18	9:30	TT @ 8700
						STATIC
1/27						STATIC 50# FT. /160# BAR /3 GAL
	11	1.458|1.420|1.417	9.670	142.85	9:22	O W 3140# 53½ R
	12	1.437|1.420|1.937	9.674	143.08	9:50	3 C 29.5 FT. TIRES
						STATIC
	13	1.423|1.417|1.425	9.631	143.08	10:10	8000 LAUNCH O W
	14	1.439|1.420|1.447	9.654	143.08	10:28	O W
						STATIC
	15	CHANGE TO WET				SUMP 11 QT. 1 BURN OUT 2 8000 IN NEUT.
1/28						STATIC
	16	1.458|1.442|1.436	9.699	142.63	12:45	O-2 H
	17	1.474|1.471|1.462	9.810	141.50	2:30	STATIC BETWEEN 16 & 17 O W
	18	1.632|1.451|1.956	9.795	141.06	2:50	3 H

4G 1510
MADE IN U.S.A.

From Ted Spehar's papers is this written register of what was recorded during one of the early 1971 tests at Irwindale. Using the new 5.38 gearset, seven areas were recorded with the results from eight runs shown in the lower area. The best time was a 9.631 at 143.08 mph using an 8,000-rpm launch. (Photo Ted Spehar, Courtesy Steve Atwell)

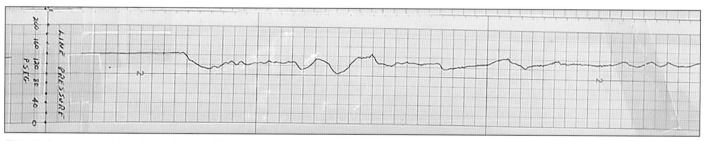

This is just a small length of the yard-long tape generated by the process. It shows transmission line pressure in the ClutchFlite during the first moment of a pass. (Photo Ted Spehar, Courtesy Steve Atwell)

at all the tapes to figure out what modifications represented real performance gains.

"But then, at the drag strip in Cecil County, I actually got a call from my boss in Huntsville. He told me Chrysler's space program would be cut back and I was being laid off. He said, 'Pile all your stuff in the van and come back to Huntsville.' That didn't go over [well] with Tom Hoover. No way! Tom countered with, 'We're in the middle of a test!' After a few phone calls to the corporate offices, I ended up working for Tom out of Detroit. I stayed at the track for the rest of the test but soon moved to Detroit.

"When I first got there, I actually worked out of Teddy's shop," Killen continued. "They set me up with a little

lab in a corner. That was the home of our instrumentation for the next several years. When Teddy moved from Performance Automotive to SVI, I moved with them."

As Tom Hoover noted, the initial version was simply feeding data to a tape recorder. At first, once the run was completed, that tape was replayed via a drive using a small printer, and a very long paper strip was the result, plotting out the data that was recorded. For the first time, in those 10 seconds a Pro Stocker went through its acceleration and shift patterns, it was possible to ascertain what was actually happening due to very specific points of measurement on the car.

"Initially, only 6. Eventually 7," Killen noted when asked how many readings from each run could be

recorded. "I would have the car set up to measure 15 or 20 performance points. Because we could only test 6 things, the guys would tell me which 6 they wanted to test. The downside was they'd have to wait for me to get the recorder out of the car and play it back on a chart recorder; then, they could look at the charts. After a couple of years, we switched to a telemetry system. Then, we actually got the data as the car was going down the track. We would be sitting in the van and we could instantly see what was going on. By the time the car came back to the pits, they had already figured out what they wanted to test next. That made a huge difference. For me, it meant I didn't have to run out and pull stuff apart between every run."

Even with the taped printouts, however, this effort proved to be crucial as work on the ClutchFlite evolved during the course of 1970 into 1971.

"We figured we might be able to do better if we could provide more gear ratios, make it into a 4-speed automatic," said Hoover at this same gathering. "And that's where Ron's instrumentation and data collection came in. We talked to B&M Transmissions and basically what resulted from that was a conventional clutch with a conventional 3-speed behind it and a hacked-up 727 2-speed splitter behind that.

"Having committed that kind of effort and budget to getting the hardware available, having cut the car up to do so, because suddenly the floor pan was too close to everything . . . 'This whole mess was how long?' Two oil pans, the whole shot. So, we didn't want to evaluate

it guessing. And what you needed was instrumentation that would provide a real trace of engine speed, what speed it shifted at, and so on. So folks such as Coddington and the rest of us would look on and look at the tape to see what it meant. There was a major motivation to bring Ron and the gear up to Cecil County to do it."

"I think we used the instrumentation in all the *Missile* cars," stated Ron. "From time to time, we'd transfer it to different cars, everything from Super Stock cars to off-road cars. The other side of my story—every now and then, Larry Rathgeb would steal me to do something in the Grand National [NASCAR] programs. So I'd load up and go there. But most of what I did was with the *Missile* cars."

Winter Racing Recap

For 1971, there was the same basic group of NHRA national events, including the change in the Summernationals location and a first-ever national race in Sanair, Quebec, Canada, announced for midseason. As noted, the former World Finals moved from Dallas to a track in Amarillo, Texas. The AHRA was also regrouping from its loss of venues to Carrier's new group, and the Kansas City–based group was in several smaller venues for 1971 as a result, in addition to its sanctioning of the legendary Lions Drag Strip in California for one final season. For the IHRA, Carrier scheduled several of his tracks to host two races each that first season.

The factory tests for 1971 began at Irwindale Raceway in California, and Ted, Dick, and Mike all went west in January for that, as did a number of the corporate engineers who flew in. The *Queen Mary* had been retired as the tow vehicle, and Ted now had a box truck with an open-air tagalong for the car.

While a number of teams built new cars for 1971, working from what they had discovered in 1970, the *Missile* was updated in appearance but retained the same basic chassis configuration. During the weeks between November and January, a new 1971 Challenger grille and taillamp panel were installed, and the paint was changed to its more visible 1971 design.

"We did not do a lot to it for the new year," Ted noted. "We changed to yellow with black lettering because we now wanted it to be more visible. We went from our schmanzy-pantsy stuff that we engineers thought people would like to see to something a sign painter would do. [laughs] It had the same suspension."

The team headed west to California with three 426 Hemi engines (numbers 24, 25, and 26), with plans to run some testing with Roger Lindamood as the driver. Lindamood, a fellow Michigan racer who was ironically a former automatic transmission specialist for Chrysler, was then still very active in the Funny Car category, something he had been involved with since the 1965 season. The tests at Irwindale were also attended by some of the other factory teams that went west for the winter season, but the Lindamood attempt had less than pleasant results.

"I was considering [Roger] Lindamood," Ted said. "Anyhow, we had three engines I put together for all of this, and two of them stuck tappets. I was over-boring the lifter bores by then, but the supplier had gone to a very slightly larger size and it was enough to jam the lifter."

As a result of that and its valvetrain destruction, the car did not appear at the NHRA Winternationals the following weekend. Ted noted to *National Dragster* writers in the event results issue that Roger would have only been in the car for that one event, and plans were already being made to hire Don Carlton and change over to a 4-speed transmission as well. Meanwhile, Spehar and Oldfield were set up to do their engine repair work at Dick Landy's shop. However, that following week, on February 9, there was a major earthquake right in the Northridge area. After wondering why everybody was driving like maniacs, the Michigan men received the answer when they stopped to get coffee and breakfast,

Funny Car pilot Roger Lindamood (center) came in to drive the car during the Winternationals, but engine trouble sidelined that effort. It is likely that talks with Don Carlton happened during this time. Ted (left) and Dick look on. (Photo Tom Hoover, Courtesy Dave Rockwell)

then headed over to Dick Landy Industries.

"We walk in the shop; the car is moved—it's knocked off the jack stands!" Ted exclaimed. "There's junk everywhere. We ask, 'What happened?' One of Landy's guys said, 'Oh, there was an earthquake!' We had no idea . . ."

With the remaining good engine, the team went to a big post-Winternationals match race at Orange County International Raceway with Oldfield driving, where they suffered another driveline breakage problem in round one. However, the use of a new Weiand ram manifold that used an open-plenum design was showing promise for all of the Hemi racers, as Oldfield clocked a great legal-weight 9.76 during his qualifying run. As they headed back east, they attended the final weekend of the trip, the AHRA Winter Nationals in Phoenix, where Ted's records note the car made eight passes total—the final one being a redlight start against AHRA regular Jim Hayter in the Fred Gibb–owned ZL1 1969 Camaro in the first round of eliminations.

At that same event, Don Carlton was Top Qualifier, running a 9.75 in Billy "The Kid" Stepp's new Challenger built by Sox & Martin. Stepp was becoming a well-known character in the Pro Stock world, though he reportedly had a close affinity with an organized crime syndicate in his Dayton, Ohio, home base, according to the *Dayton*

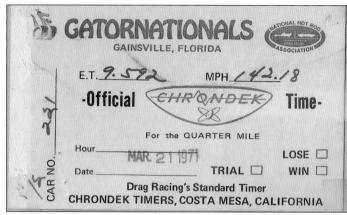

With the engine troubles sorted out, Ted and Dick took the car to a big Pro Stock race at Orange County and took home the Low ET with this 9.76 at 141 mph. (Photo Courtesy Ted Spehar)

The bite at the Gatornationals was good, and so was Don Carlton. Driving the ClutchFlite for this event, Carlton ran a 9.59 best on a Sunday morning test run. (Photo Courtesy Ted Spehar)

Daily News. Carlton was selected as his temporary driver when Dick Humbert, the car's former pilot, broke his leg during the preseason months and could not return as the driver.

"Lindamood was really still into the Funny Car deal, so after he made a few runs, we knew that wasn't going to work," Ted said. "We went home, and Dick was really frustrated. He was working all week at the shop and he hated the pressure. It was Dave Koffel who suggested Carlton, who was working for Stepp. So I called down to North Carolina, and they told me he was in church—on a Wednesday. I thought, 'Oh, crap; he's in church on Wednesday, and he's going to come to work for these guys? Ain't gonna happen.' Well, we talked a couple of days later, and I told him, 'I don't know what Stepp is paying you, but we'll match it, give you whatever you want, and this will be the fastest Pro Stock in the country, bar none.'"

Don with a Clutch and a National Event Win

Within a matter of days, the team had the chance to meet and finalize the focus. The plan was to convert the car to a manual configuration, which would not be overly

Seen here in the late-afternoon semifinal run against Reid Whisnant, Don ran a 9.60 that gave him lane choice for the final, but he lost to Sox in the money round when the trick transmission was left in second gear at the launch. (Photo Courtesy Bob McClurg)

Ted's brother took this image that is in Ted and Tina Spehar's scrapbook. This young woman prided herself as a model and was light enough to get on the fender. Of course, we are only paying attention to the GTO and Don Prudhomme's Hot Wheels hauler in the background. (Photo Courtesy Ted Spehar Archive)

The car with the 4-speed in it and Don's name in the window sits outside the shop before one of the spring trips. (Photo Courtesy Dick Oldfield Family Archive)

time-consuming because the clutch and pedal assemblies were already in use. For his part, Don then recommended a close friend to take over his place as driver in the Stepp operation. That was fellow racer Stuart McDade, another Lenoir, North Carolina, resident who had actually been Don's racing partner in earlier projects.

"We told Donnie that we would get a manual transmission into it as quickly as we could," Ted remarked. "I hired him with the promise to give him a fast car. We showed him everything we had, everything he might like. At the time, Joe Liberty was working with his clutchless [transmission] deal; he was sorting out the shifting mechanism, so he and Donnie got together and that was part of our deal as well."

The NHRA Gatornationals was only about 10 days later (March 19–21), so it was agreed to leave the automatic ClutchFlite in place for that race.

"We knew how much the automatic was giving up; we only had a competitive edge because the rest of the car was better-prepared," said Ted.

Indeed, the only other serious racer to try it was Bill Tanner, briefly noted by the racing media at the NHRA Winternationals a month earlier, and his use may have been at the direction of his factory sponsorship. It should be noted that even at this late point, the 3-speed version was still the only one to ever be used in competition.

At Gainesville, Sox was on top with a 9.57 time in the quarter-mile, with Carlton just behind him at 9.60 when qualifying had concluded. The 16-car field was primarily Mopars, 11 in all, with Hayter leading the GMs at 9.75 and Don Nicholson atop the Ford crew at 9.82. Donnie beat "Grumpy" Jenkins to win round one 9.69 to 9.94, clocked a 9.72 over Canadian John Petrie in round two, and ran a 9.60 over Reid Whisnant to get into the final against Sox.

This was the furthest the *Missile* had ever gone in NHRA national event competition, and at the green, Don let the clutch fly, but the motor bogged down because the transmission was in second gear instead of first! Ronnie Sox, driving his fresh 1971 'Cuda—nicknamed the *Burlington Missile* due to its use of many new ideas, including some the factory had released from the 1970 *Missile* tests—clocked a winning 9.60. Carlton could only muster a 10-second time.

The IHRA program began to step up as well. Carrier's first event was his IHRA Rockingham Pro-Am from April 16–18. Sox won that one as well, but Carlton and the *Missile* crew had instead towed all the way down to West Palm Beach, Florida, for the AHRA's new Grand American that same weekend. There, Don qualified the Challenger in the top spot and marched through the field like, as Koffel said in Civil War terms, "Sherman through Georgia." Being the *Missile*'s first full race with a manual transmission, the crowd saw times of 10.02 and 9.82 before Don reached a final round against the feared Dick Harrell–prepped ZL1 Camaro of Jim Hayter and Fred Gibb. Hayter broke into the 9s for the first time that weekend with

The IHRA was playing in Rockingham, but the team headed to West Palm Beach, Florida, for the AHRA's Grand American in April. The S/S 117 designated that this was not an NHRA event. The team is shown unloading the car on Sunday after taking it back to the hotel the previous night. (Photo Courtesy Tom Hoover Family Archive)

Taken from the stands, Tom Hoover captured the final round, where Don was up against Jim Hayter in the Fred Gibb–owned Camaro. This was the first ZL1 Camaro ever built. (Photo Courtesy Tom Hoover Family Archive)

Based on his season-long efforts, Hayter would become the 1971 AHRA champion, but on this day he was up against the Missile *and would have to settle for a runner-up when Donnie trailered him at West Palm Beach. (Photo Courtesy Tom Hoover Family Archive)*

Don and the team put the car into the winner's circle. Oldfield and Koran, sporting clean STP T-shirts, are behind the car; Hurstette Nikki Phillips is to the far right. (Photo Courtesy Tom Hoover Family Archive)

a 9.98 on his side of the track but was watching taillights as the *Missile* flawlessly clocked a 9.71 at 141.50. Though not an NHRA-sized race, this Florida victory was a huge thrill for the team and certainly helped morale to now have a national-event crown under its belt.

The next big appearance was an NHRA points race in Suffolk, Virginia. Located west of the tidewater military town of Norfolk, the sea-level air was always conducive to record setting, and that was the biggest reason to show up at such a small-scale venue. Donnie and the car did not disappoint. Not only did it reset the NHRA National

Record down to 9.67 in qualifying but the *Missile* also took charge of the event in what *National Dragster* referred to as a "devastating win," running even quicker at 9.63 during the race and 9.64 in the final round.

"Anything we did outside of Chrysler, we got that money," said Ted. "So, any match racing was mine, and the expenses for any national events we did was on me. My money from Chrysler was for the testing work on the *Missile* and the other cars we were responsible for. I owned the car. If we had anything in there that was under development, it had to come out before we went

The smile tells the story. Don wanted to be in the winner's circle as much as the team did. Tom Hoover was behind the camera but was certainly smiling as well to see his project finally secure the fruits of victory. (Photo Courtesy Tom Hoover Family Archive)

to an event just to avoid the idea that we had something no one else could get yet . . . politics with the clinic cars."

Politics meant that someone *upstairs* at Chrysler would get a call from a racer who had factory help but was not as fast. If the complaint was from someone important enough, that boss in turn would call Ted and scream about not giving the "stars" all the equipment under development. This scrutiny was not limited just to Chrysler rivals, either. From the other side of the fence, those calls went to the NHRA or other sanctioning body bosses. The *Missile* crew was always thinking of ideas, some of which succeeded in being legal, while others would result in a hand slap from the high sheriffs.

"Politics that first year wasn't too much," Ted noted. "Once Donnie started driving for us, it got more serious. You know, with [the] NHRA, if you had them looking in one direction, they were not looking in another one, and you could get away with stuff. The Ford guys were always complaining. I mean, [Don] Nicholson was a racer's racer. He noticed everything, and he would go and tell [the] NHRA or his bosses. One time at Indy, we put clear moon discs over the wheels to clean the air up. He complained about that. We put a ground fairing under it; he saw that too. [The] NHRA made us take it off, but we told them it was to prevent radiator overflow from getting on the track. [laughs]"

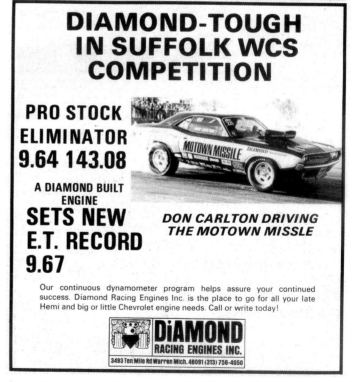

Steve Reyes took this image of the Missile *that showed up in the newspaper ads for Diamond Racing after the team set the NHRA Pro Stock national event record at the sea-level track in Suffolk, Virginia. (Photo Courtesy Steve Reyes)*

The truck was showing its miles, and the car was still being towed on a tagalong behind it. Dick Oldfield was the primary driver, although occasionally Don Carlton would drive it as well. (Photo Courtesy Dick Oldfield Family Archive)

Summertime Blues and Another Big Win

While testing continued in the middle of almost every week, the team was still working a serious event schedule. The next NHRA race was the Springnationals in Dallas the second weekend in June, and Dons crept through the starting beams in the third round to force a foul. The following weekend, the IHRA ran its first national event in Bristol. Having raced for Sox and now lined up against him in yet another final round, Carlton lost on a redlight start in Thunder Valley that afternoon. Still, the testing effort with the reworked Liberty clutch and transmission design began to wake up the car.

At the new Summernationals location of Englishtown, New Jersey, in mid-July, Donnie put the car into the top spot with a big 9.502 time followed by Mike Fons. Fons had just forsaken his well-traveled 1968 Camaro for a recently constructed Rod Shop–sponsored Challenger, another machine built with tips from the *Missile*. In a third-round battle with eventual-champion Dyno Don Nicholson, Carlton came up a tick short: 9.66 to 9.67.

Then the NHRA tour made its first trip into Canada for the first Grandnationals, where Fons topped the charts with a 9.51. He had also recently reset the Pro Stock record to 9.56, and the Dodge-associated Gil Kirk–backed Rod Shop Pro Stock crew was taking no prisoners—at least not until round one, when an oil pump failure sidelined the potent entry. Meanwhile, Ted turned up the wick and Don became the fastest Pro Stock driver ever in

This handout image is an artist rendering from new sponsor JEGS's catalog. The car was painted in a different format on the rear quarter panels of the actual **Missile**. At the time, this firm and the Columbus-based Rod Shop were the two serious speed parts sellers out of Ohio. (Photo Courtesy Ted Spehar Archive)

the history of NHRA national event competition when the *Missile* clocked a 9.48 at 146.10 during the quarterfinals. Working into the final round for the money, in the other lane was Ronnie Sox, but Don still did not shake the monkey off his back when a missed shift allowed the Burlington bomber to remain the preeminent winner in the class. A *Drag Racing USA* magazine story noted that Carlton must have been contemplating suicide based on these events, but justice was coming.

In early August, the main stars of the sport returned to Martin 131 Dragway in Michigan for the *Popular Hot Rodding* magazine event. Don was not the Top Qualifier; that went to Stu McDade in the Stepp Dodge. But when Sunday action began, revenge for the earlier losses in both 1970 and 1971 was up for grabs. After beating the Fords of Dick Brannen and Wayne Gapp, Carlton prepared for the semifinals, where he was alongside Mike Fons, the driver who won the event against Oldfield the previous season. At the green, Don went forward and Mike went upward. The Rod Shop car's wheelstand was high enough to slow down to a 10.57 while the *Missile* went 9.66. In the final round, the opponent was Dyno Don, whose victory at Englishtown uniquely made him the only driver other than Ronnie Sox to win an NHRA Pro Stock title during 1971. Dyno knew he was covered

The Missile was doing serious wheelstands when the NHRA tour came to Texas in June for the Springnationals in Dallas. Noteworthy was the huge tower behind the car. This would be the last NHRA event held at the deluxe track, which went to the IHRA later that year and unfortunately fell into bankruptcy. (Photo Courtesy Steve Reyes)

This photo showcases the new wheelie bar setup on the car when the NHRA went way north into Canada for the Grandnationals at Sanair Raceway near Quebec. This design used a vertical support and a spring-loaded lower caster to try to get the nose down without unloading the chassis. The car again went deep into the field before falling to Sox in the final round. (Photo Courtesy Bob McClurg)

This time slip from Sanair would prove to be one of the fastest national event runs of the 1971 season. It was clocked during the semifinals following a 9.49 effort earlier in the day. (Photo Courtesy Ted Spehar Archive)

Sweet revenge from the final-round loss at the previous year's running came at Martin 131 in Michigan during the Popular Hot Rodding *race. This is the final round, where Dyno Don tried to get a fast light and instead got a red light; regardless, his 9.72 was no match for the* Missile's *9.62. (Photo Courtesy Steve Reyes)*

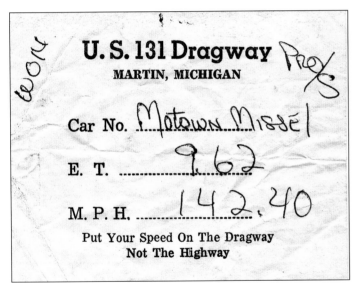

That word in the margin, "WON," sums it up. (Photo Courtesy Ted Spehar Archive)

and left a red light in his wake, clocking a 9.72 as Carlton went to the winner's circle with a 9.62 at 142.40. A big win for the team, and in front of all the Detroit faithful, this day was a harbinger of things to come.

Testing Continues

For Ted and his group of dedicated employees, this was icing on the cake. The *Missile* was originally built for testing—and testing it did. With Killen's data recorder taking it all in, the 4-speed work by Don Carlton was part

of the process, and gains were being made during that summer. The factory was able to use the results from the test work for all the racers, helping make every Chrysler driver more competitive. Fons's new car, being part of the Dodge-sponsored "super team" out of the Columbus-based Rod Shop, certainly proved this, as did Stepp, who bought the very best of everything and chose wisely when he put McDade in the driver's seat. The truth was that all the Pro Stock teams (regardless of brand) were simply getting better as the class evolved, which the record book and performances showed.

Meanwhile, Dick Oldfield was glad to no longer be the guy with a target on his back, and Donnie's driving frustrations on the national event scene perhaps gave him a little vindication. Dick was still at all of the events because he drove the transporter, and since Ted usually had the engines turnkey ready, he remained underneath the car more than anyone else dealing with driveline issues.

"Once Donnie came on board, he drove the car and he drove the transporter a few times," Dick noted. "We had the Liberty transmission stuff too. That made the factory transmission into a slick shift, and once we had gotten it all assembled, that one actually worked pretty well. Now, with any transmission we had, I could service them at the racetrack. I had to. Looking back, I think on some of that stuff, we lightened it up so much that reliability wasn't there any longer. I had to constantly take it out if only just to check it so it wouldn't break on the next pass. I had a lot of extra parts wherever we went."

Ted Spehar concurred, and both he and Dick gave credit to Donnie for going the distance.

"When Don came on board and we changed to the 4-speed manual, there were a whole lot of clutches available in the aftermarket," Ted said during the 2014 event. "Chrysler did a clutch and there were problems. So we did clutch development with Donnie being very proficient in the transmission area. He brought lots of good ideas to the team, and we all learned from him."

Meanwhile, John Bauman was also on hand at both the tests and during the events.

"He had all these carburetor tuning packages," Tom Coddington noted at that same gathering. "I think we had our chief executive finally sit him down and told him, 'You better write these down!' He was kind of secretive about the things he did. Of course, that meant job security. He was a member of the team. He went to almost all of the tests with us."

Carb expert John Bauman was a vital part of many of the Chrysler test days and proved to be invaluable to the racers when he attended national events. His background in fuel systems science was unmatched among the support people who helped the Missile *attain success. (Photo Courtesy Dick Oldfield Family Archive)*

"He [Bauman] was a real asset at the national meets because he could go through all the troops [Chrysler racers], in particular priority, and if the guys were lost . . ." said Tom Hoover. "Folks get lost when they start *helping* carburetors. That's a real issue. And they get panicky. 'I did this, and I did that, now I'm 2 mph slower.' Bauman was very helpful in that regard. He would tirelessly circle the pits with his little box of tools and get the guys back on track."

Ron Killen recalled Bauman's work ethic as well.

"I traveled with John a lot," Killen said. "I had the van with all the instruments. I even pulled our test car a few times. Once John tells me, 'I need a cabinet in your van to put all of my stuff.' I think that whoever has that van, if it still exists, it smells like carburetor bowl gaskets. 'What is that stuff, John?' [I'd ask.] It was interesting because we did a lot of testing together. Some of the manifolds he kept, such as the Edelbrock Rat Roaster open-plenum manifold. I remember a problem we worked on—Was it ignition or fuel?—It turned out to be fuel. He was relentless in working on things until he finally figured them out."

The 1971 Test Results

In the meantime, Al Adam was working directly for Tom Coddington, who moved up the corporate structure when Tom Hoover moved from Engineering to Product Planning. Al was responsible for writing up the final test results that were sent out to the racers. The first test of 1971 was performed at Irwindale during the two weeks bracketing the AHRA and NHRA Winternationals. When Adam wrote results of a test, he summarized the very best performances. However, dozens of runs may have occurred. The reports still filled several pages. Stepp and his driver Carlton were there with a 5.38 gear

in a quick-change rear (only Sox had received an actual Dana-mountable set of these gears at that point). After the *Missile* ate the two engines, Arlen Vanke's Duster was used to continue the factory portion of this test. The big issue at this moment was switching from the older IR intake design to a shortened Weiand version that featured D-shaped ports and an open plenum. These were tested with 780 Holley carburetors.

In late March, it was 1971 test number two, which was performed at a little track near Orlando with the ClutchFlite multispeed effort. Tested just after Gainesville, the plan for this trial was to compare the latest accepted-as-best Weiand intake design to various competitors' cars that remained on hand as well as to begin evaluations on hood scoop sizes, which continued later that spring at the track in Milan. Ted adopted a 13.4 compression ratio, and a Chrysler cam design was standardized for testing and sold under part number-985. The *Missile* did not show a lot of improvement with this, but over several days at Milan in late April and early May for the third test, the adaptation of the dual distributor was selected over the standard Prestolite-assisted points-type distributor setup or a single magneto. Importantly, the shift points moved up to 8,200–8,600 rpm as result of the valvetrain changes, and accuracy in the timing cycle became a problem with a points-type design. This led the group to switch to the Chrysler electronic magnetic impulse units that were being adopted in the street environment for the dual-distributor project. This meant that two coils, two ballast resistors, and two control units were used. Al noted that even a single distributor of this configuration was close in performance. The new 4820-steel alloy Dana 5.38 ring also showed minimal breakage wear after 20 hard runs in the car.

While the team was seeing real-world results at racing events, test number four in June at Milan showed that the simple switch to the manual-transmission configuration was worth over a tenth of a second and approximately 3 mph with Donnie pushing deep into the 9.50s when corrected by Al using George Wallace's charts. The added air scoop volume did not help, however, and the final test on a ring gear change was hindered when a different car broke and oiled down the racing surface.

The fifth test was even more amazing. Working with a new set of internal transmission gears probably from Liberty (going from the standard 2.45-1.93-1.39-1.00 to a tighter 2.45-1.64-1.19-1.00 combination) saw an improvement of two tenths of a second, and adding

An Outsider's Look at the 1971 *Motown Missile*

Ted Spehar recalled during the creation of this book that noted racing photographer Bob McClurg reminded him about how secretive the *Motown Missile* crew was. At the time, every run was the equivalent of a test pass. The team was hyper-focused on its work, and there was always a sort of mystique about being the factory team and not just another race car. Perhaps one of the most in-depth pieces on

Steve Reyes captured these two side views of the Motown Missile *during the 1971 season. The early example (top) shows the car in Arizona for the AHRA Winternationals with Fernwood Dodge still on it, Dick Oldfield driving, the B&M ClutchFlite installed, and short wheelie bars. The shot from Indy (bottom) shows Don Carlton at work, with "JEG'S" on the rear quarter panels, as well as a much larger number of associate contingency decals, the Liberty 4-speed in the transmission tunnel, and the vertical wheel bars design. (Photos Courtesy Steve Reyes)*

the team effort conducted by an independent journalist was written that year following the preseason test efforts at Irwindale by well-known technical writer Alex Walordy.

Walordy was a freelance writer and a photographer in the automotive field for many years, which may have been the reason he was selected for this task. The result was published in a multipage black and white story in *Super Stock & Drag Illustrated* magazine in July 1971. While Ted recounts the basic changes to the car for the new year elsewhere in this chapter, the ongoing progression of the *Missile* was laid quite bare in the period story in part perhaps to help other racers see what was going on with the factory research and development program.

First, the use of the legally allowed 2-inch engine setback that required reworking the clutch linkage and header fitment is mentioned. The radiator was smaller than the factory Hemi versions, and the car's engines at that time were all 426 ci with a 0.020 clean-up, which allowed for a weight of 3,010 pounds at NHRA events. The work by Oldfield to weigh literally every component on the car was noted as well as Ted's use of titanium for various parts. Possibly not every titanium component was unveiled to the public in this tome, although Chrysler racers may have been aware of them.

Among the chassis tricks were using Dodge Dart spindles (worth 3 pounds, with the added benefit of lowing static height by 1/2 inch), Hurst-Airheart disc brakes, whittled-away control arms, old and well-used 1966 Satellite front shocks, and a titanium drag link. A lightened reworked K-member supported the engine that was solidly tied into the car's frame with large tubular braces; engine plates soon made an appearance in Pro Stock. The cage used tubing with the rear supports and wheelbase-length lower frame connectors that tied the front and rear suspensions together. Out back were 1965 S/S rear springs and a set of wheelie bars, a narrowed Dana 60 with lightened brakes, and regular asbestos-type shoes. Firestone slicks in 15- or 16-inch-diameter sizes were selected based on track conditions.

As noted elsewhere in this book, the engine's weight changed substantially. Walordy noted that it took $200 worth of milling work to smooth off the first 30 pounds; then, Ted or Len went after the rest using a die grinder. The tappet bores were all reamed to be exactly perpendicular with the cam lobes and then sleeved. Oldfield noted that even at that time with the flat-tappet cam, the valvetrain was stable to 9,000 rpm, which was crucial due to the very rapid first-gear acceleration. The bottom end was a forged Grand National crank and a slightly long NASCAR rod to increase compression to 13.4:1 using either TRW or JE pistons.

The flex fan pulley with a Chrysler viscous drive was mounted to the crank instead of the normal fan pulley location, which allowed the upper unit to solely spin the water pump with no added drag. Aluminum heads from 1965 and an aluminum water pump housing from the 1968 program lightened it up more. Testing could find either the Weiand or a custom IR intake atop the engine working with Bauman's well-tuned 4500-series Holley carbs, two rear-mounted Carter fuel pumps, and either an 8- or 16-plug ignition layout.

It was important to note that anything Ted could remove from the engine could be moved rearward as ballast. Coupled to the engine setback, it is easy to see why the car was launching so hard.

By this point, Ron Killen used his recording equipment, and Walordy implicitly stated that Chrysler's NASCAR expert George Wallace was a part of the group at this test. The instrumentation was in the trunk and still required a printout, but someone read the weather station data at the end of each run for Al Adam to quickly write down: "Speed 139.872 [mph], wind velocity 3.2 miles northwest, humidity 43 percent, air temperature 82°F, ground temperature 74°F." Since the ClutchFlite was still in the car, Killen took readings of the band apply pressure, fluid line pressure, and measured driveshaft-to-rear-wheel speed differentials among other things. Walordy compared the overall scene to NASA's Mission Control facility in Houston.

While it was not possible to secure some of the photography taken for this story originally, the article provided an excellent analysis, often shown as part of the work Walordy was known for, especially the images of the machined block prior to buildup and details on the rear suspension layout. The 1971 *Missile* was among the most advanced efforts in the Pro Stock field of the era.

During one of the tests at Milan, Donnie launches wheels-up while Ron Killen's van in the background gets ready for the recording data. The 1971 season would be one of the most visible seasons for the Missile *in national event competition. (Photo Courtesy Ted Spehar Archive)*

Seen from behind, the car is using the earlier version of the wheelie bars, placing this test in late spring or early summer. A recording device for the rear wheel speed is visible. (Photo Courtesy Ted Spehar Archive)

Goodyear's latest-compound tire sent the *Missile* down to a 9.39/146.38 best. This was probably just before the NHRA's race at Sanair, where Donnie posted the runner-up to Sox.

The seventh test was a combination of changes done at a final July day and several in September for the first roller cam using the Crane R-288-413-R4 unit. Although performance did not improve over the Chrysler 3512725 model, this new valvetrain option was an up-and-coming racing technology that rising engine speeds would soon require. A second test regarding a larger spoiler size proved that the version on the car was adequate, and further post-test evaluation with the NASCAR specialists at the Chrysler Chelsea Proving Grounds noted that there was a point of lost benefit if the spoiler was too large, simply adding frontal area for the car to push through without any aerodynamic benefits. A third part of this

test was using new 13/16-inch Venturi 4500 Holleys with both progressive and fixed linkage; comparatively, this change showed no major differences.

At test number eight, which occurred in October just before the NHRA World Finals, Mike Fons's car was on hand as well. With Bauman's theories in play, the *Missile* tested the first of the boundary layer snorkel-type hood scoops, not yet seeing an improvement, as well as a new header design. However, Fons's car showed a solid improvement with the new 13/16-inch carbs even in an A-B-A-B test series.

By this time, the next *Missile* was also being constructed, and Fons's car actually became the primary subject for the ninth test, which was performed out at Irwindale when the NHRA Supernationals took place in November. Fons clocked a best time of 9.54, which again proved the validity of the carburetors when mounted to the 8-Barrel Plenum Ram (as the modified intake was being called). At this same test, Don Grotheer worked with a similar taper-flow Edelbrock plenum-ram design with the big carbs and went 9.50 while using a lower shift point than Fons did.

This work created real-world results, all of which went to the Chrysler racers. These results came from factory reports that still exist in the late Dick Landy's personal files. The racers could adopt the ideas they wanted. No other company from Detroit was doing anything like this in Pro Stock.

Indy, NHRA in Amarillo, and IHRA's First World Championship

The NHRA Nationals at Indianapolis over Labor Day weekend was the sport's largest event and most important weekend. Torrid qualifying put Carlton's *Missile* on

Bob McClurg was on the spot at Indy as Don launches against Ronnie Sox in the semifinals. Was Sox quicker out of the gate? Not with 0.3 dialed into the tree by mistake. When the clutch broke on this run, the Missile was not able to return and make the call for the rerun, and Sox beat Stu McDade for the event win. (Photo Courtesy Bob McClurg)

top again with a 9.559 that just bested McDade's 9.562. That latter pass was so quick that the Sox & Martin team protested Stepp's car, requiring a time-consuming engine teardown. After passing technical inspection, Billy "The Kid" reportedly tore up the $100 bills posted for the teardown and threw them at Buddy Martin, very angry that he had just lost a full day of time trials in the barn with his mechanic Paul Frost taking everything apart and putting it all back together. When it was over, those two times were tops, Sox was third at 9.63, and Butch Leal, one of the alumni of 1965 in a new Plymouth Duster, was fourth at 9.66.

The quickest 32-car program in NHRA history to that point, these top four also drove in the semifinals. Rain on Monday postponed some eliminations until Tuesday, when Donnie beat John Hagan, 1970 winner Herb McCandless, and Wally Booth before meeting up with Sox in the semifinals. At the green, Sox left first by a lot. This was because someone in the tower did not remove a 0.3-second handicap from the Christmas tree. Then, as the *Missile* went downtrack, the clutch broke.

While Ronnie and Buddy offered to wait for a rematch of the round, even with help from some fellow competitors, Ted could not get the repairs done in the time window that the NHRA allotted to rerun the miscued matchup. Sox won again, beating McDade in the final by the smallest of margins: 9.586 to 9.588. The *National Dragster* headline was "Sox Wins . . . So What Else Is New?"

However, this was the most important day Chrysler ever had in the NHRA. It won every single eliminator

from Top Fuel (Steve Carbone) to Stock (Al Corda), and Tom Hoover's effort to "crush them like ants," bore fruit, despite a huge number of Chevrolet racers on hand. This hammering was not lost on the NHRA's leadership. There

The Missile babes stand in a group. The wives came to Indy in 1971 dressed to the hilt in part to try and win Best Appearing Crew honors. Seen here from left to right are Jonnie Carlton, Carol Adam, Camille Bartush, Tina Spehar, and Sharon Oldfield. (Photo Courtesy Oldfield Family Archive)

This is the Challenger in the Rockingham winner's circle with the crew. From left to right are Mike Koran, Miss Hurst Golden Shifter Linda Vaughn, Don Carlton, Ted Spehar, and Howard Marsales. The following weekend, Don won the IHRA World Championship in Lakeland, Florida. (Photo Courtesy Ted Spehar Archive)

were not only rules changes in the Pro Stock category for 1972 but also an invasion of many lower-class entries into the Super Stock and Stock ranks going forward, which forever ended the dominance of Hemi-powered cars in those two popular divisions. Beyond that, even if the Chryslers could remain competitive, it was easy for the NHRA to add weight via factored horsepower to package cars, such as Dave Boertman's 383 Charger that was a dominant combination in 1971. Payback for Chrysler's successes in this season was brutal and, quite frankly, permanent.

For the *Missile* team, the plans were already laid to move over to a fresh 'Cuda design for 1972. The Challenger's last NHRA race was at Amarillo, the new World Finals location. The team's efforts on the regional Division II circuit actually made Carlton number one in the so-called Eastern Conference because the NHRA chose to seed the fields in Texas with a balance of cars from both sides of the country. That ideal was difficult to achieve because a number of the possible prequalified positions were empty when some qualified entrants did not come out for the event, which led to a field of only 27 Pro Stock cars for 32 positions and a first-round bye run for the

Missile and several others. Many upsets followed, with Don losing to Stu McDade in round two and Mike Fons spending his day beating Mopars. John Hagan, Butch Leal, Ronnie Sox, and finally Herb McCandless all fell to the Rod Shop entry, and Fons won it all to be named the 1971 NHRA Pro Stock Champion.

The IHRA's first full season was one of ups, downs, and growing pains. The *Missile* made several trips into the South to run events, however.

"We did not start running IHRA until [Donnie] came onboard. He wanted to do it," said Ted. "Tom [Hoover] wanted to keep him happy, so whatever Donnie wanted, Tom made happen. That was a good thing for all of us. The IHRA was a little easier, but I liked the fact it was way more laid back. It had those Roy Hill–type characters in it then, so we were more relaxed. I mean, the racing was still intense—we raced hard, but it was also more relaxed, and that made Donnie more successful in IHRA.

"Now part of that was [because] we now had a year under our belts as a team, we were more confident, and, to be honest, I always kept in my mind that we were going to these things to win. In fact, this might sound boisterous, but I was horrified if we were not [the] number-one qualifier. We were putting in all this time to be the best, and if that didn't happen, we were not doing our homework. The car was the baddest car around, and Donnie was a star driver to the IHRA."

Ted added, "You know, another thing about [the] IHRA was that we were all sort of mixed in as stars. I would talk to the fuel guys and we were like one big group, seemed to all get along, while [the] NHRA sort of had the fuel cars and the rest of us all separated."

The IHRA's big season finale was at the new track in Lakeland, Florida. Don went to the semifinals at the second race at Bristol in the summer months but had won a US Open IHRA event in Rockingham the weekend before. Despite Disney World opening in nearby Orlando that same weekend, the Lakeland facility had a large crowd.

In round one, Sox fouled to John Livingston to end his day early, and then Fons crossed the center line in his race, removing two strong contenders. Don then beat the Barry Seltzer Camaro, singled in round two when his opponent failed to show up, and took out Max Hurley's Dart Swinger in the semifinals. When the *Missile* clocked the Low ET of the event (9.71) to trailer the Duster of rising Atlanta-based driver Reid Whisnant in the final round, Don Carlton became the IHRA's first Pro Stock World Champion.

The end of 1971 was the finale for Chrysler's legendary muscle cars. Noted as the highest-known VIN for a Hemi-powered Challenger from that last year, this Challenger R/T model was history when the 1972 vehicles were announced. Street muscle was dying, and soon minicars would become dominant in Pro Stock as well.

The End of an Era

The racing news reports used terms such as "SoxNationals." Other than his round-two loss at Englishtown due to a flat rear slick and the honest trouncing he took at Fons's hands at Amarillo, Ronnie Sox won every round of NHRA Pro Stock national event competition in 1971—all six other events. With star drivers, such as Jenkins and Nicholson, making noise about parity, by midseason both the media writers and the sanctioning body rules makers began to look into creating a more-level playing field. That Sox was good was not the main issue; it was the overall ability for Chrysler Pro Stocks to consistently top every event field, and usually Sox was racing another Chrysler in the final.

Busy with the new Barracuda being built, the *Missile* did not go to Ontario for the second Super Nationals in 1971. There, Sox defeated Herb McCandless in an S&M customer's car to end the year, but that was not before lodging a complaint against Butch Leal after a semifinal loss. The rules stated the car could not have more than 55-percent static weight on the rear tires, and the Ron Butler–constructed Duster was as trick as they

came. When a set of wheel scales indeed proved that the extremely fast red-and-white Duster was at 58 percent over the back end, the SoCal crowd-favored *California Flash* was disqualified and Ronnie advanced to what was his final NHRA national event victory.

The well-traveled 1970–1971 *Motown Missile* was posted for sale and purchased by a long-time racing driver from Memphis named John Livingston. When it showed up for action in 1972, it was changed very little even in its colors, aside from its new name, *Tennessee Thunder*. For Mike Fons, his 1971 World Championship was the highlight of his driving career, but his association with the *Missile* was not over yet. For Sox & Martin Race Cars, a thriving retail enterprise with weekly ads in *Drag News*, four months' worth of back-ordered cars under construction, and a steady stream of cash-paying customers from around the nation, no other business in drag racing was more affected by the outcome of the coming two years.

Meanwhile, things were changing in other ways. Perhaps most notable from Chrysler's position was the discontinuation of the production 426 Hemi and the 440 Six Pack engines; both fell victim to changing emissions requirements and proudly died where they stood as

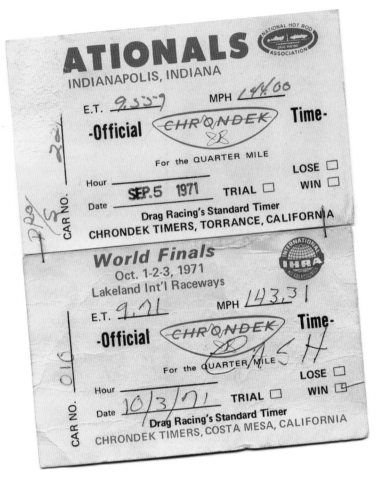

Two time slips, including the 9.55 from Indy and the final-round run at Lakeland, show that the Missile *had come to play seriously. It would be a brand-new world in 1972. (Photo Courtesy Ted Spehar Archive)*

multicarbureted engines with high compression ratios to the very end. For his part, Ted Spehar was about to find out that his business model would change as well due to his Chrysler-employed associates looking for new avenues in the test program to ensure they could keep Ted's business under contract.

Don Carlton became part and parcel of the *Missile* crew. There had been a few missteps in 1971, to be sure, but he was still all in and capable of what was needed. This was especially true from the aspect of testing. Toward the end of 1971, a number of Pro Stock racers gathered to create the United States Racing Team match-race circuit, and while there were dozens of possible members nationally, Donnie was among the chosen 16 to be booked into the nationally focused tour. To that end, he added a second car to his racing efforts as well so that he always had something to drive in that series and at match-race dates. The new *Missile* 'Cuda was reserved for factory work and Ted's event plans.

In the background, seismic shifts were implemented in the racing rules. At midyear, the AHRA had a secondary weight break for smaller engines, dropping weight if a smaller engine design was chosen. This was in part because there were a handful of racers now trying to compete in the new Chevrolet Vega. Before the end of 1971, the NHRA also looked at this and, despite having already announced its rules package for 1972, followed suit with a set of weight breaks as well. That forever changed the history of Pro Stock, so that the *Missile* team had to do whatever it could to finally get into the NHRA winner's circle.

Ted Spehar on Engine Evolution: 1970–1972

The 426 Hemi was well developed by 1971 and had proven to be very durable in all forms of racing. Ted Spehar had the unique task of taking it to the limit in Pro Stock. During 1970 and 1971, the team made hundreds of passes on the first *Motown Missile*. Whether with a ClutchFlite or one of the 4-speeds that Don Carlton used following the spring of 1971, every engine in the *Missile* program was pushed hard in this environment and found its weakest links. In 1972, the final year that Ted actually owned the car, it was more of the same. Even today, Ted admits that discussing powerplants that did not stay together under pressure is something no engine builder ever wants to talk about.

What you are about to read here has never before been publicly revealed. Keep in mind that the 426 Hemi, as it was designed, was never expected to spin at the rising RPM levels that even early Pro Stock generated, let alone survive the rigors of high-RPM shift point differentials, heavy block modification, and extreme parts stresses. As a result, main bearings were checked and replaced by Dick Oldfield or Ted himself, almost with the regularity one might expect in a supercharged application. Rocket science . . .

"Primarily, we did a lot of testing," Ted said. "It was not very romantic, but that is how you learn. So, if it seems like we failed a motor every month, you have to remember that was because of all the stuff we were doing. You'd fail a motor, you'd put another one in, you'd figure out why the one you took out was broken, rebuild it, and do all over again.

"The first engine was number 24. Remember [that] each engine, regardless of type, was given a number— whether it was a wedge, a press car motor, or a race motor. We used number 24 from April through the Englishtown [1971 Summernationals] race, then it cracked a main web and was out of service for a while. The main web issue reared its head on several occasions with these engines at the time, and 24 will be back.

"Number 25 was built as a D5-head motor; this was the first one we built with the D5 Weslake heads. That was one of the engines that was out with us for the tests at Irwindale in 1971. Anyhow, in California, it never got warmed up before seizing a couple of lifters up. The problem was a very small enlargement of the lifter diameter, less than a thousandth; it slid in the 0.030-over bore fine when it was cold, but was not so good once it got hot . . ."

"Anyhow, we rebuilt it with a light hone to the lifter bore, which fixed that problem, and it stayed as a D5. Then, in July 1971, we dropped it down to a 396-ci displacement and we put a roller cam in it; we had it through the Gainesville test in December. The Weslake design was sort of a backburner deal that never really worked out. We had carbon fiber pushrods in it; they were really cool, but I don't think they lasted a moment. It was fine in the static environment, but they never worked under compression or track load and just made a mess out of everything. So, after I rebuilt it again, it stayed a D5 through 1973 when it went to Pomona using a special premium D&D tapered steel pushrod, which took care of the flex problem; then, I noted it went into storage at Chrysler and I lost track of it.

"The D5 was actually an older design from the mid-1960s. By the early 1970s, Ford's Cleveland-style design was showing the direction things were going,

the next generation of engines. The D5 wasn't really a high-speed engine design. The head was big because the exhaust port wasn't laid over; it had very large valves and round ports; actually, those ports might not have been big enough. Regardless, the result of how the valves were laid out meant that [the] pushrods got about an inch longer, everything was heavier, so the valvetrain was very speed-limited. The intake had to be so wide [that] it needed a bend in it. Later, Landy may have had some success with the D5; the camshafts had gotten better by then. You know, we could never make that engine a priority; we had to justify the expense and had spent so much time on the multispeed transmission, there wasn't time or money to make an honest effort on it.

"A 1970 block was used for number 26; the earlier ones had been 1965–1966 blocks, and the 1970 model had a thicker web. That engine also stuck lifters at Irwindale in 1971; once we came back, we discovered the lifters were slightly bigger than they were supposed to be. We fixed it quickly, and that engine ran Gainesville, the AHRA race in Florida, and the record run at Suffolk. We swapped it over to twin plugs for the Super Stock Nationals, used it again for twin-plug testing, then at the Blaney, South Carolina, points event, a match race, and then it went fast at the NHRA Dallas Springnationals. We rebuilt it for a test in late June, but it failed a connecting rod and failed the block. We were still with the solid tappets at that time, as the manufacturers kept making better cams.

"Next, I built engine 27 in June; that one failed a thrust bearing early on, so we put a new crank in it, and that is the one we went to Sanair with. It ran in testing, match races, and at Indy that year. At the end of 1971, during the Gainesville test with the 'Cuda, it had a rod bolt issue; we later redid that engine as number 32.

"Engine number 28 was built for 1971 and started out with a 180-degree flat crank early in the year; we had it at Irwindale too. It needed a special cam and gear, but I turned it back into a conventional 90-degree engine and, according to my records, that engine did not go in the car again. That engine likely went to Don Carlton for his new match-race car.

"Engine 29 was built in September of 1971 as a California car test engine with some of the bottom-end parts from engines 24 and 26. No racing—it was

Testing in late 1971 at Gainesville involved making run after run with the new car. (Photo Courtesy Ted Spehar Archive)

Engine 27 ended with a rod bolt failure. Speed costs money; how fast do you want to go? (Photo Courtesy Ted Spehar Archive)

The team looks at the carnage; then, it is back on the trailer for surgery. All in a long day's work. (Photo Courtesy Ted Spehar Archive)

used to figure out the real difference between compression ratios of 12.5:1 and 13.5:1. In the end, 12.5:1 with more spark made about the same power, and we settled in at 12.8:1 to 13.2:1. We serviced it, and in February 1972, that engine became the Crane R290 roller-cam/twin-plug test engine that we used in the Lakeland, Florida, hood scoop tests. The speed picked up; it went 9.56 at 145 mph and we also got something from all the hood scoop testing we did there as well.

"That was just before Gainesville. On that Saturday morning, it cracked the number six cylinder, so we removed the engine. I later rebuilt it and used it for testing. We ran it in June at the spring IHRA race

in Dallas and got 9.40s at 142. By then, we were trying a lot of roller cams. We put on fresh heads and a new cam, but it broke another crankshaft. We rebuilt it to go to Tulsa for the boycott race—again high 9.40s at 145. We put new heads on it; my notes say it had an Edelbrock intake on it there, but I remember having a new magnesium intake on it. It ran 9.30s at 148 at the IHRA Finals in Dallas, then we tested with it. It never failed at the track, but when we went to rebuild it, we found that the block had cracked at the number four main web, the whole saddle from the crank to the cam, and it had cracked another crankshaft.

"That was three crankshafts in a row. The failure

was on the number three journal in the fillet area, and the problem could have been the radius diameter. We tried some different things, we probably went to a larger radius later on, and I didn't record whether that was a 1966 crank, a Grand National crank, or a new one. Regardless, it was a good crank. All of them probably had 100-some runs on it, but they still should not have been breaking, not these ones.

"That brings us to engine 30. That was the replacement short-block we had at Gainesville [that] we built during the race. We took everything off of the old one and put it on this one. We had the dry sump on the car by then, so it was a real fiasco with all those AN high-pressure lines with Teflon inside, the sump, everything. It won the race on Sunday, best of 9.55, and we tested with it in Gainesville afterward. We used it in April and May; then, [it] cracked another crankshaft. We rebuilt it, put it back together, and ran it for the rest of the year. Engine 31 was not a Pro Stock engine, it was a 440 6-barrel engine, probably a magazine test car engine.

"In April of 1972, I built engine 32 using the block from engine 27; we ran it from April to July; then, it went to Carlton. He was running his own car by then. Clyde Hodges worked for him, Donnie flew home, and they raced. He was going back and forth; he did not move up here until late in the year when we did the A-Bodies in Michigan. We might have kept the wet sump in Donnie's A-Body as we worked up some oil pans with this engine, doing anything to get oil away from the bottom of the engine. One had the sump rearward under the transmission; it was pretty exotic, and a pain in the butt to take on and off.

"August 1972 was engine number 33. This was a test engine; it ran fast and was always a good motor. We ran it from August to October; we put new heads on it and that went into the new A-Body for the Gainesville fall test. That might have been the Butler car, but man, that thing went fast—9.20s at 148 mph, and we finally had the Lenco behind it by then. This one had a very unique oil pan because I had cut the skirting from the block way back. It had a two-piece oil pan that went up next to the bores, again to get the oil away from the engine. The sealants back then were not real oil-friendly, but if you could seal it up, that engine always worked pretty well. We built two engines like that.

"When we did that, we had to work hard to keep the block in alignment but figured it out. We picked a block with really thick bores because of that intention and then stressed the bores enough to make them stay straight. It took a couple of times to get where it seemed happy, but then each time after we rebuilt it, it always seemed to want to get better. There are better ways to do that now, but that was how it worked then. A big machine at Kramer Boring Company always took about 30 pounds off of them and we did the rest by hand. I think I had one of the blocks down to 215 pounds after we finished working on it.

"On the ignitions, we A-B-A tested that twin-plug deal a lot and figured out the B-position alone worked best for power. To be honest, some of that was driver preference. Donnie never seemed to care either way. Later, with the A-Body, he might have felt differently. You have to remember, it wasn't difficult to go back and forth between single- or dual-plug with the D4a aluminum heads.

"The D4 version, the fourth Hemi head the company did, was an iron head, and it was very good. When Bob Mullen was doing the porting work for Chrysler, he came up with the D4a design. While it still had a rectangular instead of D-shaped exhaust port, it was higher and just as good. Once Chrysler had done the run of the D4-type heads in aluminum, it came ready for twin-plug openings; you just closed off the one side if you were not going to use it. They were ported to create the D4a. We tried everybody's heads—Diamond-Elkins, Mullens, [and] sometimes Butch [Elkins] came up with a good set, but we probably used the Mullens more than anything else.

"You know, having that lightened block created its own set of challenges. You had to change the front cover and the lifter bridge, and even the 3/16-inch you milled off the pan rail was a big chunk of metal. It was all solid iron, and we did a lot of hand grinding in the beginning. Then, I came up with the idea to get some of it milled away. You then had to make it all fit together and not leak too bad.

"At the first big race we went to at York [July 1970], we had a lightened engine, and Jere Stahl was all over this thing. The people who were paying attention could see the changes and knew what to look for. We had cored out a 1.25-inch hole in the front pad where the engine number gets stamped on and put a freeze plug in there. He picked up on that right away. [laughs] He and Jenkins talked a lot."

Photographer Steve Reyes was in Tulsa over Labor Day in 1972 as Donnie attentively launched the Missile *'Cuda during ferocious qualifying. Wheels-up, the car had become one of the most visible in the nation thanks to great publicity and victories on the NHRA and IHRA circuits that season. (Photo Courtesy Steve Reyes)*

Chapter Four

1972: The 'Cuda, Conflicts, and the Corporation

The dramatic election year of 1972 was an appropriate backdrop for what was happening with the *Motown Missile* program and Performance Automotive during this season. The cultural changes initiated during the turbulent 1960s began to emerge, and the nation's biggest political battle pitted the "law and order president" Richard M. Nixon as the traditionalist against the more liberal policies promoted by former bomber pilot turned flower-power champion Senator George McGovern. Top 100 hit music ranged from Don McLean's "America Pie" to the

thunderous metal of Argent's "Hold Your Head Up" and Alice Cooper proclaiming, "School's out forever!" Drama was part of the moment.

By the year's dawn, the era of the American supercar had passed, although there remained a very strong public interest in automotive performance. For its part, Chrysler continued to offer a line of full-size cars and sporty mid-size models, utilizing imported Crickets and Colts from Japanese manufacturer Mitsubishi to meet the growing demand for so-called minicars. Of the Big Three, the Chrysler Corporation always made do with less. After Dodge and Plymouth again won NASCAR, USAC, IMCA, ARCA, and NASCAR West championships in 1971, the company announced that it was done with circle track racing research projects as a corporation amid tightening budgets. The development role was now assumed fully by Petty Enterprises. Indeed, all of motorsports was in a state of flux as a result of Detroit's tectonic shifts away from muscle. Among the rules announced for NHRA Pro Stock as 1971 wound down was a ban of all Hemi-type engines as non-production powerplants by January 1, 1973, with a more radical rumor of nothing over the 366-ci 6-liter margin being part of this.

Nonetheless, in all the drag race sanctioning bodies, Pro Stock continued in its popularity, and many changes occurred in the 1972 season. For Ted and his crew, as well as the engineering guys at Chrysler, it was both a change in focus and a change in race cars.

Performance Automotive to SVI

While testing efforts with both the *Motown Missile* and the Sportsman drag packages continued as part of his work, Ted's business model morphed from being simply race- and performance-car oriented into one that performed specific vehicle projects that Chrysler assigned. The result was a name change to Specialized Vehicle Incorporated during this year, and by the end of 1972, driver Don Carlton became the actual owner of the *Missile* racing business.

"Another thing played into how much we could do here at our shop after 1972," Ted remembered. "You know, by the end of that year, they [Chrysler] wanted me to do a lot more stuff; it was not just Pro Stock anymore. There was a push to be sure that the bean counters did not cancel us out. You know, 'Why are we paying this guy? We could be doing this stuff in-house with the union guys.' Bob Cahill wanted to justify our existence, so we did projects. The parts for the featherlight Duster, we did that, and we did development on the *Lil' Red Express* truck. So, as my duties changed, that was the biggest reason Donnie took the drag car program over. He got the car deal and I stayed on board under SVI to do engines for him.

"At that point, SVI was actually getting bigger because we were doing more," he continued. "The engine deal was now a part of that whole thing. We were still doing the Sportsman stuff. I hired a guy, Ross Smith, who was like Jimmy Addison, a very bright young guy. So I gave him a list of what we would be testing, and he would get things ready and get whatever car to the track. I was busy with other stuff by then. Eventually, he ended up at GM in Advanced Engine Development; he was very smart."

Of course, this happened later. Ted owned the then-under-construction *Motown Missile* Plymouth 'Cuda for the 1972 season, and Donnie continued on as the driver working for him. This new car garnered more publicity than any prior *Missile* iteration by the team. Since he wanted to continue in the racing program, Dick Oldfield

went to work directly for Carlton until 1977 when Ted hired him back.

The Motown 'Cuda

Of course, Mr. Hoover continued to be the de facto champion of the *Missile* cause, and with basically 18 months of flogging the Challenger, many lessons were learned. That, in turn, meant a new car was going to be needed soon enough. The sport evolved during the two racing seasons, and while the original *Missile*'s testing schedule was still very aggressive, it fell on Tom Coddington under Hoover's direction to execute applying some of that fresh knowledge to a new vehicle that was already chosen as a Plymouth Barracuda.

"Well, we had used the 1971 car for two years, including all the test runs on it, and you could watch it do the watusi as it went down the track," Ted laughed. "It was time for a change. It was worn out for testing too, as you could see the whole car shift when you let the clutch out.

"The factory told us [that] if we did build a new car, it would need to be a Plymouth because we had just run two years as a Dodge, and it was a Chrysler promotional program," Ted said. "The biggest change from a construction standpoint would be a better chassis, a better roll-bar design, and we went to the leaf-link rear suspension. Pete Knapp, Dan Knapp's younger brother, came in to work for me and he was a good welder. We got another body in white, but we did not need a street car this time to convert the car."

The NHRA had been reworking the rules during this period as well. Editor Jim McCraw of *Super Stock* magazine opined that there was likely not a single "legal" car in the sport based on some of the current rules. The racers always were creative in their interpretation, and the next *Missile* was as trick as anything else out there during the era of its construction.

"All [of] the titanium stuff we had figured out with the Challenger was part of that build," Ted noted. "It had been an evolutionary process to get there. For instance, we went with some titanium bolts, but we found out they could not constantly be taken in and out; they are just not as strong. We learned you would sometimes need to sacrifice weight for durability, especially after you have broken a few bolts off. You say, 'Well, this isn't going to work! It didn't save time or money! Then it was useless because they changed the rules and you had to put that 400 pounds back into it anyhow.'"

The acid-dipped 'Cuda body was in the shop by early April, seen here with a 1971 grille fitted to it. The team would spend a good part of the 1971 year completing the car. (Photo Courtesy Dick Oldfield Family)

Now with a fresh valance, the new 1972 grille was in the front end by mid-year, glass was installed, and trim was installed. Primary to the physical construction was Dick Oldfield and Pete Knapp, directed by Tom Hoover and Tom Coddington. (Photo Courtesy Dick Oldfield Family)

The earliest images of the car under construction date to April 1971, showing it with a 1971 'Cuda grille. There already was some magazine reporting that the team was getting a second car ready, but as noted from the race and testing schedule in the last chapter, the time in a day could only go so far.

"We started building that car in the late summer of 1971, August or so," Ted recalled. "I don't think they had announced the weight changes yet. The car was done by December. We knew we would not be going back to the automatic, so it was set up as a manual car from the start. It had the rear suspension changes done and we added a dry sump as well.

"The car would still be used for testing, but there was not a lot of extra stuff we did for that," Ted continued. "It was still pretty spacious in the engine compartment, and we may have made the inner fenders easier to remove. We did make the tunnel bigger so we could access the bellhousing and transmission quicker for in-between-rounds changes. There was no removeable front end, and the doors did not come off easily yet, like they do now."

Nonetheless, it required quite a bit of re-engineering. In the front suspension, that included a switch to a Cam Gear rack-and-pinion layout similar to what was being employed by the new Ford Pintos. By fabricating various parts from lighter materials, the net result freed up a considerable amount of weight as did the removal of 20 pounds related to the OEM steering layout. Inverting the steering arms from side to side with accompanying changes to the A-arms also allowed the car to maintain positive caster under acceleration, improving stability at speed.

The rear suspension was a leaf-link design that offered substantial improvements from the prior car in adjustability as well. The leaf link used a conventional bias-design Chrysler Super Stock leaf spring set, moved inbound onto the factory frame rails. At its front, a round bar ran perpendicular to each spring. This was located directly above the back half of the spring between a brace on the narrowed Dana rear housing and a multipoint-drilled and vertically positioned mounting bracket that was welded to the car at the roll cage's lower crossmember. This bracket also held the front eyelet of the leaf spring. The design allowed either the bar or the spring to be adjusted via a set of possible bolt positions to optimize track conditions and desired rear suspension height without changing the pinion angle. Even with the car kept with its proven standard two-degree rake, the team had a lot of possible adaptations here. The rear eyelet of the spring was held in a static, nonadjustable position. Also, the rear frame longitudinals remained in their stock location, although wider wheel tubs for tire clearance were also installed. Working in conjunction with a custom roll cage designed by Coddington that used multiple triangulations to increase rigidity, the overall suspension package was a big step forward from 1971.

Of course, the new dry-sump oiling system was another crucial part of the car's reworking, as its adaptation allowed a significantly lower nose stance over a conventional wet-sump oil pan beyond the more obvious benefits of oil evacuation away from the crank. The tank for the dry sump was located in the front of the

As seen during the initial work, holes were drilled for mounting the leaf-link bracket solidly to the frame support. Note the large round hole through which a section of chrome-moly tube would enter from front to rear. (Photo Courtesy Dick Oldfield Family)

Here is the first leaf-link installed. Though offering only modest adjustment points at this stage, the design was a big advance at the time over the factory rear-bias-based leaf spring pack. (Photo Courtesy Dick Oldfield Family)

Tilted up on one side, this construction image showed the tubes running between the front and rear sections of the unibody. Light gussets have also been applied, and the cut-open transmission tunnel would allow for very easy servicing as needed. (Photo Courtesy Dick Oldfield Family)

engine off to the passenger's side. The car was equipped with front disc brakes, rear drums, and two associated line locks, one to hold the front wheels for the burnout, the second to hold the rear firmly on the starting line.

The car began as an acid-dipped body in white with fiberglass components where the rules allowed. After its construction, the choice was again for black paint, this time it was augmented with gold-leaf lettering, all painted by the same people who had done the Challenger. Ted also garnered a nice sponsorship program from Lee Filters as the car went together.

"I hated having a lot of decals on the car," Ted admitted. "Lee was a bunch of companies—Lee Filters, Cyclone Headers, Fenton Wheels, Eelco Linkages. Then we had Liberty [transmissions] and Trick Titanium, which was Apollo Welding's growing business in race car parts."

With the 'Cuda just completed at the end of 1971, *Hot Rod* magazine did a major photo shoot resulting in the cover story for its January 1972 issue. One of photographer Bob D'Olivo's images showed all the team members depicted in various positions of responsibility and spare parts positioned all around. Meanwhile, writer John Dianna gave an excellent seven-page analysis of the car's construction, using D'Ovilo's work and images taken during construction. Testing began in Florida in December, and the *Missile* crew did not attend any of the sport's early-season events leading up to the first weekend of February, when the NHRA hosted its season-opening Winternationals in Pomona, California.

Before Pomona: The Shape of Things to Come

I noted earlier that the American minicar had arrived in the form of Chevrolet's sporty Vega, the Ford Pinto, and AMC's little Gremlin. The NHRA heard an earful from anyone not named Sox about how boring the class

During the Hot Rod *magazine photo shoot, this image of the just-completed car was taken in the studio. The resulting seven-page story was a very large commitment from the publishing firm that, at the time, regularly limited car features to a mere page or two. (Photo Courtesy Dick Oldfield Family)*

Even decades later, the January Hot Rod *cover story that showed a dapper Ted and serious Mr. Hoover was being used to market diecast toy cars. Barely visible, Don Carlton was sitting in the car. (Photo Courtesy Ted Spehar)*

seemed to be. While not exactly true, what was fairly usual was at least one Chrysler A- or E-Body of some sort in every final round, and Sox had won most of those during 1971. Indeed, as a brand, Plymouth won *every* NHRA Pro Stock event title for two years, other than one by Landy [Dodge], one by Nicholson [Ford], two by Jenkins [Chevy], and the World Championship pass of Mike Fons [Dodge]. With Detroit no longer offering big-inch performance motors in their models, the NHRA was also concerned about the class's future relevance.

William Tyler Jenkins of Malvern, Pennsylvania, was never anybody's fool. While short in physical stature, his Mensa-level mindset was always working something out. His nickname, "Grumpy," even allowed for his temperament, which could be terse, pointed, and often noted in print ending in the term, "hrmph!" Jenkins was shut out of the NHRA's final rounds since his two wins in early 1970. It is still not known how much influence he put on the powers that be, but the result was the first of the NHRA's true tube-frame Pro Stock cars that emerged from his shop for the 1972 season.

The Vega was Chevrolet's car for the 1970s—sporty but economical. Jenkins, who had a backdoor research and development budget from a company that was never revealed but is well known, took all of his lengthy knowledge of the small-block Chevrolet to create a 331-ci engine that would allow the car to weigh a mere 2,234 pounds. That was because the NHRA had adopted new sliding weight ratios with inline wedge valvetrain designs, such as the Chevy small-block set at 6.75 pounds per inch.

The team was surely a serious contender for an event title going into the 1972 NHRA Winternationals, as one of 20 Mopars in the final program of 32 qualified entrants. Some earlier testing had already been done in both California and Florida, but this was its first big national event. (Photo Courtesy Steve Reyes)

Other groups were at 7.0 for canted-valve designs, such as the Chevrolet big-block and Ford Cleveland, and then an increase to 7.25 for Hemi-style big-blocks or other designs. This meant the new 'Cuda with its 426-plus 0.020-ci had to now weigh 3,098 pounds. That's almost 900 pounds more.

"I give Jenkins credit because those guys did a good job," said Ted. "But when we got to Pomona and saw it, the handwriting was on the wall. There was not much more we could have done to our car to change it by then. We stayed about a month on the West Coast and tested. We only ran the NHRA race, and I don't remember if we even did any real testing before the Winternationals. Remember, we did not do a lot of match racing with the *Motown* car.

"I guess, thinking about it now, the shock really came after that first race," Ted continued. "It was first, 'Wow, did we take a wrong turn,' followed by, 'Why weren't we allowed to do this stuff?' Why weren't we (meaning Chrysler Corporation, and to the same extent, Ford) in on making this decision? Why did GM get to do this stuff? We had just built this car, spent all this time and money, and it's already obsolete. It could still win a race—we won at Gainesville the next month. But the writing was on the wall."

In Jenkins's defense, he had followed the letter of the law. The tubular frame retained the semblance of the "stepped frame accepted/stock frame retained," though little remained of what came from the stamping plant.

The real benefit was two-fold: the small high-winding displacement coupled to the weight and the use of the semi-adjustable coilover shock absorbers. The NHRA allowed for a somewhat unsafe 2,000-pound minimum that year for all 94- to 99.9-inch wheelbase minicars; 2,400 pounds was the minimum of any American-built vehicle with a wheelbase of 100 inches or more. Incidentally, the Colt and Cricket were both less than 94 inches in wheelbase, rendering them illegal for NHRA Pro Stock from the start, and they were not American-made, either.

Winternationals of Discontent

When the tour rolled into Pomona in early February, the rules were settled for the moment and it was time to go racing. In *Super Stock* magazine's logical coverage of this first race, the writer broke it down as Group 1 (7.25 maxi cars), Group 2 (7.0 wedge cars), and Group 3 (6.75 mini cars). The field was still led by Mopars: McDade in Stepp's car at 9.59, then Leal, Sox, and Grotheer. Next was Dyno Don's Maverick, then Landy, and then the new *Missile*, but basically all the top 16 cars were Group 1 Hemi Mopars or SOHC/Boss Fords. In 17th place was Bill Jenkins and his just-built Group 3 Vega, powered by its 331-ci Chevrolet small-block with an ill-handling 9.90. The final car in the field of 32 was clocked at 10.74, creating a program of 20 Mopars, 6 Fords, and 6 Chevrolets.

Bill Jenkins proved to be a serious contender, running a 331-ci Chevy small-block in a just-finished Vega that was under the 2,300-pound legal weight in the latest Grumpy's Toy. *Jenkins beat the* Missile *in the semifinals, then topped Don Grotheer's 'Cuda for the event title. (Photo Courtesy Steve Reyes)*

Though the Vega passed tech, a number of competitors immediately asked questions regarding its letter-of-the-law eligibility. The NHRA tech inspectors from Jack Hart down basically shrugged off those concerns; the newest and smallest-ever *Grumpy's Toy* was going to run on Sunday no matter what.

Since the qualifying result put Jenkins against McDade in the first round (number 1 versus number 17), the Vega was figured to be a novelty. However, after some suspension tuning, Jenkins was suddenly fast, hitting a big 9.63 to trailer the 9.74 entry of Billy "The Kid." Next was a quicker 9.62 over Bill Bagshaw's Challenger, a 9.73 over Melvin Yow's Dodge, and a semifinal meeting with the *Missile*. Carlton was consistent all day, beating the S&M-built Ronnie Lyles 'Cuda with Joe Fisher driving in round one, a 9.78 win over "Fast Eddie" Schartman's Ford in round two, and a wonderfully scripted holeshot victory over Sox himself, 9.68 to a faster 9.64, to get a chance to stump the Grump.

Before the semifinals, Jenkins reportedly thought his engine was badly damaged and was said to be almost ready to forfeit the event when his crew discovered it was a simple valvetrain problem. The NHRA gave him time to repair it, and at the green, against the *Missile*, the Chevy headed to a 9.70. Carlton rowed through the gears, but a head gasket gave way. He slowed to a 9.84 to watch the Vega move closer toward its first event win of 1972. In the final, Jenkins raced multitime event finalist Don

Grotheer's Plymouth, and the "mouse that roared" won handily: 9.68 to 9.82. It was indeed a new era.

Testing 1-2-3

The team immediately moved to regroup, and testing was a serious matter. One development that arrived in this era was the Crane R290 roller cam, named for its 290 degrees of duration. Harvey Crane designed it for Chrysler on a computer in his Hallendale, Florida, shop, measuring several features from the factory's proven P9512725 flat-tappet design and then adopting them to the rollerized valvetrain. When he was done, it created a true 0.700 intake valve lift with a 1.57-ratio rocker, and 0.678 on the exhaust side with a 1.52-ratio unit. In testing, this cam and the attendant change to the roller tappets proved to be very beneficial.

Meanwhile, the code D4 Hemi head castings found major advantages with this cam profile as well. Chrysler produced a 500-unit run of aluminum heads set up to be easily milled for a second plug, but one downside was that they kept the basic 1965 S/S port configuration, figuring that porting was needed regardless. Still, just the weight difference (116 pounds for rare cast-iron D4s versus 46 pounds for newly cast dual-plug designs with the 1965 ports) required an immediate response when the benefits were confirmed on the original D4 port configuration.

Hard at work in Florida during the Lakeland test session, Don looks over the new scoop designs that John Bauman came up with. The snorkel on the right won in Gainesville a week later and was adopted by most major teams, regardless of brand, by the end of the year. (Photo Courtesy Tom Hoover Family)

This is where Bob Mullens came in. A former Chrysler employee working in the California speed equipment business, Hoover contracted Mullens to find out if the 1965-style port in the new castings could be recontoured to match the flow rates on the D4. He did just that, actually bettering the best iron-head D4 flow numbers and averting the problems that those castings presented in their as-created form. Through porting efforts, he and other specialists used the fresh aluminum castings for additional development work and sold them to the racers. As a side note, Mullen actually decreased the OEM Hemi valve sizes (from 2.250 to 2.200 on the intake side and from 1.940 to 1.900 on the exhaust) to prevent clearance problems from overlap on the new Crane cam design. This was in lieu of the more disruptive effort required by sinking the valve deeper into the head.

With the cam and heads now reworked, focus returned to the hood and carb airflow issues. With Mr. Killen's *Missile* science recorder in attendance, the team went down to the IHRA track in Lakeland, Florida, to work on several scoop designs that Bauman had been playing with, again running lap after lap in A-B-A fashion. When the team arrived at Gainesville Raceway in 1972, the first of the snorkel scoops became part of its appearance, but thanks to the black paint, this was not an exceptionally visible change.

Chomping at Gainesville

When the NHRA tour hit Gainesville, Florida, in early March, Jenkins showed that he had been doing his homework as well. A stellar 9.44 at 144.69 was the best time ever recorded in an NHRA-legal national event competition. He was followed by Ken Dondero in Don Nicholson's SOHC Maverick at 9.46. In fact, when qualifying was over, the *Missile* 'Cuda was well down in the program at 9.70, bracketed by Irv Beringhaus and Dick Landy, who also ran exact 9.70s at varying MPH. There was a good reason for this, though, when engine number 29 blew up during a Saturday morning time run.

"We split a bore at Gainesville with the *Missile*," recalled Tom Hoover at the roundtable gathering. "That

After an all-night thrash to build a fresh engine and a before-dawn test on a nearby country road with permission from the police department, the Missile went to the final in Gainesville. Melvin Yow had the big jump . . . and a red light! Don Carlton now had an NHRA title under his belt. (Photo Courtesy Steve Reyes)

Tom Hoover is not in this shot because he is holding the camera as the test team celebrates in victory lane at the Gators. From left to right are Koran, Bartush, Spehar, Killen, Bauman, and Carlton. Dick Oldfield is not shown. (Photo Courtesy Tom Hoover Family)

Steve Reyes took some images for ad clients as well. Don poses with the Valvoline oil rep and Miss Gatornationals, a young coed from a nearby university. (Photo Courtesy Steve Reyes)

meant change the motor. We had rent-a-cars, and Ted and I and the guys got the engine changed. We thought we better see if it ran okay."

With all the effort expended to get the engine rebuilt, there was a need to make sure there were no leaks or problems prior to the event beginning. However, the NHRA was not going to reopen the track for this, so the *Motown Missile* was instead going to get some "run time" out on a local public road.

"We called the cops and they said, 'Right! If you go on this little road out through the bayou someplace, go ahead,'" Hoover remembered. "It was pitch black. I volunteered to drive one of the rent-a-cars so we would have headlights, and Donnie followed me. That was one of scariest experiences of my life. I didn't know whether I would survive that night or not! Whaaaaa! [engine noise] behind you. No lights! Pitch black."

Mr. Hoover survived, and the car passed its road test. Sunday morning, Jenkins was the odds-on favorite. The Grump put "Mr. 4-Speed" Herb McCandless from the Sox & Martin team on the trailer in round one but fell due to handling problems against Reid Whisnant in round two. Meanwhile, the fresh "highway" engine was now seasoned enough for Donnie to put his foot in it. The result was a round one 9.58 win over Sox, who uncharacteristically missed a gear shift. Next, a 9.56 in round two took out the Camaro of Bruce Walker, and Carlton then dramatically won the semifinal over Dondero's fast Ford,

9.56 to a quicker 9.54. On the other side of the ladder, Melvin Yow, the 1965 NASCAR Ultra Stock drag racing series champion, had quietly been working his way up to make it an all-Mopar final.

At the green, the Yow car was already gone; a red light in his lane negated his 9.71 time. Don Carlton launched the *Missile*, slightly wheels-up, and thundered to a 9.56 at 143.54 to get the team its long-desired NHRA "Wally" trophy. *Super Stock*'s Jim McCraw wrote, "The crew of Carlton, Spehar, Oldfield, and Hoover, et al., walked on air for the rest of the day, while non-racers tried to reconcile their spending of two years and $200,000 to win $10,000."

Spring and More

The spring months did not see the team return to the track for any big events, although Donnie and Clyde Hodges now raced the Demon on the match circuit and at the events Donnie wanted to run. It is likely that he signed a contract with the IHRA's Larry Carrier to be paid for attendance at that series. Although they missed Lakeland, the car appeared to make its first formal appearance at the IHRA's rain-delayed Pro Am event in Rockingham in late April, where the Demon fell to Sox's 'Cuda in the final, 9.42 to 9.54. The IHRA's rules were 7.0 for Hemi engines, a reason why the times were quicker. Still, this

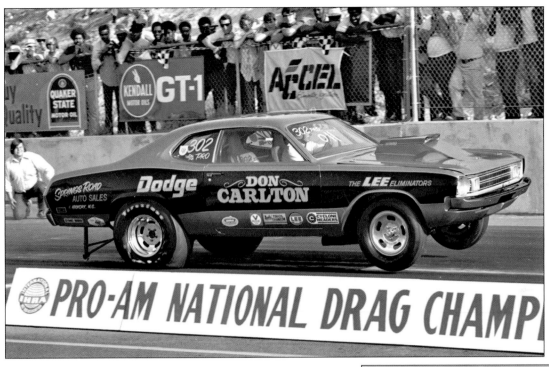

By the late spring, Don had his own Demon running based out of his shop in North Carolina and maintained by mechanic/builder Clyde Hodges. Anything that was found in *Missile* testing was applied to this car as needed. Don was runner-up to Sox during this spring weekend in Rockingham. (Photo Courtesy Steve Reyes)

was one of the few matches on the 1972 IHRA tour where Donnie had his own car running because Chrysler officials quietly began to boycott NHRA races that summer. The Demon was seen on the match-race and United States Racing Team circuits, often run from the North Carolina shop until Don established his own home base in Troy.

Super Stock magazine's rumor mill "1320 Notes" for the July issue asked cryptically, "What's 16 feet long, red, white, and blue and probably obsolete?" With the advent of Jenkins's Vega business and promising efforts with Don Nicholson's Pinto, the answer was Sox's new Duster, and both Ronnie and Herb McCandless would debut fresh new A-Body cars for the upcoming event cycle. The NHRA circuit was back in action for a new Springnationals race in Columbus, Ohio, while the IHRA now had two events: a new event at Dallas called the Longhorn Nationals and its traditional Spring Nationals in Bristol, Tennessee, two week later.

The freshly paved National Trail Raceway on US 40 outside of Ohio's capital city was untried, and Don qualified at the NHRA Springnationals in second (just behind Jenkins's 9.63) and then cranked out a huge 9.51 test run on Sunday morning. However, the *Missile*'s clutch linkage broke against Don Grotheer in round one and ended the team's hopes for back-to-back NHRA event titles. As at Pomona, Grotheer's 'Cuda again advanced to the final

A few months later, Reyes was at it again as Don receives accolades from a representative from Firestone tires. This was after the win at Dallas International Motor Speedway on the IHRA circuit. (Photo Courtesy Steve Reyes)

round and again fell to Jenkins's little beast.

However, Carlton won the new IHRA Longhorn Nationals in Texas in convincing fashion. Driving the *Missile* in Texas, after qualifying at 9.43, he backed that up with a 9.50 to start things off on Sunday morning while racing against the team's old Challenger, now the

Round one at the Dallas IHRA race pitted old and new as Don raced John Livingston in the former Missile, *now called* Tennessee Thunder. *Livingston, a long-time racer out of Memphis, had nothing to top a 9.50 from the new car on that day. (Photo Courtesy Bob McClurg)*

Ace shooter Bob McClurg was up on his ladder as the final round of the Longhorn Nationals was underway. Beating Ronnie Sox was always a big deal; beating him in a final round was exceptional. The Missile *also ran low ET of the event with a 9.42 on this pass. (Photo Courtesy Bob McClurg)*

John Livingston–driven *Tennessee Thunder*. Round two was a 9.52 single; then, Carlton beat Mike Fons with a 9.48 in the semifinals to meet Sox, who was now in his final racing appearance in the Sox & Martin 'Cuda.

At the green, Don was gone, and the timers rang up a Low ET of the event 9.42 for the win, while Sox followed at 9.63. Of all the races, this was a crowning event, beating Sox in the money round and having the field covered by well over a tenth of a second on every pass. Indeed, Sox's second-place 9.58 in qualifying was the only other pass below 9.60! Soon after, Don ran the Demon at Bristol but fell in round two.

Other dramatic action was happening at this moment off the racetrack as well. On May 9, Don Garlits and a group of Fuel racers organized their new Pro Driver Association (PRA) group. The goal of the racer organization was to begin demanding better purses and treatment for the racers, and memberships to the legal corporation was via a stock purchase of $100 for two shares. Classes included Top Fuel, Funny Car, and Pro Stock. The group then laid down the gauntlet. With help from the AHRA's Jim Tice, and sponsored in part by the Navy, PRA intended to host its own national event at the track in Tulsa, Oklahoma, directly opposite the NHRA Nationals

USRT: A Season of Gold Dust

Over the course of Pro Stock's first two formative years (1970 and 1971), popularity in the "factory hot rods" knew few boundaries. The dragsters and Funny Cars were still a huge draw at national events and on the match-race scene, but many fans fondly remembered the heyday of door car racing from the mid-1960s, when the factory Super Stockers and FX machinery ran in heads-up class battles. The Pro Stock class met and exceeded that thrill in terms of close competition and overall professionalism. Riding on this wave of popularity, the biggest names in Pro Stock decided to compete in a series of Wednesday night match races with the factory hot rods being the sole attraction under the title United States Racing Team, or USRT for short.

Gold Dust POWDERED ROSIN

"Made by Champions for Champions"—that is the claim of SOX & MARTIN for the new "GOLD DUST" powdered rosin. Developed by Ronnie Sox and Buddy Martin through years of Southern Style drag racing. "GOLD DUST" is the best traction aid available when use is permitted on starting line. Packaged in 25 pound drums, "GOLD DUST" is a must for the traveling professional driver.

From the 1970 Sox & Martin Product catalog, this was the notorious "gold dust." Made from a rosin normally used on dance floors, the material was shaken out and broomed onto the starting line. The car would conduct the burn-through to make it hot and sticky, pulling wheelstands on each attempt. It was part of the show, and the fans loved it.

OFFICIAL PROGRAM 1972

UNITED STATES RACING TEAM

$2.00

This is the program issued for the United States Racing Team in 1972. Sold at the events, the 16 drivers were shown on the cover. This series would be a career highlight for many of the Chrysler racers in the Pro Stock category. Don is on the second to bottom row on the right side.

Unlike the normally booked-in match-race programs that a track would organize with local cars as fill-ins, the new USRT special would guarantee literally all the biggest names in Pro Stock to be on hand for a single night of heads-up action. The team coordinator was Al Carpenter, a former Hurst public relations employee. Carpenter arrived a week early and organized driver interviews by contacting the local papers and TV stations, working with sponsors such as Coca-Cola distributors, and managing race car displays in shopping malls or related automotive businesses.

For their part, each USRT member put up a portion of the initial funding to get the program off the ground. The 16 cars attending each event then attempted to qualify for one of three four-car eliminators, or "place" groups. First Place was comprised of the fastest car from each of the four manufacturers: Dodge, Plymouth, Ford/Mercury, and Chevrolet (plus Wally Booth's new AMC Gremlin in the Chevy group). Second Place was given to the next four qualifiers

Here is Don Carlton, wheels-up in the gold dust at Great Lakes Dragway in Union Grove, Wisconsin, during the USRT race. These Wednesday night events led to near sold-out crowds for the tracks that participated during that first USRT season. In this series, Don made ample use of having a personal drag car at his disposal as the Missile 'Cuda was still primarily for testing parts. (Photo Courtesy Mark Bruederle Collection)

regardless of make, and Third Place was filled with the final four qualifiers. The four cars that did not make one of the three eliminators were kept in reserve to enter the program under the break rule if a qualified competitor could not race.

The track had a guaranteed purse with the winners and runner-up finishers earning additional money. In the best-case scenario, there were four cars each from one of the four manufacturers at every event, although that did not always happen. Non-members of the USRT could try to qualify, although they were granted a spot within the program only if there was a problem with a USRT member's car and no other replacement was available from the touring teams.

The top guys for Group 1 were often the usual suspects: Ronnie Sox for Plymouth, Bill Jenkins for Chevrolet, a Dyno Don car for Ford, and either Landy or Sox teammate Herb McCandless for Dodge. These stars didn't make Group 1 at every event—Jenkins was ousted by Wally Booth's Gremlin at Atco, New Jersey,

on July 13, and Wayne Gapp took the top Ford slot at Englishtown in August. McCandless was the most consistent runner on the USRT once his Sox & Martin Dodge Demon debuted in June. After winning the race at Atco, he won at Epping, at Englishtown, and at Union Grove, Wisconsin, to take four straight Group 1 titles.

"That Dodge was the strongest car I ever had," Herb said. "It was the quickest car in the country for about three months. We had gotten a set of Mullen heads right before that Atco event, and it would really run. Chrysler had decided that Sox & Martin needed to have a Dodge out there, and I was happy to do it. It flew."

Don Carlton, Dick Landy, and Mike Fons also took honors for Dodge in Group 1 before McCandless made his move to the White Hat crew; Herb then qualified for the top Group 1 spot for the remainder of the 1972 series. However, he had missed Capital's event because the car wasn't ready yet, which allowed Sox, the most

Young fan Dan Williams was in the pits at Minnesota Raceways near St. Paul when the tour made its stop there in June. He took this image of the Carlton Demon, the only color example we were able to locate for this book. (Photo Courtesy Dan Williams)

After its late-spring debut, Herb McCandless's new Sox & Martin Demon was a dominant player in USRT action, taking home several Group 1 titles in a row thanks to a set of 14 x 32-inch Firestones and excellent prep. During one of Chrysler's test days that year, he came in to make some runs. (Photo Courtesy Dick Oldfield Family)

consistent Group 1 qualifier and winner, to take home the individual crown. Dodge, for its effort, won the manufacturers' title thanks in part to Donnie's efforts in the Demon, as the Don Carlton–lettered car won Group 2 honors at a few of the events where McCandless won Group 1.

The fans supported it big time. According to the period newspaper stories, in some cases the USRT Factory Showdown event was the largest midweek crowd in the track's history. Atco hosted 10,000 fans, and Union Grove had even more than that; Herb remembered there being at least 5,000 to 6,000 people at each event. Since qualifying was limited to one single shot, it was anyone's game once it began; a loose plug wire or poor traction setup could mean you spent the next few hours hoping someone broke so you could get back in. Once underway, the race was run on a fairly quick basis, with just a semifinal and final round to determine the winner in each of the three groups.

"Because of the rules problems, Englishtown [the NHRA Summernationals in mid-July] was the final 1972 NHRA national event for most of the Chrysler factory teams," noted McCandless. "I ran a few AHRA Grand American races, but we did enough match racing and USRT events that I never missed it."

Of course, the time-honored ritual of laying down gold-dust rosin and doing multiple burn-throughs was also a regular part of the action. Wheels-up in the increasingly sticky powder and some massive crowd-pleasing wheelies had no small effect on the occasional clutch and rear-end problems that competitors suffered during the USRT races. Veteran mic jockey Jon "Thunderlungs" Lundberg came in to announce every event.

While the Chrysler entries were the most abundant and were all Hemi-powered, the Fords were a combination of 7-liter SOHCs, 429 Boss "shotgun" mills, and 351 Cleveland small-blocks. Chevy had Jenkins and the MIMI Vega entry of Bill Blanding (driven by Rick Mirarcki) with Chevy small-blocks, Dave Strickler in his ex-Jenkins rat-motored Camaro, and Wally Booth's AMC-powered Gremlin. Booth changed manufacturers after the team was formed and remained part of the Chevrolet associates. When Nicholson won the final USRT bout of the year after McCandless had clutch problems, Ronnie Sox was still the king.

There were nine USRT events total in 1972: Phenix City, Alabama; Capital Raceway near Baltimore, Maryland; Minnesota Dragways, St. Paul, Minnesota; the rain-delayed Atco, New Jersey, event; New England Dragway, Epping, New Hampshire; Raceway Park, Englishtown, New Jersey; Great Lakes Drag-O-Way, Union Grove, Wisconsin; and National Trail Raceway, Columbus, Ohio; plus a point-gathering appearance during the Super Stock Nationals at Pennsylvania's York US30 in mid-May.

The only series title that Sox won in 1972 following his 1970–1971 dominance was the USRT crown. He is seen here in the gold dust, wheels-up for a hot lap at Union Grove, Wisconsin. The Sox Duster proved to be a stellar machine, but even he could not match Jenkins's onslaught in 1972. (Photo Courtesy Steve Reyes)

For 1973, things changed on the USRT program but not for the reasons you might think. First and foremost, Chrysler pulled the plug on much of its Pro Stock program, so there were many drivers no longer traveling like they had been before. Vanke, Grotheer, and other names were soon semi-retired. McCandless believed that there were only a few events for 1973, including one in Canada, before the team itself sort of imploded partway through the season. Post-event publicity was minimal, and little record was found to verify locations or results.

The sport changed as well. The new Lenco transmissions were in, and the cars were becoming more complex. The weight-related rule hassles that plagued Pro Stock in 1972 were even more pronounced in 1973. Finally, soaring gas prices and the nation's economics may have played a role as well. In the end, just as in 1965 (the first year of Funny Car racing), changes such as these perhaps ended the United States Racing Team tour a little sooner than many had hoped. But the memories of the wheels-up glory days remain.

over Labor Day, an extravaganza that would pay $25,000 cash to each of the Fuel class winners and $10,000 for Pro Stock. A majority of the bigger names, including Jenkins, Sox, Carlton, and Landy, joined the group.

Missile Tests Continue

A full set of Chrysler's 1972 drag testing paperwork was not available to review for this volume, but 1972

was a very evolutionary year for the class. As Ted Spehar noted, cam and valvetrain designs were constantly evaluated. Suspension redesign work was ongoing, especially the desire for a wheelie caster design that could withstand the effects of hard, clutch-driven wheelstanding without unloading (losing the fulcrum benefit of the chassis or rear tires). However, one of the biggest advances of the 1972 year was the advent of the 14 x 32-inch Firestone drag slicks in the late spring months. This product release

Testing at Gainesville continued after the race was over. Seated here, Tom Hoover (left) and Al Adam get tires ready for another day of hammering on the car, looking for more power and results. Tom looks none the worse for wear following his late-night "street light" runs on a local road. (Photo Courtesy Dick Oldfield Family)

Vacation time? Not when you spend the day servicing the race car in the hotel parking lot. By now, the box truck was large enough to carry the car plus the parts. To the left are the Don Grotheer and Mike Fons race cars. (Photo Courtesy Tom Hoover Family)

of a new-width Pro Stock tire was more important than realized at the time because the broader face of the tire's tractive footprint at the launch, coupled with the continued adaptability of the rear leaf-link suspension layout, allowed for much more solid traction when track conditions were lacking. Prior to its arrival, this challenge was one reason why the USRT events made use of the gold-dust rosin.

Of course, since the A-B-A testing analysis was crucial to further understanding these and other developments, there remained the need for extensive on-track testing, and the 'Cuda was subject to the same workout the Challenger received. One area of testing included the data-recording efforts of Ron Killen, but at that time the car was still wired up without radio telemetry and required the removal of taped media for downloading after each pass. Beyond those variables, there was also the focus on weather analysis, a factor rarely considered at that time by drag racing participants.

"If you're looking for five-hundredths [of a second], you better have weather capability, or you're going to get lost. It's that simple," noted Tom Hoover. "God knows there are enough variables to deal with that you can't control, but you better be able to keep track of the weather. The track temperature changes, especially when you are running with other cars. People spill oil and drop water. The tires start to wear out. It'll drive you nuts. For *Missile*-program-like activity, you've got to be able to track the weather."

Nonetheless, to engineer Al Adam, it was part of any day's work, and the drag tests often noted these atmospheric changes.

"The toughest part is to follow the barometer," said Hoover in 2014. "We put a mercury column in the van; that's the right way to do it. That eliminates all the guesswork. What we do today is, for each strip in this country, there's a reference table on the internet that tells you which weather station to call. It's usually a local airport, hopefully very close to the drag strip. They can give you the barometer at that airport close to the drag strip, within about a half hour.

"That's only half of it, though. They're in the business for airplane pilots to get an idea of what the weather is going to do. They take the mercury column they're looking at in the airport, [and] they correct everything to sea level! Okay? So, I've got a little plot to get back to so-called absolute, what Killen's mercury column would say.

"The most potent factor is the ambient air temperature," he added. "I'm talking about the air that goes into the carburetors. You can get a little meter that'll read the relative humidity very accurately; you have to figure that in. It's not an easy calculation to make. The 0.28 root of a complex equation. So you need the right calculation to do that. Years ago, one of the times I first went back to Indy to watch some Pro Stock racing, the GM cars had humidity correction charts that they were tracking the

Round-one action in Englishtown found Don beating the 'Cuda of independent racer Alban Gauthier. Don fell to Herb McCandless in round three. This mid-July event technically ended active participation by the Mopar factory cars for the remainder of the 1972 season in the NHRA series. (Photo Courtesy Steve Reyes)

Herb McCandless did not win but got his picture in every magazine when he did this towering wheelstand against Jenkins in the semifinals after a wheelie bar broke and both bars were removed. The Mopar troops left E-Town with Mike Fons too light, Herb too high, and Dick Landy too broken when he sheared the wheel studs and lost a rear slick right off the starting line in the final. Jenkins won again. (Photo Courtesy Steve Reyes)

weather with. They had my name down in the corner, baby! Warren Johnson, those guys . . ."

Meanwhile, work continued on the science of clutches and transmissions. Joe Liberty worked with Carlton directly on some of this development, while Dick Oldfield continued his at-event efforts to dial up the driveline for durability and performance. Still, Don-

nie was never a guy who was afraid of tools or getting his hands dirty.

"By 1972, he [Carlton] was doing the stuff on the Liberty models," recalled Ted. "No, Donnie was more than a driver. He understood what was going on, and he pursued things to get answers—like the clutch eyebolt problem that was going on right then where the bolt would pull through. He was always figuring things out. He could do that stuff himself. He had Tom Hoover's ear, and he also listened to Hoover."

"Donnie was a cool head," Tom Hoover said. "He was a stabilizing influence. You know, a lot of young guys just get excited and all. But Donnie was cool—stable."

Tom Hoover was a true scientist, and all the guys who comprised this racing team at this point were working in unison.

"Mr. Hoover and I got along real well. It was never a problem," said Oldfield during our 2018 discussion. "Dave Koffel and I, that was another story. The fact was, he had his own ideas, and I did not always agree with them. Then Mr. Hoover would make the final decision in those cases."

Of course, travel was still part of the business, and Dick had the responsibility of getting the box truck down to wherever the event was held. In July, it was time to go to Englishtown, New Jersey, where the NHRA hosted its Summernationals.

Oh, Boy(cott)

Bill Jenkins actually bettered Sox's win record from 1971, and with the desire to see Chevrolet take as many wins as possible, "The Grump" began helping out his fellow racers. Associates from his shop crew began a car construction business called Speed Research & Development (SRD) and quickly began putting a lot of competitive Vega Pro Stockers on the racetrack. Jenkins Performance could provide horsepower as well; and as an engine builder, Jenkins also worked with these new Pro Stock clients as he had his Stock Eliminator customers in the 1960s, helping them sort out problems at the racetrack.

For the Sox & Martin team, the switch from E-Bodies to the latest A-Body Duster and Demon at midseason had not proven obsolete after all. Both cars responded well to the moment: Sox won his first time out at the IHRA's Bristol race, and Herb's Demon was especially potent during the summer of 1972. One reason he gave for this was the Firestone tire improvement. After a test session, he was allowed to keep the company's prototype set and was the only driver for about a month to have the bigger stickies.

Still, Jenkins came into E-town fresh off his victory at the Super Stock Nationals. He qualified in first position with a 9.50, then ran a 9.40 in round-one action to set the Low ET of the event. For his part, Carlton broke a differential during round one of the York US30–hosted Super Stock Nationals event, but the Missile was doing well at this NHRA race with round wins over Alban Gauthier and Bruce Walker. In the third round of the 32-car eliminator, he lost to Herb McCandless's Demon but more telling was Jenkins running 9.44 to Mike Fons's 9.50. At the scales, Fons's Rod Shop Challenger was proven to be 300 pounds light, in an effort to convince the NHRA that the current half-pound-per-inch difference between the Hemi and wedge-head engine designs was quite unfair. Another Dodge, Dick Landy's, had an amazing day. He beat Roy Hill, Arlen Vanke, Ronnie Sox, and Don Grotheer to meet Jenkins in front of the roaring crowd for the final, only to shear a rear wheel off and watch Jenkins win another NHRA crown.

For Chrysler racers now facing an onslaught of the minicars and their favorable weight rules, the frustration was palpable. On the other hand, the NHRA was thrilled to see Jenkins taking wins after two years of Mopar dominance at their races.

"In 1972, we planned to run the entire NHRA circuit, even though you knew you were going to lose," Ted noted grimly. "Donnie might have tried to do the IHRA circuit as well, but some of that was with his car. I don't remember the Missile pursuing that whole series when I owned the car. Anyhow, we figured we would be in third or fourth place, but that was the year everyone began to boycott, and we went to the race in Tulsa instead of Indy."

When the NHRA's tour rolled north of the border to Quebec again for the Grandnationals soon afterward, a handful of independent Mopar racers participated, but the big Chrysler names were all absent. Donnie qualified the Missile at the Popular Hot Rodding race but became physically ill and could not drive on Sunday, forfeiting the defense of his 1971 title.

That left the upcoming NHRA Nationals, which were on the traditional Labor Day weekend but now with the PRA's Nationals Challenge event as well. It was rumored that Chrysler racers would boycott the traditional Indianapolis race to go to Tulsa, and that was the case. At Indy, the Vegas dominated the class, with Dyno Don Nicholson's Pinto playing the spoiler, and one magazine wag actually calling it "a Moparless field." Not quite true, but all the Chrysler racers who showed up were gone by the end of round two. Ray Allen, who had been a Hemi nemesis in 1970 Super Stock racing with an LS6 Chevelle, took the event title in a Vega that Jenkins's guys built less than two months earlier.

In Tulsa for round two, Don gets ready to race John Hagan. Don lost this round, and Hagan fell to McCandless after a controversial semifinal race that was rerun due to a timing challenge by Buddy Martin. Jenkins was the only minicar on hand; he won. (Photo Courtesy quartermilestones.com, Jon Steele Archive)

In 32 spots at Tulsa, it was Jenkins followed by a slew of Chryslers; and it must be noted that Jenkins's 9.395 best was closely matched by Landy's 9.40 and Sox's 9.41. In the *Missile*, Donnie was in 6th at 9.481, beating Charles Lamarr's Camaro in round one but falling to John Hagan in round two. Incidentally, the Carlton Demon was also on hand at this event, being driven by Melvin Yow. Like the *Missile*, however, it did not go far on this ladder, and Jenkins won that fat $10,000 prize on Sunday night, beating McCandless's Dodge and wrapping up a stellar weekend for SRD's minicars.

The NHRA hosted two final events in 1972 after Indy: the World Finals and the Supernationals. The *Missile* and most of the other factory-associated cars opted to not attend those events in continued protest of the rules. Of the independent Chrysler racers, Ken Van Cleave went to the semifinals at Amarillo's bash, and no Chryslers got past round one at Ontario. The winner at both these races as well, Jenkins grossed over $200,000 in 1972, but the fact that he won over Pintos at both of these events was a foreshadowing of 1973's continued challenges for the Pro Stock class.

Meanwhile, the IHRA Continues On

In addition to testing, the latter half of the year found Don Carlton racing back home down South. Sox's new Duster came into its own by the time the IHRA's US Open Nationals in Rockingham took place that fall,

clocking a legal 9.27 for the top spot. Meanwhile, the Don Carlton–lettered Demon, now well-seasoned thanks to USRT races and the summer tour, was second at 9.33 and looking for another IHRA victory. Don beat Hubert Platt, Linson Kendall, and Bobby Yowell to reach a rain-delayed Monday afternoon final against Sox. There he ran a 9.33 at 146.57 for Top Speed honors, but Sox was the champion with a slower 9.39 as Don had left a red light at the start.

That left two events for the 1972 IHRA season: an event simply called the Nationals at Dallas, and the season-ending All-American Championships at Bristol, where the single race victory determined the overall champion for that season. Ted and the crew towed back to Texas, only the second time the *Missile* 'Cuda appeared on an IHRA track that season. Newly released wide Goodyears and engine number 29 were coupled with the tuned suspension, and the car flew to the top spot with a blistering best-ever time of 9.29. The 16 cars ranged from that and a 9.32 by Sox to a 10.02 by Dave Atkins's Camaro.

By this time, the mini Chevys were now boycotting the IHRA to try to get a better wedge-head weight break from Carrier, leaving only big-inch Camaros on hand for the Bowtie faithful to cheer on. In previous 1972 IHRA action, Jenkins won the Spring and Empire Nationals titles, Lee Edwards's Camaro won once, and Sox and Carlton split the rest of the victories. Carlton strung up the best round numbers all day on Sunday in Texas, beating Max Hurley (9.38), Charles Lamarr (9.40), Reid Whisnant (9.34), and then an ill-handling Sox (9.32) in the final to

go undefeated in Dallas International Motor Speedway action for the season.

At Bristol two weeks later, it was the Demon back in action. Carlton again put the car into the program on top, but Sox would get Low ET of the event with a 9.35 during eliminations. In the final round (and technically for the IHRA World Championship—there was no additional award posted, just the event championship prize money), Don got the leap and clocked a 9.39 (to Sox's close-but-losing 9.46) to claim his second IHRA championship in a row. The IHRA was in its heyday by now with solid Pro

classes and exhibition cars ranging from rocket-powered go-carts to noted celebrity "Big Willie" Robinson of the Street Racers of Los Angeles. Promoter Larry Carrier parlayed his go-it-alone risk into major status in the sport. As it turned out, both IHRA and AHRA Pro Stock fans benefitted from the NHRA's rules packaging for 1973.

A Final Look at 1972

"The whole weight thing drove you crazy," Ted said. "It became a joke. How much weight will you put on us

Butch Leal took a significant leap in involvement with the testing focus for 1973 and ran an amazing 9.11 late in the season in a match race against Jenkins. He is seen here at the AHRA Finals in Fremont in a low-down view by race photographer Steve Reyes. (Photo Courtesy Steve Reyes)

Don Carlton talks with a handful of people during either a very early or very late appearance at the legendary Detroit Auto Show in Cobo Hall late in 1972. Normally, the car was thronged, but Tom Hoover waited to take this uncluttered shot. For the team, the year had been a season of ups and downs; 1973 would not prove to be any different. (Photo Courtesy Tom Hoover Family)

this week? We began to feel Chryslers were never going to win again. Tom said, 'If one car weighs 2,800 pounds and the other one weighs 3,200, who do you think will get there first? The lighter car is better, regardless of how much power you make.'"

NHRA rules changes for 1973 allowed for a decrease in car weight for the Hemi/SOHC powerplants back to 7.0 pounds per inch, but it also allowed for a decrease for the Wedges to 6.5. Minimum car weight was raised to 2,300 pounds. Two other major changes were the allowance of any transmission, which quickly legalized the 5-speed Lenco design that a number of racers now employed elsewhere, and a new measurement for engine setback that was based on an alignment of the front spark plug to the front spindle. This meant that a 6-inch setback for Hemi engines was possible, and the NHRA had rescinded the originally scheduled idea of banning the Hemi Chrysler or Ford powerplants for 1973.

"At that point, we couldn't just give it up. Since it was being done by rules, look at the weight break," said Ted. "Dave Koffel would have been dealing with that. I am sure they wrote a letter to Wally Parks telling [the] NHRA that this was not fair, but it was legal. Hoover would say, 'We're still getting repaid for running the Mini Nationals in 1969.' That stuck in their craw for a long time. Eventually, even Wally admitted to somebody, I think Sox, that they had not treated us right. To be honest, did it change my life? Luckily, no, because I had other things and was getting paid to do this, but if you were a competitor, and

going faster and faster . . ."

Indeed, this showed on the match-race scene where Sox, running at 2,900 pounds, went 9.16 using gold dust, and Leal, running his new Duster in a Southern-style match race against Jenkins at Orange County late in 1972, not only hammered the Grump but ran an amazing 9.11 in the process. In the meantime, a number of teams and car builders nationwide began to look at the mechanics of wedging a Hemi down into the confines of the Colt for match-racing purposes.

"[The] NHRA got so sick of us winning everything; it was like a Red Army marching through East Germany in 1945 almost!" Tom Hoover recalled during the 2014 roundtable event. "They told Jenkins, and he told Chevrolet engineering, 'You guys do anything you want to beat the Mopars.' The outcome of that was a tube-frame car, which was a little spooky. And all Wedges had the most favorable NHRA ratios of car weight to cubic displacement factor. So Jenkins brought out his Vega. The 1972 'Cuda car represented about as well as you could do with the NHRA rule book still in your hand. Suddenly, we were confronted with a whole new ball game. Now we build a whole tube car and skin it; that was the purpose of that stage of the *Missile* program."

In mid-1972, Tom Coddington and Dick Oldfield made a trip to California to find out the secrets that went into the building of Leal's Duster and Bagshaw's Challenger. When 1973 rolled around for the *Missile* men, it was a new car, a new name, and a new owner.

Even with ever-tightening rules, Don Carlton's ownership of the Missile continued with more winning in 1973, including the event victory at the NHRA Springnationals, appearances in every final round in the IHRA tour, and a third consecutive IHRA World Championship, plus IHRA's 1973 Pro Driver of the Year honors. (Photo Courtesy Bob McClurg)

Chapter Five

1973: The Duster, Decisions, and Don

Extremely popular, the first three seasons of Pro Stock drag racing saw growing pains, and this reality manifested in both racing politics and expensive technological advances as the most serious and better-funded teams steadily pulled away from the rest of the pack. Nonetheless, 50-plus entries could still show up on occasion to try for one of 16 or even 32 open positions as a handful of the NHRA's larger events were still holding fields at that level.

What 1973 really showed was that nothing ever stands still. Indeed, this was certainly true in popular culture, where movies ranged from *American Graffiti* to *The Exorcist*; barcodes and fiber optics were invented; and vans everywhere were playing *Dark Side of the Moon* by British rockers Pink Floyd. Politics were dominated by the end of the Vietnam War, the start of the Senate Watergate hearings, militant Environmental Protection Agency (EPA) mandates, and (late in the year) the Organization of Petroleum Exporting Countries (OPEC) oil embargo, which all provide context to place the similar upheavals in auto racing into better perspective.

For the NHRA, this era perhaps became best known as one of increased performance when traction spraying of the racing surfaces resulted in record times in the nitromethane categories. For fans of the Detroit hot rods, there was a quite rapid transition from the muscle car body designs to the mini-compacts following Jenkins's ultra-successful efforts of 1972. The result led the sanctioning bodies to begin to consider factoring in wheelbase length along with the ongoing effort to police the parity of cylinder head configurations.

Bill Bagshaw's Red Light Bandit was the first-ever drag car Ron Butler built and took Best Engineered honors after its debut at the 1970 US Nationals.

Still, 1973 began with Chrysler entries again becoming competitive. This was in part due to rules revisions to help balance weight differences and fresh science being applied to cars such as those in the *Missile* program. Before getting into the nuances of the racing and research efforts for the year, much led up to the 1973 Winternationals from the position of car creation, engine configuration, and—perhaps most importantly—the reworked, renamed *Mopar Missile* team effort now owned and managed by Don Carlton.

That Butler Guy

By the time the 1973 rules were being announced in mid-1972, a number of shops had sprung up nationally to take over the construction aspect of Pro Stock vehicles on a professional level. Former Funny Car and dragster chassis builders Logghe Stamping Co. of Detroit and Don Hardy Race Cars of Texas were among these, as was the new Pro Stock–focused, Jenkins-associated Speed Research & Development in Pennsylvania and M&S Welding in California, the latter handling a number of the new 351 Cleveland Pintos. However, for Hoover and Coddington, their choice was a man in Culver City, California, named Ron Butler.

Butler grew up in New Zealand and worked for Carroll Shelby's competition team as a fabricator. When the axe fell at Ford for 1970, he opened his own fabricating shop, coincidentally sharing space with a drag racer named Bill Bagshaw. Butler did not know anything about drag racing but knew all about chassis design, weight balance, and car construction.

Meanwhile, Bagshaw, who was a Dodge contract racer, already had a new Pro Stocker planned, getting an acid-dipped body in white and a real Hemi Chal-

lenger from Dodge much the way Ted Spehar received parts to construct the first *Missile*. So, Butler's new shop quickly had work, Bagshaw now had a car builder, and the result was the next in Bagshaw's line of *Red Light Bandit* Dodges. Despite being Butler's first drag car, it was so well designed and built that this Challenger took Best Engineered Honors in its debut at the 1970 US Nationals at Indy.

Butler's approach to car building was based around creating a rigid "tent" design that employed triangulated bracing throughout. According to a profile in *Car Craft* magazine's April 1973 issue, Butler was also very concerned about safety, and, unlike a lot of drag racers with bogus muffler pipe roll cages, he didn't skimp on that in the interest of weight savings. Moreover, he was among the first to recognize the severe-duty impacts that multiple wheels-up launches and violent suspension travel created during gear changes on the car's actual structure. The very things that made the first *Missile* "do the watusi going downtrack," as Ted Spehar noted toward the end of 1971, were actually constructed out of the race car when a Butler chassis was built.

Tom Coddington created the basic ideas for the next *Missile*, which was an A-Body Plymouth Duster. Tom Hoover, having apparently received a legal letter from Motown Records boss Barry Gordy about the name usage, decided the next car would be called the *Mopar Missile*. Since Ted technically owned the *Motown Missile* name, this did not present any issues but averted any legal noise from upstairs at Chrysler. When Ted later sold the 1972 'Cuda to Mike Fons, Fons continued to use the *Motown* name as a race moniker even on his subsequent cars.

"Yes, I was in charge of having those cars built," Coddington said during a question-and-answer session recorded by Yetter. "They were built in California by Ron

Butler. My boss at the time thought I was going to go to work out there permanently. I think I was out there every other week, under Tom's direction, getting those cars built. The chassis were highly modified A-Body Dart chassis."

His role became more prominent by this point, again as things shifted at the corporate level.

"I was the head of engineering testing and all," Coddington continued. "Al [Adam] worked for me, and we all worked for Tom Hoover. Actually, I had taken over Tom's position. He moved over to planning and promotion. And Al and I worked on engineering. We were the ones [who] farmed out the work to the engineering departments to get support for the car builds. And we ran the testing program."

So, Coddington and Dick Oldfield traveled to California to watch Butler apply the Chrysler Engineering–suggested touches that were asked for, as well as follow the basic car construction. The Duster was something Butler already had proven his expertise with, as his follow-up to Bagshaw's Challenger was a new Plymouth Duster for

Butch Leal. This vehicle, under Leal's capable tutelage, was a serious contender from its debut, and Butch was promised additional financial factory support by Chrysler's Bob Cahill himself after the late 1971 incident at Ontario, California, when this new car was protested by the Sox & Martin team. Butler, who normally had just one or two cars being built in his shop at any given time, also built A-Body Pro Stock Mopars for Jim Clark, Bob Lambeck, and Ken Van Cleave, then cycled back to fresh iron for Leal and Bagshaw as soon as the next *Missile* was completed.

After Butler's basic construction was finished, this latest *Mopar Missile* was delivered in 1972-model trim during the final third of 1972. Built of fiberglass and lightened metal, the skinned chassis was brought back to the SVI shop in Royal Oak to be completed because Donnie did not yet have his own place in Michigan. Again, Oldfield was the primary player in the actual fabrication, using his tricks in lightening and vehicle blueprinting to complete it. The car was painted in black and orange, and the paint featured four separated rear segments to denote it being the fourth version of the *Missile*. It was again sprayed at Tignanelli's Shadowoods Automotive, and the lettering applied by Jim Stadinski's Advanced Sign for the first time proudly called attention to the company's own trademarked *Mopar* name.

Florida Flyer Cover Car

Testing began late in the year, and freelance journalist Jon Asher penned a cover story on the new car for the March 1973 issue of *Car Craft* magazine while the shakedown effort took place at Gainesville Raceway. Though not as extensive as the *Hot Rod* story from the year before, this feature provided an excellent breakdown of the car.

The rules for 1973 were still giving advantages to the inline and canted-valve engines. With the NHRA, it was

Acid dipping, done by only a handful of firms commercially, was how the 1972–1973 Mopar Missile *A-Body began before Ron Butler started on the chassis, which was designed with input from Chrysler Engineering. (Photo Courtesy Dick Oldfield Family)*

This was the end result, seen testing in Gainesville at the end of 1972. (Photo Courtesy Tom Hoover Family)

Ted Spehar (right) and John Bauman work on getting the new 396-ci engine package ready during the 1973 tests. (Photo Courtesy Dick Oldfield Family)

With Jon Asher setting up photos for the 1972 Car Craft story, this shot was taken by Joe Pappas showing the whole group. From left to right are Ron Killen, John Bauman, Len Bartush, Dick Oldfield, Don Carlton, Tom Coddington, Al Adam, and Tom Hoover. (Photo Joe Pappas, Courtesy Dick Oldfield Family)

Here is the car as configured for the start of 1973. The rear panel was lettered for sponsor Lee on the Duster model. The paint continued the gold-and-black theme from 1972, but it was updated with more color when the remainder of the 1973 front body parts were added. (Photo Courtesy Joe Pappas)

now 7.00 Hemi versus 6.50 canted or inline; in AHRA it was 6.85 versus 6.50; and in IHRA, it was 6.75 versus 6.50. The 0.5 difference in NHRA weights was a primary factor in the Chrysler boycotts of 1972, but through Ted's efforts, the team found that losing 30 cubes did not lessen horsepower. The resultant combinations used a lightly stroked (0.250) NASCAR-grade Kellogg crank, a change in piston pin location, a NASCAR rod, and the newly cast Mullen-ported aluminum heads with the D4-initiated runner changes. Bauman continued his efforts on carburation and intake designs while his sci-

ence-proven snorkel scoop became de facto equipment on most Pro Stocks.

One additional engine advance was the adaptation of the crank trigger ignition. Because of the way the OEM Hemi drove the distributor via a shaft and gear on the cam, the shaft could flex between under-power and normal operation, especially at gear changes, resulting in a condition called "spark scatter." This occurred when ignition events were not kept in sync with the reciprocating assembly's actual position. The cure was developed by Killen and also applied to circle-track applications. This used four steel blocks as triggers mounted exactly at every 90-degree location on a wheel that then mounted to the crankshaft behind the harmonic balancer. Each time one of the steel blocks passed over a magnetic field created by a sensor mounted to the block, a brief pulse was carried by wire to an amplifier (rebuilt from the normal black box Chrysler electronic ignition) mounted under the car's dash. The amplified signal then passed from the box to fire an Accel coil to spark the plug in perfect unison with the crank position itself. If using twin plugs, a second sensor could be applied. It greatly eliminated the problems associated with scatter, which became even more amplified by the Hemi's increased RPM level.

Noteworthy in Butler's construction was the elimination of the Chrysler rear leaf design for a four-link rear suspension setup. This used Koni adjustable shocks and an angled side-to-side track bar mounted forward on the driver's side and rearward on the passenger's side to keep the suspension squared and true. By using a linear transducer position created by Killen to measure shock and suspension travel as one of the recorded measurements, the team now had an exacting view on how the car was reacting both under the severe transitional conditions of launch and during shift changes. During testing, other readings taken at the same time could take into account prop shaft and rear wheel speeds to determine if the car was spinning the tires anytime over 1,320 feet. The narrowed Dana 60 used a 5.57 gear and was equipped with lightened Lockheed disc brakes.

"A four-link suspension basically uses two separate bars, an upper and a lower, creating a box," said new crew member Joe Pappas during a later interview. "They are much shorter than ladder bars and offer tremendous adjustability. You just had to know what you were doing to make the four-link work. You have some variability in how you position the lower bar, and that gives you different kinds of 'bite' in the rear end. You can make the car rise in the rear, make it squat, make it remain neutral as the car leaves the line. You can finesse it in smaller increments than with ladder bars. I think most modern Pro Stock cars run four-link suspensions because they are just the best."

Up front, Butler used a tubular crossmember, titanium and magnesium-based rack-and-pinion steering components, an engine plate for mounting support to the chassis front end in place of traditional motor mounts, and he similarly refitted lightened front disc brakes. A set of coilover Koni shocks eliminated the need for torsion bars, which freed up space for headers. Based on the current weight needs, the optimal plan was to lower the front-end area's weight (including the engine) to 1,400 pounds or so, allowing for a little additional weight to be put where it mattered the most, which was over the rear axle. It fell on Oldfield to mathematically ascertain the static weight of the combined pieces and adjust the specific weight of components as needed to find the optimal balance. So, the phone line to Apollo Welding's growing Trick Titanium racing part business was always nearby. In fact, with Apollo just a couple of doors away, anything they created as a prototype part for the *Missile* could immediately be marketed to other racers once it proved to be successful. It was an excellent arrangement for all.

Like those used in the rear of the car, Killen's transducers for test recording dealt with front wheel speed and measured things such as airflow into and around the hood scoop and the G-forces generated inside the car. The team was still relying on a recorder in the car (mounted in the location of the passenger seat) to tape these events, which required the time-crunching output of long tapes and analysis. However, it worked, and this level of research was groundbreaking in a drag racing application.

A Little Less Engine, Please

Tom Hoover and Ted Spehar both saw the benefit of running the Hemi in destroked form when it became obvious that the NHRA was not going to change the 1973

This was the configuration of the car for the first three months of 1973, when it still wore a 1972-type "sharktooth" grille that came on the 1971–1972 models. (Photo Courtesy Dick Oldfield Family)

With the idea of weight savings continuing, the team moved toward destroked engine packages, getting one Hemi down to 366 ci to take more weight off the vehicles. (Photo Courtesy Dick Oldfield Family)

Costly pieces, such as this magnesium differential and lightened driveshaft, were among the exotic parts developed for weight savings by Trick Titanium. Near Carlton's racing shop in Troy, Trick Titanium could also market successful items that were initially prototyped for the Missile *to other racing teams. (Photo Courtesy Joe Pappas)*

weight breaks. Engine 33 was the primary catalyst in this process and was still being referred to as a "sweetie" by Tom years later.

"The real benefit to destroking an engine is not simply the moving reciprocating weight, or what is known as rotating inertia, but friction reduction," Tom said during a conversion we had. "You are not moving the piston as far. One thing people talk about today is pis-

ton speed; this is the mean amount of travel the piston makes in a given amount of time at a given RPM level. When you can reduce the stroke, piston speed can be safely increased, but friction is probably the most important factor. Reducing friction means reduced heat, which ups the thermal efficiencies. However, if the destroking exposes more surface area in the combustion chamber, you lose some of that.

"A good example would be to compare the 225 and 170 Chrysler sixes," he continued. "They made about the same amount of power; the longer stroke and larger displacement may have meant more torque, but it did not mean the engine was more powerful. Some of that was the frictional loss of the larger displacement, but what you want is the least amount of stroke and the highest possible RPM. That is what makes today's 500-inch 11,000-rpm Pro Stock engines so amazing. The biggest challenge then becomes making the valve gear work with the potential RPM levels."

Ted noted that the effort in building smaller-displacement engines did not take any longer than the time required to meticulously build a standard 426-ci Pro Stock Hemi. Careful measuring was still needed, but additional preparation was actually only impacted during the outside machining operations prior to assembly. There were a number of ways to reduce displacement, but Ted settled on using a light overbore on the standard 4.25 cylinder size and then pulling some of the stroke out by using a lesser rod length, crank throw size, and repositioned piston pin height. With the new roller cams and the ignition issues addressed, it was possible to get more RPM from the package.

"As [the] NHRA started to factor the Chrysler cars, we developed the 400-ci or 396-style motor," Ted recalled at the 2014 round table. "Which was a little shorter stroke, so we could have that little bit better weight advantage and it allowed us to run a higher engine speed. So, of course when you raise the engine speed, then you have to have better valve springs, better cam—it's a vicious cycle, as we all know. But that proved to be a good package right up to the end, when they decided to get out of Pro Stock racing."

That was still in the future, and the ability to reduce the engine significantly more was limited primarily by the technology of the original 7-liter Hemi engine design.

"It was a big wallop to go from 7 liters [the 426] down to 6 liters [which was 366 inches] without making major changes to the block dimensions," Hoover noted.

It was later in 1973 that the group seriously looked at the possibilities of using the LA-series small-block, such as what the 1970 Trans-Am 340 engines had been based on; but for now, Chryslers continued as Hemi Pro Stockers.

That Pappas Guy

By the end of 1972, Don Carlton took over ownership of the race car and its team management and rented a shop not far from the rest of the players in the Troy area. Dick Oldfield went to work directly for him when this change happened at the start of the next calendar year. He needed another crew member because Koran and Bartush remained employed by Ted doing the engine and shop work at SVI. To that end, Don and Dick turned to a young man who had been around the entire time but was working for the other guys—Joe Pappas of the Mike Fons crew.

Always a car guy, Joe leaped at the chance that the exploding professionalism of the sport offered, having dropped out of college to become a highway vagabond like many of the other young racing support staffers of the era.

"I grew up right off of Woodward Avenue and liked cars from the start," Joe recalled. "In the early 1960s, we would go out on our bikes and find a place to watch the street racers. I got to know Mike Fons because he was dating my best friend's sister, whom he later married. Mike had a Corvette for the street race stuff; he was serious about it. I graduated from high school in 1966 and was busy just doing car stuff. I decided to not finish college and was busy with cars; once Mike got busy actually drag racing, I began helping him with that."

Joe was involved in the building of the World Championship–winning 1971 Rod Shop Challenger, and he and Mike were both familiar insiders at Ted's shop as they took extensive measurements of the existing *Missile* Dodge to build the new car that spring. In fact, the first big trip for Joe over the road with Mike was when the car won the 1971 Pro Stock World Title in Amarillo, where Joe bore witness to the successful freeing of a Native American icon that instantly became a legend in drag racing circles as well.

"The Rod Shop deal in 1971—that team was one of the biggest things going. It was huge," Joe noted in a Yetter-recorded interview. This referred to Dodge's wholesale backing of the Rod Shop team across multiple classes. "The problem was, Mike and Gilman Kirk did not get along too well. They were both big personalities; not bad guys, just bad chemistry, and Gil was sort of stuck with Mike after he won the World Championship. There was a lot of friction between them."

The result could not continue indefinitely, and as 1972 wound down, the sparring personalities seemed soon to part ways. By this time, Fons already was involved in some of Chrysler's testing efforts, and travelin' Joe had shown himself there to be someone who would work hard, could drive the transporter, and even followed instructions, a crucial reality considering the personalities of Mr. Hoover, Mr. Coddington, Mr. Cahill,

Joe (left) and Ted work on the car at Gainesville's second test in 1973 after the new front end was added. (Photo Courtesy Dick Oldfield Family)

Joe was part of Mike Fons's World Championship effort in 1971. Fons was captured here by Steve Reyes climbing the pinion gear at Martin during the 1971 Popular Hot Rodding *meet. (Photo Courtesy Steve Reyes)*

Fons had a box truck similar to this one that Don Carlton later used. The Oleynik conversions were the machines that Joe Pappas and Dick Oldfield drove thousands of miles each year. (Photo Courtesy Joe Pappas)

and Mr. Spehar. Don Carlton agreed, so Joe got a new job.

"We would all take the week between Christmas and New Year's Day off; that was our actual vacation," said Joe. "We were finishing up the last week's work in the late part of 1972, and Mike figured his [Rod Shop] deal was done. He was eventually right. Anyhow, he made some calls before that happened and then he came in and said to me, 'Go ahead and get your tools ready to move; when you come back, you'll be working over at Don Carlton's place.' That was how I first got involved."

Pappas and Oldfield proved to be compatible. Some of this was the result of a shared sense of humor. They also had similar war stories from those hours between races when the highway miles are disappearing under the nose of the truck. One in particular stood out in Joe's mind before even changing bosses.

"Yes, stuff could happen. When I was still with Fons in 1972, we were headed over to the first USRT race at Capitol Raceway," Joe said. "That famous photo on the steps of the Supreme Court in DC with the 16 drivers had to be taken that same morning. So we started out from our shop in the brand-new Dodge truck Mike had just gotten. It was the first big one we had; it was an Oleynik conversion with a box in the back, and our first one with air brakes. As soon as we got it, we loaded it up and left. It was raining sideways the whole way down, and we drove out on the Pennsylvania Turnpike before heading south toward DC.

"Outside of Breezewood, we got on the next road and turned into this Esso station for fuel," Joe continued. "There was this chicken place up the hill and a Howard Johnson's below it, all in a row. I told Mike, 'Listen, just put fuel in it and don't touch anything; I'm going to walk up to get some chicken for us.' So it's still raining, Mike gets the gas going, and I don't look back.

"Well, the wipers were still running and squeaking, so Mike decided to try and turn them off. He doesn't realize he took the air brakes off as well. So, while he is standing there outside, suddenly the truck starts slowly rolling forward. Remember, it is brand new. He can only watch as it goes right through the posts of the station sign and slow-rolls down a 30-degree embankment, stopping nose-first about six feet from the window of the Howard Johnson's.

"Meanwhile, I'm waiting for the chicken, and this large black woman walks in, and says something like, 'Oh my, oh my! Did you see that big truck just roll down the hill? Oh, my.' I didn't think twice about it. I get the chicken, walk out the door, and start [walking] down toward the gas station. No truck. Just Mike standing by the pump sort of wringing his hands. I look ahead through the rain and can just barely see the roof-mounted lights of the box just at the edge of the hill. Oh, crap!

"So Mike is looking sort of embarrassed, and I go down and look, and there is no way we are getting it up from there ourselves," Joe said. "Now, luckily, Breezewood has got truck wreckers, and we make a call and tell them where we are and what happened. About an hour later, still raining, two of the biggest wreckers I've ever seen show up to get it moving, as well as a pretty good size crew of guys. They have to use house jacks and cribbing to get it angled well enough to drag it back up. It's now way after midnight, but we get back on the road and get there in time for the photo shoot. It was all part of life."

Seen here in the pits at Pomona before the weather went south, the new Mopar Missile *was already considered one of the toughest entries in the field and proved it by later qualifying number 1 with a 9.22 time. (Photo Courtesy Joe Pappas)*

When the race finally happened in mid-February, the Missile *never equaled that 9.22 qualifying time. Seen here racing another Ron Butler car, the Duster of Bob Lambeck, Carlton went to the final round but lost to Don Nicholson when the* Missile *broke traction. (Photo Courtesy Steve Reyes)*

On to the Races

The 1973 season began with the new *Mopar Missile* already dialed in thanks to the initial late-1972 Florida test work at Gainesville Raceway. In fact, a number of fresh 1973 Chryslers were ready to go by then. Dick Landy teamed up with Fuel car chassis builder Kent Fuller to create a handful of Dart Sport Pro Stockers out of his shop, cars that proved to be very competitive that year, and Butch Leal's newest car, another Duster, was already being built at Butler's shop. Ronnie Sox was in his updated car from 1972, showing strength. However, in late February, he crashed that Duster during a sandy Florida match race with Jenkins, and Buddy bought a Don Hardy car that had been recently built for Don Grotheer. Sox used this Hardy car for the remainder of

his A-Body efforts during 1973, and the Sox & Martin chassis/race car business began to fade.

But that all happened after the marathon that became the 1973 West Coast tour. The racing started at Beeline Dragway, where Sox ran a legal 9.17 in his updated 1972 car to pace the field. He beat Jenkins in round one but had problems in the semifinals against Don Nicholson's new Pinto, which grabbed the season's first big event title by beating Billy Stepp's car driven by Melvin Yow.

The racers headed west to Pomona, California, for what truly became the Winternationals when both rain and a rare SoCal snowstorm postponed the event on two consecutive weekends. Nonetheless, during the few qualifying sessions in those earlier sessions, the newest *Missile* showed up for the first time and came to do business with a very strong 9.22 that held for Top Qualifier by almost two-tenths of a second.

One of the primary reasons was because Carlton already decided to use the new Lenco planetary transmission. Designed initially by Leonard Abbott as a 2-speed for nitromethane cars, this worked similarly to the ClutchFlite in that the clutch was only engaged for the initial launch. After that, a series of single-duty shift arms on the floor allowed the driver to move through gearsets (each mounted in separate housings) without ever truly disengaging the engine.

The Lenco could easily be built into a 4-speed configuration by bolting three modularly fitted units together with an added section to operate as the legally required reverse gear. The Lenco also offered a large selection of possible gear ratios to place the engine into its favored RPM band. The one big drawback to the Lenco was simply cost. It took more than $2,500 to buy one for use in Pro Stock when things were added, such as magnesium cases. Since the tires were not disengaged between shifts, its big benefit was immediately proven on the unusually even-for-Pomona slippery track conditions due to the weather. The new *Mopar Missile* did not lose traction between shift points the way that most of the standard clutch–equipped cars did, and Lenco's production became very busy that spring. The result was a time of 9.22.

On the other hand, this was also the first race where the team tried racing the fresh 366-ci Hemi that was carefully built by Ted Spehar. Engine 35 came to this displacement with a destroked crank and was primarily cre-

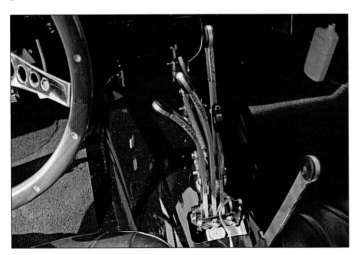

It looks busy, but since each gear had its own handle, the Lenco design made everything easier: pull, grab down; pull, grab down; etc. It quickly became a part on most competitive Pro Stock cars, even when someone as talented as Carlton was the pilot. (Photo Courtesy Joe Pappas)

ated to allow 210 pounds to come off the car (compared to a 396 displacement at the 7.00 NHRA break). The 9.22 performance was quite stellar, but the issues associated with the 366-ci design did not really leave any room for making more horsepower, and the team was quickly back to the bigger but more conducive-to-success 396-398-ci sizes. Ted noted that engine 35 was turned back into a 396-ci version soon afterward. Actually, it is not noted in any of the race reports if the team even used it when race day finally came to Pomona. It is possible that engine 33 went back into the car for eliminations.

One other thing happened at Pomona: The NHRA tossed a large number of cars of every make during the initial tech session due to rules interpretation on the new packages. This enforcement fell by the wayside as the sanctioning body realized it would not have enough legal cars for 16 places, let alone 32. In the end, with slight changes, most entries were allowed to return with an already-announced plan to formally adjust the overall rules package following the Gatornationals event in March given as the reason for the allowances.

Nonetheless, due to the weather delays, only 22 cars were still on hand when the actual eliminations began. Scribes rumored that the *Missile* was deliberately slowed down to give the company reason to continue pushing the NHRA for better weight breaks on the Hemi engine, but it was officially attributed to an ignition issue. As a result, Carlton ran 9.70 against Barrie Poole's Ford, took a 10.20 bye run in round two, and ran 9.50 against Hemi racer Bob Lambeck. That left three cars. Dyno Don Nicholson's Pinto, solidly in the 9.40s all day, got the single, while Carlton showed his hand with a fast 9.34 victory over Jack Roush's Pinto. In the final, Nicholson drove into the winner's circle, running a National Record–legal 9.33 to Carlton's traction-foiled 9.64.

NHRA and IHRA:
Florida Follies and Their Aftermath

Though AHRA racing was now an afterthought, Carlton and the *Missile* crew intended to pursue the IHRA points trail in 1973, where the lesser 6.75 break was an excellent way to remain competitive. Despite the weather, the team spent approximately six weeks out West, testing extensively. It then went to Florida to prepare the follow-up to its 1972 victory at Gainesville.

Before that, on March 3–5, the IHRA season opener occurred in Lakeland, Florida. Another track the factory

As a shirtless Dick Oldfield keeps it in the water, Don does a burnout during the Gainesville tests. Alas, a repeat victory here was not in the making for the Missile *in 1973. (Photo Courtesy Joe Pappas)*

Still at Gainesville for post-event testing, Tom Hoover and Don Carlton discuss the car as Joe gets to work under the hood. The level of garbage on the ground attests to the race's popularity the previous weekend. (Photo Courtesy Dick Oldfield Family)

used for testing, the *Missile* qualified second there, running 9.29 behind a 9.25 by Mike Fons (who managed to stay with Kirk's Rod Shop operation as a Chrysler contract driver into early 1973). With the closer weight rules, Nicholson was fourth at 9.37 in the middle of 7 Mopars. Without 16 cars, Fons and Carlton had first-round singles. Then, the *Missile* beat Reid Whisnant with a 9.25. That set up a semifinal meeting with who else but Nicholson, and the *Missile* took revenge for Pomona, the Plymouth running its best time for the day, a 9.17 at only

141.50 to the Pinto's losing 9.28 at 146 mph. That set up a final-round meeting with Ronnie Sox, who was still in the 1972 S&M car, having been quickly repaired after its match-race wreck earlier that same week. The red, white, and blue Duster went 9.29, while Don Carlton scored his first IHRA victory of 1973 at 9.19.

By this point, it was obvious that the Ford contingent was going to replace the Jenkins Vega armada and be a serious concern for 1973. The big-port canted-valve 351 Cleveland in smaller-displacement trim pushed Dyno, Gapp, Roush, and Glidden down to the 9.0 ranges in NHRA-legal trim. Bill Jenkins, for his part, was having an uncharacteristic run of bad luck at this moment. Although performances were formidable when the Vega stayed on course for all 1,320 feet, the Grump was not a big factor the first half of the 1973 season. Incidentally, his car was being driven by Modified-class ace Larry Lombardo.

With a glue on the track strong enough that *Super Stock* magazine entitled their Gatornationals story "The Sticky Nationals," Wayne Gapp served notice for the Blue Oval guys with an amazing 9.02 best in qualifying, followed second by the *Missile,* a whole tenth behind at 9.12, and then the normal cast of players. In round one, Don drove by Rufus "Brooklyn Heavy" Boyd to set up a round-two battle with Nicholson. Everyone watched as the two Winternationals finalists again paired up, and Dyno hit both his and the NHRA's best-ever performance at 9.01 at 150.00 to win the round. Don Carlton was close behind at 9.06 at only 139.75, but the day was over, and eventually Nicholson beat Gapp for all the money to take three wins in a row between his AHRA and NHRA efforts.

When the factory funding was cut back in early 1973, Mike Fons was out at the Rod Shop and subsequently purchased the 1972 Motown Missile Barracuda from Ted Spehar, seen here later in the 1973 season. (Photo Courtesy Steve Reyes)

Nothing Changes

Editor Jim McCraw noted in his editorial in that same issue that the NHRA held its Pro Stock rules meeting immediately following Gainesville with Dick Maxwell and Dick Landy on hand for Chrysler. There was no adjustment to weight break to either help the Chryslers or slow down the Fords, which was something Jenkins also wanted. The goal was to try to get the current rules more in line with how the new cars were built, so the meeting's focus was actually more on safety and appearance. While Ron Butler had kept fairly to the "letter of the law" for the *Missile*, several other cars featured pronounced windshield adjustments and recontoured noses. However, this issue of moving away from stock was not addressed in the meeting, and further liberality was also given to suspension designs, a ruling that ultimately played into the most radical *Missile* project the following year.

Truth be told, the NHRA had heard enough from the other guys in past seasons that they had little incentive or intention of allowing Chrysler products to again be seen as dominant in their hottest door-car division. After all, a large number of Funny Car drivers, including Don Prudhomme, Tom McEwen, and Gene Snow, among others, continued to campaign Chrysler bodies in 1973. While dragster pilot Jim Bucher ran a fast 6.07 in a Chevrolet-motored Top Fueler at the Gators, most of the nitromethane class cars were running Chrysler engines as well. Any Chrysler victory going forward was hard-earned in NHRA Pro Stock.

For the team, swapping engines before race day in 1973 sometimes proved to be a lot easier than reworking the powerplant in the car and ensured there was a fresh motor for eliminations. (Photo Courtesy Joe Pappas)

There was one other result of this meeting in Gainesville that had serious repercussions to the Mopar troops. After a painful but honest meeting about the class's future, Dave Koffel was given the undesirable job of telling a lot of Chrysler-assisted racers that the factory money and parts pipeline to the faithful was closing up immediately. Five were left standing—the *Missile* as the development car, money for one Sox & Martin entry, Leal, Landy, and one car with the Rod Shop. A terse uncredited quote was that it was easier "to race with 5 noncompetitive teams than 12 or 15." After all, if the rules remained as they were, the volume of factory competitors was inconsequential.

As figured, Gil Kirk dropped Mike Fons, keeping long-time Rod Shop associate Bob Riffle as his sole Pro Stock driver. Fons called up SVI and immediately bought the moth-balled 1972 *Motown Missile* 'Cuda from Ted Spehar that was sitting in the old shop. Herb McCandless needed to find someone else to drive for, and it ended up being "Brooklyn Heavy." Billy Stepp kept driver Melvin Yow but took "Dodge" off of his car and replaced it with "Independent." Later that year, he even added a second car with his own funds. As noted earlier, Don Grotheer sold his almost-new Hardy Duster to Buddy Martin to replace the damaged Duster and ordered a new Pinto from Don Hardy. He crashed it (thankfully without harm) on its maiden pass at Manassas, Virginia, but he and several other Chrysler stalwarts such as Arlen Vanke would simply quit Pro Stock racing by season's end.

This announcement came to the fanbase from another McCraw editorial in *Super Stock* magazine, and he further revealed that a new run of D5 heads were coming. This was true. An aluminum version was created at that time by Keith Black Racing Engines, which simultaneously worked with former Chrysler Engineering specialist Bob Tarozzi on an aluminum 426 Hemi replacement block for fuel racing (iron blocks remained mandatory in legal NHRA Pro Stock racing). However, by the time the fresh head called the D6 finally got into the racers' hands, developmental focus by the factory had shifted quite dramatically.

Tricks of the Trade

Joe Pappas and Dick Oldfield were the hands-on crew, and Joe revealed some things that helped make the *Missile* so competitive. These were things that every major Pro Stock team played with at the time. Every team looked for that little edge to get to the winner's circle on race day.

"Between the E-Body and the A-Body, I really liked the A-Body better," Dick noted. "The car was easier to work on, and I had actually been out at Ron Butler's place when they were building it. I did not build the car itself, but I was out there to learn. We did not take a lot of pictures. The car was really easy to adjust; I could do it pretty quickly. I do remember when we were out West, some guys told me the track was really greasy. So I set it

up that way. When Donnie launched it, it went right up in the air! It almost went vertical!"

Joe also analyzed the 1973 car from a mechanic's perspective.

"The Duster had frame rails that came forward," Joe noted in his interview with Yetter in 2009. "Its K-member, a.k.a. a light-end crossbar, was highly modified and it had Pinto rack-and-pinion steering with no torsion bars. The upper A-arms, so-called 'clamshells,' were swapped side for side. That theoretically kept the front wheels 'in the lights' longer as the nose lifted on launch. That is, the front wheels actually kicked rearward before breaking out of the staging lights. We used either a modified lower control arm or a fabricated lower control arm. I think we fabricated the spindles, and we used Koni-type coilover suspension in the front."

There was a little more to that front end as well.

"The *Missile*'s wheels were positioned slightly forward compared to a stock chassis," Joe continued. "Look at the front of Pro Stock cars in the 1970s; look at the distance between the edge of the front wheelhouse and the bumper. It's only a few inches, and you know it's not stock. I have to say, you never wanted to park your race car near a stock model so no one could see the difference and say, 'Hey, what's wrong with this car?'

"In drag racing, a light beam at the front wheels triggers the clock," he said. "When you stage the car, your wheels are barely up to the light beam. The longer you can keep those front wheels from breaking the beam, even while the back of the car actually starts to move, you have an advantage, even if it's only a few milliseconds. You don't want to redlight or break the beam too soon.

"Actually, the wheelbase could even be different from side to side—staggering the front wheels slightly, where you have one wheel slightly ahead of the other," he continued. "In that case, they stay in the lights longer. That's approximately how it works, anyway."

The wheelbase tricks practiced by Chrysler racers were already well-known throughout this entire era, once again pointing to the value of an engineering mind-set and rule book creativity.

"As a matter of strategy, you wanted to 'cheat' the wheels as far forward in the vehicle as possible or shift the body as far back as possible, without breaking the rules regarding wheelbase measurement," Joe explained. "There was a plus-or-minus factor you could get away with. The rear tires are huge and you need plenty of space so you can get them on and off the car. It was the common practice to section the rear quarter panels and open up the wheel housings. In the process, you could actually move the rear wheels forward a little bit."

Coming off of the Gainesville event, the team needed to update the front end to the 1973 design. This gave Joe and Dick the opportunity to be creative on the outside as well.

"Besides the work on the wheel openings in the quarter panels, we took a section out of the nose of the car to make it narrower," Joe stated. "We took maybe a couple of inches out of the width of the car at the nose, and we sectioned the grille. They didn't use templates at that time, and if the car looked okay, they didn't say anything. I don't know that they ever threw anybody out for doing anything special to the bodies. If you look at an old Landy car, they look like they were broken in the front, like they were pushed down in the nose, and the sides [were] pushed in. We used to kid Landy, 'Hey, Dick! Who sat on the nose of your car?' He'd just ignore us."

Test Time

The first big test notes on file came out on April 3 and were primarily focused on the most crucial change of 1973, the use of the Lenco. The factory engineering crew scheduled what would be checked on each day, and none of these development efforts were unorganized. With the *Missile* testing both while on tour and regularly at the Milan track when at home, there had been time to try things out with the multiple ratios the Lenco offered. With the Lenco, the best results at the NHRA 7-pound rate with a 400-ci Mullen D4A-head engine package was 9.00 at 151 mph. This time was achieved from a combination of very steep 2.96 first, 1.90 second, 1.31 third, and 1.00 fourth/final gearsets working with a 32-pound flywheel and the tight 5.57 final gear. The latest reworked Liberty-modified A833 examples broke under the same strain, and frankly the Lenco design was already becoming the weapon of choice; even 4-speed star Sox quickly used one.

It was further noted that replacing the standard aluminum Lenco hubs for steel versions was recommended for consistency, and tests with an 11-pound flywheel showed more promise. Loading different quantities of discs into the clutch packs inside the Lenco was also experimented with, and a fresh Goodyear tire design did not improve over the currently preferred Firestones.

"You know, the Lenco was not really built right," Dick noted later. "I felt it was totally wrong. I remember when we first got it, I could not even turn the input shaft by hand. I did a lot of stuff to make the ones we had work better. We had to change the clutches, rework stuff inside, and [it] made a lot of adjustments. We only had one, and I was always having to service it. It was over-designed as a Pro Stock unit, so I made spacers, took out some of the clutches, did whatever we could to make it lighter.

For this test, primarily done at Gainesville, the team conducted the first of the tuft tests with yarn; read the "A Tall Yarn" sidebar for more information. Meanwhile, by late June, plans were laid to get the new 396-ci D5-head program going. Tom Hoover released a series of recommendations on June 25 regarding engine prep and noted that required porting work needed for use with the larger-diameter D&D tapered pushrods was likely to break through into the port area, therefore requiring port repairs. A just-released R294 Cam Dynamics roller cam was selected for the D5, but in the meantime, Donnie and the *Missile* were busy with winning.

Late in the year, a little additional Hemi info was released by Tom Hoover, mostly regarding durability and oil issues, and there was also the latest advance in ignition science thanks to the new firm MSD. The initials stood for multispark discharge, and the result was a way to eliminate the need for dual distributors because the MSD box (which was wired opposite of the normal Chrysler electronic unit) threw a lot of spark out to truly clean up combustion. However, that would be in October.

The midyear announcement of Chrysler's new kit car program for circle-track racing was not dramatic except for one thing: it noted that the factory was working to get the LA-series small-block ready for competition. By now in Pro Stock racing, it was basically only the Chrysler Hemi and a few of the big-block Chevrolets still in action at over 366 ci, and only the Hemi came in at the heaviest weight breaks.

For all purposes, the competitive Ford racers (most in the process of building new Mustang IIs by midseason) were using the Boss 302/351 engines, and a majority of the Chevrolets were small-block Vegas. The NHRA had no reason to preserve Chrysler's legacy, but spring racing events showed the King Kong Chrysler Hemi was not dead yet. Not by a long shot.

A Tall Yarn

Of everything the *Missile* did in this era, the tuft tests were perhaps the most visually interesting. The team took a good portion of one test day and placed short lengths of yarn down one side and on top of the body. Killen set up his recording equipment at the desired points on the car, and someone else took photographs of the yarn as windspeed directed its positioning. Unlike a wind tunnel, where smoke was used to determine aerodynamics, this was something that simply required the effort to apply the tufts and a willing cameraman to take the images.

"You'd be surprised how important some little facets of all that were," noted Tom Hoover when asked during the 2012 Yetter roundtable discussion. "We tried to keep in mind all the information that had been collected by Chrysler over the course of a number of years. I'd call the most significant thing that had been done in that regard was that before the introduction of the 426 Hemi at Daytona in 1964, Cahill and Thornton and the aerodynamics guys took a car to San Angelo, Texas, to the Goodyear track. From that, [they] developed a list of recommendations for what you need to do to make a NASCAR car smoother aerodynamically at a 160 [mph]. Little things like the A-post trim because it determines whether or not the air coming off the edges of the windshield is turbulent going back

Here is what the car looked like for its "tuft testing" in Gainesville in early 1973, after the Gatornationals had been completed. (Photo Courtesy Joe Pappas)

By using pieces of yarn, the team would shoot still photos and video to determine the airflow over the body. This was in addition to anything Ron Killen was recording electronically on the pass at the same time. (Photo Courtesy Joe Pappas)

With no seat belt (or seat for that matter), Tom Hoover told Joe Pappas to wear a helmet for this shot, which was taken from the rear of the passenger area at speed as Don Carlton headed downtrack for one of the yarn-based "aero recordings." Through the windshield, Dick Oldfield can be seen shooting from the passenger-side windowsill. (Photo Courtesy Joe Pappas)

along the windows—stuff like that. And they were also very specific about the flow of air through the engine compartment and out through the wheelhouses around the front wheels. We kept all that in mind."

The reason for not covering the entire car with yarn was that all things were essentially the same from side to side. "You draw a line down the middle," Hoover continued. "The right side's the same as the left. So you only have to do half the car. You determine where the air is turbulent. The little gizzies are going like this [pointing finger curved], instead of lying straight back."

The team tuft tested at both Gainesville and Rockingham in 1973 in part because the nose of the car was updated following the return from Florida.

"We tufted the car," Ted remembered at that same gathering. "Mr. Hoover was overseeing everything. We were going to send the station wagon down with everyone filming with their 8-mm cameras. Terribly unsafe, but this is what you did back then. And I remember Mr. Hoover explaining to Donnie how fast he was going to go and how he was going to accelerate the station wagon. And Donnie said, 'Well, you go ahead and I'll catch up!'"

Carlton bombed by at about 150 while Hoover drove about 80 in the other lane and Dick Oldfield was sitting on the rear doorsill with elbows up on the roof, shooting film with an 8-mm movie camera. Mean-

Shooting from multiple angles also helped. Here, Joe takes this photo while Dick focuses from the back on this hard launch during the Gainesville session. (Photo Courtesy Joe Pappas)

while, a few other images were taken from inside the car as it went down the track. Joe gets credit for them.

"To know how the picture was taken—I took the picture!" Pappas laughed. "I was behind Donnie with my arms around the roll cage at 150 mph. And, God bless Mr. Hoover, he told me to wear a helmet, so I wouldn't

Following the update to the 1973 nose, more testing was done at Rockingham, with the team trying out some under-nose chin spoilers to see what could help airflow. (Photo Courtesy Joe Pappas)

get hurt [laughs]. But I really thought it was because they thought I was going to bump my head again. Because I always bumped my head when I got in the car!"

The results were quite conclusive. No area of the car showed significant resistance to the air except the hood scoop. Tuft testing focused on various other aspects going forward, sometimes still requiring at-speed photos. However, Joe Pappas, for his part, did not continue as the rider wearing a helmet in the back-seat area holding on for dear life!

Spring Has Sprung

The IHRA scheduled big national events in Dallas; Rockingham; Muncie, Indiana; and Bristol that spring, while the NHRA had its Springnationals event in Columbus, Ohio, in early June. The IHRA tour that year proved to be Don Carlton's most successful season to date. Most tellingly, the IHRA went to a cumulative points system already, meaning it was how well someone did all season long rather than the simple luck of winning on the final day of the racing year to be crowned World Champion. The NHRA finally followed suit for 1974, when car counts for their 1973 World Finals were again short.

In Dallas at the IHRA Longhorn Nationals, Don was the defending champion, and although the magazines did not cover the event, veteran announcer and researcher Bob Frey provided the details.

"Don was the number-one qualifier at 9.10, followed by Bob Riffle, Dick Landy, Irv Beringhaus, and Dave Strickler," Frey said. "Grotheer, Royce Freeman, and Max Hurley finished the first eight with Charles Lamarr on the bump at 10.01. Don beat Ken Van Cleave with a 9.20 in round one, Strickler's Chevy in round two with a 9.143, Landy in the semifinals with a 9.12/148.51, and Riffle's Rod Shop Demon in the final round 9.10/149.25

to Riffle's 9.32/142.40. The 9.10 was an IHRA ET record, and Don had also set the IHRA speed record in qualifying with a 150.55."

That precluded what happened next at basically Don's home track, Rockingham Dragway east of Charlotte.

In the spring, the team worked on getting the 1973 redesigned nose onto the car that is seen here inside Don's shop with Ron Killen's new recording van in the background. (Photo Courtesy Joe Pappas)

Back from the paint shop and ready to load up, the team asked a local police officer to act as if he were writing tickets for the car, sitting in the street near the shop. The paint was changed at this point from its basic gold letter to a two-tone design with brighter striping. (Photo Courtesy Joe Pappas)

Again, the front angle demonstrates some of what had been learned during scoop testing via scientific application of height off the hood. (Photo Courtesy Joe Pappas)

Inside was a wooden steering wheel, fire extinguisher, Butler cage structure, and racing gauges and gear. (Photo Courtesy Joe Pappas)

The *Missile* qualified with a series of 9.10 times, swapped out the engine overnight, and proceeded to run a 9.04 shakedown pass. On Saturday evening, the *Missile* ran a legal-weight 8.98 that was technically the first-ever 8-second drag racing run made by anyone anywhere in a national-event Pro Stock setting. Over the scales, the car was displacement-pumped, fuel-checked, weighed, and found to be 25 pounds over the minimum!

The Carolina track was fast that weekend, with Landy at 9.04 in second, Nicholson at 9.07, then Sox et al. The *Missile* made a check-out pass on Sunday morning to record an even better (but unofficial) 8.92. Don went 9.02 in round one, then used a 9.04 to beat his old Demon, now being driven as a team car out of his Lenoir shop by Stu McDade.

Back in the 8s in the semifinals, he beat "Rapid" Ronald Lyles with an 8.99. In the other semifinal pairing, it was a classic Landy/Sox match, and Dandy Dick upheld the SoCal honor with a 9.08 to Ronnie's 9.11.

In the final, Landy would have normally been happy to see a 9.09 come up, but Carlton was already way ahead, winning the race at another 8.98. Dick's only consolation was that Landy's Dodge and the *Mopar Missile* were tied for Top Speed at 152.28. One week later at the new IHRA event in Muncie, Carlton did it again, taking out Don Grotheer (now back in his 1972 'Cuda before the Pinto

Seen here doing a massive burnout, Don won the IHRA Spring Nationals in mid-June to remain undefeated in IHRA Pro Stock for the 1973 season. (Photo Courtesy Steve Reyes)

With Don running the Missile out at Detroit, Stu McDade was racing this Dodge in Pro Stock match races and events down South and would loan it to Dick Landy for the NHRA Springnationals. The nose, fabricated by Clyde Hodges, was considerably more "massaged" than what was on the Missile. (Photo Courtesy Dick Oldfield Family)

was delivered) for his fourth consecutive IHRA title of 1973 and sixth since Dallas in 1972.

The IHRA Spring Nationals was a flagship event at founder Larry Carrier's own track, but rain is part of mountain living and made for a long mid-June weekend. Butch Leal came east with his newest Butler-built Duster, and the *California Flash* was rapidly becoming the most serious Mopar contender outside of the *Missile*. Butch qualified on top but fell to Sox in round two on a holeshot. As usual, Carlton did his own thing with identical 9.28s in rounds one and two, before beating Sox in the semifinals.

In front of near-empty stands on a Monday make-up day, the *Missile* was in yet another IHRA final. Nemesis Don Nicholson was in the other lane and had run consistent 9.30s in his Pinto to trailer three Mopar entries. At the green, Dyno was gone. Actually, he was already gone with a redlight start, while the *Missile* pulled a slight wheelstand, took off, and ran a 9.25 weekend best to finish the day. That was despite the IHRA's new weight adjustments (6.80 Hemi/6.45 everyone else).

The record number of consecutive wins to be undefeated on the IHRA circuit for the year was certainly a rewarding effort, but the *Missile* also won the NHRA Springnationals in Columbus, Ohio, the same month. This was an event plagued by heat, not rain, and Carlton used the Hemi weight to his advantage for traction. He qualified first at 9.32 (Nicholson was identical but in second by virtue of a lower speed), and the team installed a fresh engine on Sunday morning and proceeded to run Low ET of each round: a 9.46 to beat Jack Roush, a 9.48 to trailer Jenkins, a 9.38 at 147 to stop Melvin Yow in Stepp's car (which broke in their semifinal match), and a final-round meet with Butch Leal.

Leal jumped too soon, going red to run a 9.44, while Carlton calmly launched, wheels-up, and went 9.40 to get another NHRA Wally for the shelf. However, the *California Flash* made it to the winner's circle soon afterward in August, taking an NHRA victory in Canada at the Grandnationals, and then winning the big *Popular Hot Rodding* magazine–backed race in Martin, Michigan, to come into Indy as king of the hill.

That's the Scoop

One part that the 1973 testing focused on was hood scoops. Thanks to Killen's recording apparatus, there was some true science applied to the inside of the scoop—how the air went over the carburetors and the signal it sent the carbs, how much opening was optimal, and so on. Coupled with an exact height measurement noted for the intake plenum, and very explicit instruction from John Bauman on the carburation tuning, it worked well. Nonetheless, this area was discovered to be problematic when it was checked via the tufting method. Bauman and the team already created a number of scoops throughout the 1970–1972

The tufts at speed showed that turbulence around the scoop area was one place to potentially tune for better aerodynamics. Sensors in the scoop were recording air speed as well. (Photo Courtesy Dick Oldfield Family)

Hood scoop designs had never truly been evaluated before the Missile did it. This is the car in 1973 with a twin-opening ram design. (Photo Courtesy Dick Oldfield Family)

This test looked into whether there was any benefit to using windshield air into the cowl. Nope. (Photo Courtesy Joe Pappas)

Angling the sides in and bracing the rear in a temporary fashion to ensure the rear was not being pulled down by air pressure didn't do much either. (Photo Courtesy Joe Pappas)

Here is the scoop from the front. (Photo Courtesy Joe Pappas)

This little tag tells how the fabrication was done. It reads "Another factory rebuild by Laid Back Lenny," referring to Len Bartush at SVI. (Photo Courtesy Joe Pappas)

era to figure out what worked the best, and that work continued in 1973. One solution showed up on the 1973 *Missile* as well as Leal's new Butler car: having the rear of the scoop abutting the windshield, which, according to a feature on the latest $25,000-cost *Flash* in *Drag Racing USA* magazine, relieved the turbulence around the cowl area where the rear of the scoop formerly dropped down to the hood. Meanwhile, other ideas were tried that didn't work.

"We put a lot of effort into hood scoops, which yielded the 'Bauman' boundary layer bleed-off," Tom Hoover noted amid the banter at the 2012 gathering recorded by Gene Yetter. "A&A or somebody made the first one. Look at the BF 109 G next time you are at the German technology museum on the Rhine River in Speyer, Germany, and you'll see the original. There's a Gustav [Messerschmitt] in there; that was a whole new ball game on hood scoops. That was the way to do it and everything else wasn't even close. I had one trick thing! Boy, this is the golden hope. But it didn't work for diddly. Little trap doors."

"We had taken a boundary layer bleed-off," said Ted Spehar. "It was kind of a rectangular-shaped box on top of what covered the carburetors, and we made little 'side doors.' The idea was, when [a car] was on

Donnie and Dick look into the "coolest" of the scoop experiments: the version with trapdoors that opened from the sides. (Photo Courtesy Joe Pappas)

The doors would have opened and closed like this. When it didn't work, it simply was tossed away like other ideas that did not show dividends. Efficiency was the only goal. (Photo Courtesy Joe Pappas)

the starting line, the vacuum would open the doors; and when he mashed the gas, they would automatically close. It had to work, right?"

"Didn't do a damn thing!" laughed Tom.

"Looked cool, though!" said Ted.

"Yeah," Tom concluded. "That would have kept the enemy all confused."

Spehar went on to note that the team even tried to mount a scoop on sideways to see the effect. Even the

cowl designs once favored by the Bowtie enemy were tested.

"If your boundary-layer bleed-off scoop is right, it's better than anything you can do on the cowl," Ted said.

After reminiscing a moment longer, Ted continued, "The little 'trap-door' thing was pretty cool. We should have saved that scoop. It went in the trash."

Tom replied, "Yeah. We should have mounted it on a little board or something."

Getting past the Grump had been a problem in 1972. In 1973, even as Jenkins finally got his new car running well, Don trailered him in round two on his way to the Missile's big win at the NHRA Springnationals. (Photo Courtesy Bob McClurg)

The young race queen and Don celebrate in the winner's circle at Columbus. It would be Don Carlton's final win in an NHRA Pro category, though he would take future Sportsman-level crowns. (Photo Courtesy Steve Reyes)

Bob McClurg was on the line at Indy as Donnie launched against Sam Gianino in round one. Donnie won this round on Monday, then was up against Melvin Yow in the Stepp Dodge. (Photo Courtesy Bob McClurg)

Indy 1973 and NHRA Season End

During Labor Day weekend, the NHRA's US Nationals in Indianapolis took on a new flavor after the 1972 PRA boycott—particularly, better purse money. So, the PRA event was moved forward a week still under AHRA sanction and again held at Tulsa. Bill Jenkins, whose only big 1973 weekend prior to it was dominance at the NHRA Summernationals in Englishtown, took home Pro Stock's biggest event prize of 1973 ($25,000) to win his second PRA title. Carlton went to the semifinals in Tulsa before mechanical woes ended the *Missile*'s day, and Leal was runner-up at both of the events that Jenkins won.

However, Jenkins's planned day in the sun at the NHRA Nationals was marred by the latest of the Ford runners, Bob Glidden. A native of nearby Greenwood, Indiana, at that time, Glidden's Pinto dominated Pro Stock at Indy from day one to his victory, repeatedly topping Leal's then-current 151.77 national record. For the *Missile*, it was one of the worst qualifying positions ever, a 9.24 (two-tenths slower than Glidden's 9.03) and the 14th spot. With 32 cars in the program, Don beat San Gianino's Vega with a round-one 9.23. Rumors were flying about nitrous oxide all weekend, and in round two, Carlton faced Stepp's *Independent* Demon with Melvin Yow driving. Both cars flew to 9.05 times, but Joe Pappas admitted that, had it stopped over the scales, the *Missile* was probably 300 pounds light. Yow fell to runner-up Wayne Gapp the following round with a more reasonable 9.23.

"After our race, Stepp drove down there in his Cadil-

This is what the Missile *trailer sometimes looked like during the test sessions. It was probably even more disorganized that day as Dick and Joe headed for the gate at Indy. (Photo Courtesy Joe Pappas)*

lac," Joe recalled. "He parked right in the middle of the return road while Donnie was getting his time slip. He said, 'Donnie, we're going to weigh your car!' Now we had already figured on trouble, and Donnie replies with a question, 'Weigh my car?' [He] fires it up and drives fast right over the scales back to the pits. We already had the ramps up on the truck; he drives it right up into the

The **Missile** *is shown in Bristol for the Fallnationals. By this date, Don Carlton had pretty much sewn up his third IHRA season crown. Though victory eluded the team at the last three events, the car was still in every final for the entire season. The next time Carlton appeared in the series, however, the* **Mopar Missile** *was no more. (Photo Courtesy Bob McClurg)*

trailer, jumps out the side door, and disappears into the crowd. Meanwhile, Dick and I basically brace the car quickly and we are gone out the gate before Stepp shows back up. The truth was, everyone was scared of Billy, including the NHRA officials."

Pappas, a young man with a bit of an attitude at the time, remembered that year at Indy for another reason. Later that week, Joe took a call at the shop from Mr. Stepp, whose reputation was not to be trifled with. Billy "The Kid" began with small talk and then asked why the team had pulled so much weight from the *Missile* because it made it look like the Mopars were cheating.

"Oh, Billy," Joe deadpanned. "We never cheat any more than you would."

Fuming, Stepp stuttered momentarily and then released a string of expletives, followed by threats to come to Detroit and do permanent harm to him and every person associated with the Detroit-area Chrysler racing circle from Bob Cahill down. The conversation ended there, but Joe kept a shotgun close by at home for the next several weeks just in case.

The Indy race heralded how the remainder of the season went. Shortly afterward, Jenkins tumbled the Pro Stock record to 8.91, and Wayne Gapp, driving the team Pinto of Gapp & Roush, won the NHRA's World Championship in Amarillo and the final running of the Ontario Motor Speedway–hosted NHRA Supernationals (the two events were combined at Ontario for 1974). With Wally Booth's factory-backed AMC program that had its inline heads coming on strong and the Vegas also close to the Pintos in performance, the Mopars were shut out after early rounds at both events. Adding insult to injury, the

NHRA also tossed both Leal and the brand-new Dart Sport of Bill Bagshaw for so-called wheelbase infractions at Ontario to end the 1973 NHRA season.

IHRA World Championship #3

Though an NHRA championship was not in the offing, Don Carlton stuck to his guns in the IHRA and was in every single final for 1973. However, the final three events of the season did not yield another victory because the Fords were on top in part due to the small but effective (for the other guys) reworking of the weight breaks that summer.

In the fall racing schedule, the series returned to three tracks it previously raced at in 1973 with Nicholson winning in Bristol, Gapp winning Rockingham, and Nicholson repeating at Lakeland. Nonetheless, due to the points system, Don Carlton was named the Pro Stock World Champion and also beat out the likes of nitro racers Don Garlits and Richard Tharp to be named IHRA Pro Driver of the Year. Like Carlton, Dick Landy's strong and steady AHRA efforts had made him that series' World Champion even before the final race was held. For world championships, two out of three was not bad.

However, things were not perfect. The NHRA challenges continued to be serious enough to warrant more boycotting, and this time, the factory decided to do more than simply sit out. With so many Hemi cars and other Chryslers already competing in the Sportsman ranks, the remaining factory-sponsored racers built and debuted a series of cars to run in Super Stock and Modified Eliminator for 1974. This helped to market the factory's growing

Dick Landy's Dart Sport built with help from Kent Fuller allowed him to dominate the 1973 AHRA series points chase, much like Don Carlton dominated the IHRA series. Though Landy was not in every final, he won enough events and round wins to be crowned as the AHRA Pro Stock World Champion before the season-ending race in Fremont, California. (Photo Courtesy quartermilestones.com, Publishing Archive)

Direct Connection parts program, for which Leal was tagged as the spokesman, while giving the racers a continued competition presence even if they were not in Pro Stock.

As a result of this change in focus, the 1973 *Mopar Missile* was sold to a racer named Stewart Pomeroy at the end of the 1973 season. Leal's winning Butler car went to IHRA regular Roy Hill. Meanwhile, at Don's small shop in North Carolina, Clyde Hodges was busy prepping two new cars for Don Carlton to run the IHRA circuit, but the focus for early 1974 was testing, testing, testing.

This is a last look at 1973 in the sunset as the team tests at Milan. As this was such a regular occurrence, there are not a lot of images from these sessions, but Joe was by the finish line as the Missile slowed down from another run. Testing, not racing, would be the factory focus from here forward. (Photo Courtesy Joe Pappas)

The 1974 season would see only minor racing activity, but the team relentlessly flogged this yellow Dart Sport with a developmental Pro Stock small-block engine. (Photo Courtesy Joe Pappas)

Don did a little Sportsman racing in this B/Altered Dodge, which won the Molson Grandnationals that August. It is seen here at Englishtown the month before. (Photo Courtesy Bob McClurg)

Chapter Six

1974:
Fly by Wire,
Less Is More, and
Cha-Cha Changes

This is how the Carlton B/A car appeared at the 1973 Popular Hot Rodding *meet at US 131 in Michigan. Formerly raced by Stuart McDade, Joe recalled that he had just removed the lettering, and Don wanted to see if it would run as a Competition Eliminator car. Built by Clyde Hodges in the North Carolina shop, this car became the basis for the yellow test car the following year. (Photo Courtesy Joe Pappas)*

The end of 1973 was a time of intensity now faded from the memory of most people. When the Middle East's major oil-exporting nations determined to punish the United States following its support of Israel after the Yom Kippur War in October, the subsequent gas shortage was a major blow to an already challenged economic moment. Gas lines and rationing, something unheard of since World War II, became the focus of every car owner, and the biggest immediate beneficiaries were the imported Japanese and European imports that did not guzzle gas.

Meanwhile, pressure from the nation's press—even the racing press—was ginned up by the debacle, and in response, even the sanctioning bodies pushed toward a reduced schedule of events for 1974. The new year arrived with greater uncertainty and had a reorganized focus for the people formerly associated with the *Missile* as well.

First, the IHRA Championship–winning Butler-built Duster already had been sold by the start of the new year. Don joined the rest of the factory-associated drag racers in avoiding the Pro Stock class to focus an effort in the Sportsman ranks. Unlike Sox, Landy, and Leal, he and the remaining "name guy" from the Rod Shop, Bob Riffle, focused mostly on Competition Eliminator.

The ongoing boycott for 1974 found Ronnie Sox back in Super Stock in this 1968 Barracuda, one of the first Mopar Super Stockers to get a four-link conversion. This was thanks to recent NHRA changes to the rules, due to the class's Corvettes going quicker, meaning they could no longer utilize the factory IRS design safely. (Photo Courtesy Bob McClurg)

Although this category had record-based indexes like the Super Stock division, the rules allowed for changes much more in line with Pro Stock, and Don's eventual B/Altered Dodge actually ran quicker than the NHRA-legal Pro Stockers! Butch Leal rotated among a variety of cars in both SS and Modified categories during the 1974–1975 era. However, with the fuel crisis affecting both new car sales and the simple convenience of driving around, money was tight everywhere—racing or not.

"Well, the first thing that happened is that Mr. Cahill, Mr. Maxwell, and I were all standing in the same unemployment line in Pontiac, Michigan!" Dave Koffel recalled. "What actually happened is that we were all laid off from Chrysler and running the race program out of our homes. We did it for free; there just wasn't any money there. I went to the 1974 Winternationals in Butch Leal's new truck, which I was delivering to him. Inside it was John Tedder's 1968 S/S Barracuda, and another Super Stock car was on a trailer behind that. Larry Shepard and I drove that to Pomona for vacation because we were laid off. When we got back, I remember going to Gainesville, going to the unemployment office and telling them I was an unemployed engine builder for Chrysler who had come to town looking for work because there was a race nearby. That's the way it went until things settled down. Once we came back to work, we moved around a lot in the company, and we all eventually became part of the marketing department."

The gas crisis canceled the big 12 Hours of Sebring sportscar race that year, the Daytona 500 became the Daytona 450, and it also caused some belt tightening on the NHRA and IHRA circuits, both of which reduced their season-long race schedules. Indeed, now lost to history is that the nation's racing sanctioning bodies made an actual commitment to the federal Department of Energy to reduce race-related fuel uses by 25 percent. The result for the NHRA involved eliminating some qualifying days and reducing most fields to the present 16-car number except at the Indy Nationals. Thus, Koffel and his compatriots' problems were an early part of a larger overall focus shift due to federal posturing that eventually forced manufacturer-assisted racers to physically remove all vehicle brand names from their cars.

However, the real change at Carlton's Troy-based *Missile* shop was a refocus on solely testing for the coming months, which was why the successful Hemi-powered 1973 car had been released. Because the Hemi engine continued to be handicapped for Pro Stock racing by the sanctioning bodies, Chrysler's focus beyond the Sportsman class effort involved lighter car construction, small-block engine development, and the first regular Pro Stock uses of the company's own Japanese imports, the little Mitsubishi Colts.

Wild Horses

For Dodge, the imported Colt was never considered a good answer to the Pro Stock problem. First and foremost, it was never considered much of a sales tool for the Pro Stock audience that the company was trying to reach.

These two images were taken of the original Knapp-built Colt at Ron Butler's shop before the tinwork was done. They show the D5-head Hemi engine and the extensive chassis reworking to support the differential in the little monster. (Photo Courtesy Joe Pappas)

Moreover, at a 93.5-inch wheelbase it was not legal for NHRA Pro Stock. However, teams associated with the brand began to look at it more seriously for match racing because competing-brand drivers, such as Jenkins and Nicholson, started racing bigger engines in their "run whatcha brung" match-race mini cars, and the Colt body was still legal in the IHRA and AHRA's rulebooks.

"Why didn't we go to a Colt right away?" Tom Hoover asked. "It was a question of whether or not you really want to push the imports out of the showroom, or if you want to push Dusters out of the showroom. So we bit the bullet and did the A-Body. 'Course, it wasn't another year later and the Pintos show up with a porcupine engine. They were really tough, and meanwhile they kept adding weight to us all the time."

The Colt work was ongoing, however, even from 1971, and one example was already used in competition form. The Dodge-associated Rod Shop received a handful of the rare Weslake-designed small-block cylinder heads from the short-lived Plymouth Indy car effort of 1969, the year that Richard Petty had gone over to Ford. While this technology made no impact on open-wheel racing, when the Rod Shop's ribbon-painted Stickel & Noltemeyer Colt station wagon showed up in 1971 running as an altered in Competition Eliminator, it was soon wheelstanding its way into most of the nation's best hot rodding magazines. That stated, this engine was also a very exotic package for the most part, eventually hindered by parts availability frustrations. In 1972, Koffel sent one Weslake-headed engine down to the Tennessee team of Dwight Arrowood and Roy Johnson, who did some covert work on it camouflaged in their 1962 Sport Fury. Roy, of course, became best known as the crew chief of son Allen's later Pro Stock Dodge effort.

Nonetheless, at this same time, fabricator Dan Knapp welded up a few regular Colt sedans as possible Pro Stock cars under corporate direction in his Wyndotte, Michigan–based shop. Dick Maxwell later admitted in print that these were a sort of "doomsday machine" like the legendary A925 dual overhead cam (DOHC) Hemi engine of 1964. That engine was created primarily to dissuade NASCAR from allowing Ford's use of its SOHC design, and the Colts were reportedly being displayed as top secret in the racing press to push the NHRA toward more favorable weights on the American-bodied Hemi competitors.

With input from engineers such as Tom Coddington, the idea was to build a basic car structure and cage based on then-current chassis principles and set it up to

The first Colt raced with factory help was the wheelie-prone Stickel & Noltemeyer wagon seen here at Indy. It was powered by the Weslake-headed small-block from the short-lived 1969 Plymouth Indy car effort. (Photo Courtesy Steve Reyes)

be equipped with the performance D5-head race Hemi, in part perhaps because this engine did not look like the standard version. The first spy images of this car showed up in late 1972 in *Car Craft* magazine.

Joe Pappas took this car out to Ron Butler in the summer of 1973 to have the tinwork installed and some final prep work done. He then drove back to California that fall to pick it up and brought it back to the shop with the possibility that it would be a *Missile* in 1974.

"Oh, it was about ready to race," Joe said. "I remember that Mike Koran was getting married that same weekend I was coming back, so I missed the wedding but made the reception. It was at the shop for a couple of weeks. Then, they pulled the plug for racing in 1974 and we watched it go over to [Brian] Schram's Direct Connection warehouse, where the people picked it up with this huge forklift and put the car on a shelf about four stories up. Bye-bye."

Between 1972 and into 1974, several other teams played with Colts for match-race purposes. Notable racers were former Funny Car drivers Terry Hedrick and Bill Flynn. Both found that the little body was far from aerodynamic as the pair wrecked their cars on consecutive weekends in mid-1973 during testing. Flynn, whose injuries from this incident were significant enough to warrant a lengthy hospital stay, noted that at about 142 mph, the body seemed to simply want to flip over. In the end, this and a rash of other mini car Pro Stock accidents, some fatal, would soon have the first rear deck wings added to these squirrelly machines.

The Dodge-backed Rod Shop team also raced a regular Colt sedan, which was simultaneously being used for high-RPM small-block engine development in 1974. It is seen here at Bradenton. (Photo Courtesy Joe Pappas)

Dave Koffel looks on as the Rod Shop Colt gets worked on between runs. Koffel helped spearhead much of the small-block engine effort and later developed the B1 head that was used in the Wayne County team's Pro Stock program. (Photo Courtesy Joe Pappas)

Some of these cars received more ink than on-track fame. For instance, a Colt was built for the Mr. Norm team by Chicago-area car constructor Romeo Palamedes. The racing press depicted it with a well-endowed young woman, but in reality, it did little actual racing. In this same era, a Colorado-based Colt with Hemi power was highlighted on the cover of *Car Craft* magazine with the word "outlawed" overwritten on it. That car was basically never seen again.

At any rate, going into 1974, the Colts made only a few competitive appearances, but wrecking or not, the cars trickled onto the racing scene that season. In fact, at the same time that the factory tooled up its development program with an A-Body Dart Sport, the Rod Shop had a Mitsubishi-built bomber they were also testing with small-block power. Still, it was with Hemi motivation that these little cars would attain their greatest notoriety.

The Yellow Car

The *Missile* team was already aware that it would be focused on developmental testing in 1974, so one of the Dodge Demon/Dart Sports that Don and Clyde Hodges had built (formerly driven by Stu McDade in 1973) was converted to a testbed for the upcoming small-block development program. This process had started even before the final round of the 1973 racing season was over.

"In 1974, our *Missile* program went into 100-percent test mode," noted Joe Pappas to Gene Yetter. "That's when we built the yellow car. We did not competitively race as the *Mopar Missile* at all in 1974."

There was no *Missile* car ever run again from the Chrysler camp, officially, from that point onward.

"Don Carlton had some match-race cars painted in the *Missile* black, yellow, and orange colors with his name replacing "Mopar Missile" along the side," Pappas said. "They came out of North Carolina. Meanwhile, Dick and I continued with the test program for Chrysler."

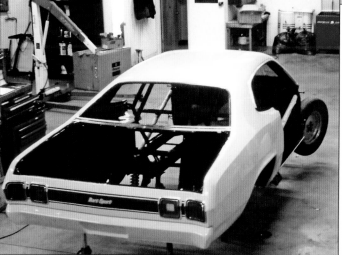

Once the car had been stripped down to the bare frame, a new body painted yellow with minimal lettering was installed. This car would not be raced in competition during the factory program year. (Photo Courtesy Dick Old-field Family)

The initial motor plate installation with a partially assembled engine in place is shown. This design would allow for fast camshaft changes and adjustments by removing the water pump. Note the crank trigger reader near the lower balancer. (Photo Courtesy Joe Pappas)

The idea behind the yellow car was to get a lightweight chassis/body package ready to be able to take advantage of the weight possibilities of an inline-valve LA-series small-block engine. The LA stood for "Late A" in Chrysler nomenclature, as the early polyspherical-head design of the 1950s was not a thin-wall casting. Introduced in 1964, the LA series was its replacement, ranging from a 273-ci configuration to the final 360-ci designs. Durable in many ways, it was pressed into street performance packages early on but had not been designed with truly serious racing in view.

That stated, the cost of the engine development effort coupled with the ongoing overall financial situation at Chrysler may well have been a secondary point beyond the rule book problems in not paying anyone to race as a factory Pro Stock for 1974. While Dick Landy had a Super Stocker, his shop assisted an independent Pro Stock effort paid for and driven by flamboyant businessman Larry Huff, but many other Mopar entries were parked when 1974 began. At any rate, there was no major road time for Pappas and Oldfield to venues beyond the

The entire car was constructed in-house. Joe and Dick built the headers from custom-bent tubing to adapt to the custom engine location. (Photo Courtesy Joe Pappas)

Notable here is the scoop's design (all the way to the cowl and windshield) and the angle of attack, which gave an idea of how the car itself would sit and ride. Scoop development took a back seat to the new engine program, but the height of the carburetors remained an important consideration due to the engine's size and location. (Photo Courtesy Joe Pappas)

Saving weight applied to every component. Note the diminutive size of this disc brake caliper mounted to the rear housing, itself of an exotic metal construction. (Photo Courtesy Joe Pappas)

A slightly later view shows additional front-end accessories being added during this time, including the experimental remote horizontal mounting of the distributor from the front. (Photo Courtesy Joe Pappas)

testing locations for the new year, and the yellow car was an exercise in process.

"The car was stripped down to the bare bones, and every weight-saving trick we could think of was incorporated into the build," Joe said in a speech he gave at the Mopar Hall of Fame banquet in Carlisle, Pennsylvania, years later. "Plenty of magnesium, titanium, fiberglass, and Lexan was used to reduce weight. We needed to get the car down to a little less than 2,000 pounds so we could put weight back in where we needed it. Despite some early issues due to building it a bit too light in certain areas, the car proved to be a reliable testbed for the A-engine development."

One minor benefit was that Hodges already did a lot to make his homebuilt cars, such as this, fairly light during their original build-up in North Carolina. The body was chemically milled (acid-dipped), and the cage was a design less structurally advanced than the Butler car had been. Athough, as Joe admits, he and Dick Oldfield stripped everything out they could to get the weight to a bare minimum. Of course, since testing was the focus, Ron "Electrocat" Killen's recording equipment was also onboard, but there were some changes to that as well.

In this pre-fuel-cell era, the trunk would get this small tank and twin pump to feed the engine. There needed to be room enough left for the data acquisition equipment. (Photo Courtesy Joe Pappas)

While Joe and Dick were responsible for the car, in the trunk area it was Ron Killen's job to prepare the equipment for recording each run. (Photo Courtesy Dick Oldfield Family)

During early initial testing, here is the car in Florida minus the fiberglass nose and hood that was constructed in one solid piece for ease of maintenance. The B-Body Charger is seen behind it. (Photo Courtesy Dick Oldfield Family)

By 1974, the team had this full-size "Vehicle Performance Planning" Dodge van, which housed the receiver for transmission of real-time data from the car, assorted other instrumentation, any spare equipment, and even some of John Bauman's carb tuning pieces. As can be seen, it also served as the home base for the team's personal items. (Photo Courtesy Joe Pappas)

Real Time Data Recording

"It took a couple of hours to get from the run to a tape you could look at and see what happened," Tom Hoover recalled at one roundtable. The biggest change in that process was the adaptation of a radio transmitter inside the car itself. "An outfit named Schembechler down in Florida someplace built a transmitter/receiver. So the car transmitted back to the van radio and it would put the paper out with the ink trace in real time. Big improvement."

That occurred in 1973, eliminating the need to download a tape, print out long streams of paper, lay them out on the pavement, and then comparatively analyze that data. Now the data was a real-time number that could be immediately output, analyzed, and then used to address immediate changes before the car had cooled down. Al Adam remained in the role of recording weather information as well, eliminating that variable from the test results, but Tom Hoover soon assigned Al with a bigger responsibility.

Regarding the electronic equipment itself, not a lot changed from the earlier testing beyond the new transmitter. As in the era when the team raced, the bulk of the equipment was simply installed temporarily where the

Here is a transducer mounted to read wheel speed. Coupled with data taken from the front wheel, engine, and prop shaft, this location could gauge wheel spin and acceleration points coupled to shifting, denoting exactly what was actually getting down to the pavement. (Photo Courtesy Ted Spehar)

This is the trunk layout and recording equipment with transmitter in the yellow car; the combined weight of all of it was about 100 pounds. (Photo Courtesy Joe Pappas)

A secondary group of components was located on the passenger's side in the car itself. The advent of the real-time data transmission equipment had moved a number of things back to the trunk. Note the light metal shield mounted over the Lenco, replacing the OEM trans tunnel. (Photo Courtesy Joe Pappas)

passenger's seat would normally go. The NHRA required two front seats at the time, and it was a simple effort to remove the seat from that side and put the equipment in its place mounted on rubber donut-shaped supports to minimize vibrations. A multipoint junction unit used input plugs and female receptacles for each channel cable, and those parameters to be recorded for each particular test were plugged into it. This unit was mounted on the trans tunnel inside the car's interior, while the recorder (and later the combined transmitter/receiver) was located in the trunk. Unlike the raced *Missiles*, the yellow car did not need to go through the continual removal of these devices when preparing to run a sanctioned event.

Recalling any actual challenges to getting ready to test, Joe noted that at the track it was easy.

"Ron would wire the car," Joe said. "In a lot of the pictures, you see the wheel speed indicators front and rear so we could monitor wheel slippage and wheel speed. We had pressure transducers and temperature transducers. We had a linear transducer to measure suspension travel. So, whatever you wanted to monitor, you just plug in and take the data. So if Mr. Hoover said, 'Okay, today we're going to be looking at engine data,' we would connect to the sensors for fuel pressure, oil pressure, engine speed."

"It was a hundred pounds of equipment," said Oldfield.

"Killen's van had a complete weather station," Joe told Yetter. "Before the first pass in the morning, we would make adjustments for weather. Then Donnie would make a baseline run, followed by as many passes as necessary. Finally, we would 'close the loop' with a last run in baseline mode. This way you test one change at a time and you'll know if a change makes a difference. This is known as design of experiments, 'DOE' for short.

"At the end of day, the engineers would study the strip charts to determine what were good and/or bad results, and then plan the next day of testing," explained Joe. "Oldfield and I would get the car set up and ready all over again, sometimes changing motors. We had a lot of motors; usually had three to five motors with us when

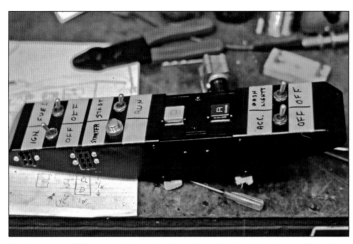

Perhaps a little crude by today standards, the team fabricated this small control panel so that Don Carlton always had everything close at hand. (Photo Courtesy Joe Pappas)

A final look shows the clear Plexiglas top that allowed for verification of what was being recorded. Three large bundles of wires extended from this box to the inside of the car and out to the permanently wired recording locations. (Photo Courtesy Joe Pappas)

Obviously, this switchboard was left to Ron to connect. Showing the myriad of possible recording positions that could be chosen, the feed from the transducers being recorded would then be bridged via this board to the recorder/transmitter. (Photo Courtesy Joe Pappas)

we traveled. They'd be different. Like with various pre-installed camshafts. We could quickly swap motors for testing different camshafts."

The early testing with the yellow car took place in Florida with all subsequent testing done at Milan, often on an intensive schedule.

"The computer equipment was crude by today's standards!" Joe continued. "But it was effective. Later on, when the car came back to the shop after testing at the strip or a race, it came all apart. We would always go through every nut, bolt, and screw on the car, make sure

everything was correct, and then get ready for the next test run. We had our 'tick list' that we worked from. We would write all of our tasks on a piece of paper, tape it to the car, and as we got them completed, we crossed them off to make sure we didn't forget anything. Dick and I worked wonderfully well together. It was easy for us to communicate, and we each had our own level of expertise.

"SVI cranked out great engines with the first W2 heads, and they cycled through the car in a constant flow. The entire year was spent with the engine. We did not have to flog the chassis or the rest of the driveline. We had a target and that was to make this engine fly.

"It was our mule. We beat the heck out of that car for a year in developing the A-engine. I don't think Dick and I were ever really privy to all the numbers because they were pretty close to the vest, but the car was pretty darn quick. Ted and Mr. Hoover were working on developing the engine. Later, as the wire car idea was developed, Dan Knapp was then contracted to build a very, very lightweight chassis."

At the Shop

The level of effort that was expended on behalf of sorting out the car and new engine package could likely not happen today. Joe recalled that the summer thrash was pretty brutal, but not without its humorous moments.

Testing the Yellow Small-Block

Once completed, the team spent much of 1974 thrashing on this car as rebuilt in the Troy shop by Joe Pappas and Dick Oldfield. It employed numerous lightening tricks to try to get it down to reasonable weight in line with the NHRA small-block/longer wheelbase rules. These photos were shot at Desoto Memorial Dragway in Bradenton, Florida, during that year by Joe and Dick; most of the testing actually occurred at Milan. The overall results of the yellow car are published in the following engine section by Ted Spehar, as well; this was the final testing program associated with the *Mopar Missile* as an actual factory race car. In later years, though testing was under the auspices of the factory on occasion, there was never again this level of direct factory involvement in the process. *All photos by Dick Oldfield, Joe Pappas, and Tom Hoover.*

We know it was Dick Oldfield who shot this image at Bradenton's Desoto Memorial Dragway, as Joe is seen behind the car as Don Carlton makes another run in the yellow car.

During one pass, the windshield cracked. Rather than stop the testing, this rudimentary repair was done. After all, no one was in the passenger's seat!

These notes from March 1974 were still with Dick Oldfield more than 40 years later in 2017, showing explicit data on the suspension tuning on the yellow car. This may have been written during the construction phase or when the first tests were done.

"Laid Back Lenny" (left) and Joe get after it with a second engine going into the car. From the trees blowing in the background, Florida weather may have played into this opportunity.

Joe Pappas, when not riding in the rear seat area or swapping engines, was up close at 1,000 feet as Don drove the Missile by at 140 mph during the Bradenton test.

Tom Hoover is looking a bit less professional after the Bradenton thrash, though his slight smile hints that the team was finding ways to makes the LA-series engines run.

Lenny Bartush is underneath while Joe works on details up top. It is likely that the science guys are in Killen's van looking over data, and somebody is probably repairing that blown-out Plexiglas windshield, which is missing here.

"In the real heyday of the factory testing, we actually went to an around-the-clock schedule," Joe remembered. "Oldfield and I would switch off every week, with one of us with the car and one of us in the shop. The car was out about five days a week at the track.

"It went something like this: the team going to the track would come in at about 7:30 a.m. to get ready for the day. Whoever was working on the 'day shift' would go with them and do whatever was needed at the track. Basically, though, everything was all set when they came in. They would make runs all day, record the info, try

new stuff out, finish up in the late afternoon, and bring it back there, getting back at about 6:30 p.m. The 'night shift' guy would have arrived by then and would get the list of work for that night written up by Mr. Hoover. 'Put a cam in this motor, rebuild that motor, fix this item, have so many of this or that ready for the next day,' and so on.

"The night guy would then work all night getting that done. If it all went well, he would leave at about 6 a.m. if there was nothing to report and go home, and the process would repeat. Normally, we would have had

Here is Joe Pappas (right) and Clyde Hodges (left) doing some work on the Altered car that Don took to the win at Sanair. The ability to add spoilers like this was one of the benefits of running in the Sportsman Gas division, though they would soon be part of Pro Stock as well. (Photo Courtesy Dick Oldfield Family)

A shot taken during the same thrash at Bradenton shows Don using tools as well. This car would eventually become an IHRA Pro Stock entry but remained in NHRA Sportsman racing until the team shifted to the Colt designs. (Photo Courtesy Dick Oldfield Family)

Showing the wire car under construction in 1974, this was the inside of the Carlton Enterprises shop in Troy during the team's heyday. The office area where the trailer tongue made an unexpected visit is in the background. (Photo Courtesy Dick Oldfield Family)

to do that between the other things that were going on, but when it came to testing in that way, that was pretty much all we were going to be doing."

Of course, though a first aid kit could be found quickly, safety was sometimes secondary to convenience. Joe recalled an incident during this era when the shop was visited by the local Troy fire marshal.

"Well, we never wanted to be out of what we needed, and we began buying racing and av-gas in bulk and just storing it in 55-gallon drums right in the shop," Joe said. "There was a wall between it and the shop, and we got pretty good at parking the truck in there, but there was very little room from wall to wall. Anyhow, we had enough fuel in there at one point that it was stacked about three levels high, maybe 15 to 18 barrels of it. We mixed the two types the way we wanted it.

"One afternoon, the Troy fire inspector showed up," Joe said. "He saw the stack and said to me, 'So, what's in the gas barrels; are they full?' I thought, 'Oh, boy, here it comes,' and said, 'Uh, yes.' He nods and writes something on his pad. He keeps walking around and looking at stuff. He gets ready to go, looks at me and Dick, and says, 'Yeah, you guys probably want to get some extra fire extinguishers,' and then he just leaves. Either he liked racers, or figured, hey, if we were going to get in trouble, that was our problem!"

Don Carlton, now responsible for the whole thing, could also maintain calm under pressure.

"One afternoon, Don was in the office with his insurance guy," Joe remembered. "Al Adam had brought his old 1966 D-Dart over for work, but we had no way to get it off his trailer. So picture this: Dick and I started jacking on it to roll it off, and in the process, the trailer itself got loose and shot across the shop floor. The tongue then hit with enough force that it went right between the wall studs and burst into the office wall, just missing the insurance guy's legs. Donnie never missed a beat; he looked down, pointed at it, and deadpanned, 'Is that covered?'"

Invariably, a thrash such as this could result in possible missteps. Due to the rigor that factory guys put on being thorough with the race car prep, it was other things that were forgotten.

"We never had problems with neighbors, but I'll tell you one story," Joe once recalled in 2009. "Oldfield, Carlton, and I would often work late into the night. I can't tell you how many times we went home and left the doors wide open. The guy who had the shop next door, he used to grind carbide cutters. He'd come in at 5:30 a.m. and see all of our overhead doors open. Our personal cars were missing from the lot. The lights were on, the radio playing with no one in the shop. He'd go ahead and lock the place up for us. That was 35 years ago. It was a different world!"

LA-Engine Efforts

The work expended during 1974 to develop a fresh Chrysler Pro Stock engine should not be underestimated. By this time, even Wally Booth and Dick Maskin had made AMC's engine live and win in NHRA Pro Stock. However, there were some serious realities to any comparison with Chrysler. AMC had paid Roger Penske handsomely to develop this engine for the NASCAR environment, and

Between Dave Koffel chasing hard-to-find parts and the engine-building skill of Ted and Lenny, the team had a number of Chrysler LA-series engines to experiment with that year. Note the very tight distributor position in relation to the intake plenum. (Photo Courtesy Dick Oldfield Family)

those fresh parts trickled over to drag racing. Efficient cylinder heads were a different matter, and Booth later noted that they required enormous splicing, cut-and-weld work, and further hand-wrought modifications to be functional on the quarter-mile.

As noted, the LA-series Chrysler block as designed in the early 1960s had never been an overly durable high-RPM design. Castings being acquired for use in the drag testing program had to be very carefully inspected, then machined for this purpose. The block itself, being the major component for keeping the rest of the parts in proper placement, was actually the weakest link in the process. Ted and Lenny were assembling the engines. Dave Koffel, whose background as a trained metallurgist was crucial to understanding why these problems were transpiring, stood in the middle of it throughout the 1970s era from the factory's standpoint.

"The A-motor had been under development, and I was involved with a lot of that research and development," Koffel said. "We had a version with Weslake heads, and the Trans-Am program we were involved with for that one year resulted in some good race parts. We tried very hard to run that engine as a modified engine. One ran in NHRA with the Rod Shop, and Francis Crider had a small-block Colt as well.

"We started making enough power that blocks just couldn't take it," Koffel continued. "But with the energy

Another attempt at the distributor mounting process is shown. Note the lines for the swinging pickup in the oil pan. A challenge here was the heat from the headers in association with the electrical components. (Photo Courtesy Joe Pappas)

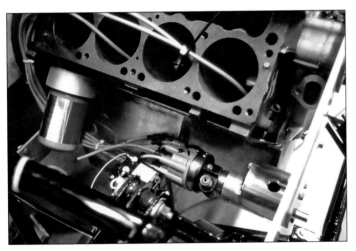

The use of an external-mount distributor was tried, placing the unit on the engine plate. This was never a simple operation, but the crank trigger eliminated some of the difficulty associated with the cam-crank relationship due to the distributor's rear-mount OEM location. (Photo Courtesy Joe Pappas)

crisis and the whole situation with the drag racing program, we couldn't get the approval or funding to make a new block. The only ones that were usable were out of the T/A-AAR program, and there just weren't any around. Anything worthwhile was going to NASCAR. In fact, I had to help Harry Hyde out with blocks for his NASCAR effort, and I ended up going out and buying 1970 AAR and T/A cars, bringing them back here, and stripping

them. I would sell the bodies and components and then sell Harry the blocks. It was pretty ridiculous.

"The factory didn't have money to make a new block," Koffel said. "Harry still had to race. We were making enough horsepower that we were splitting the stock blocks right at the number-four cylinder. We tried everything to fix that problem, but it was inherent to the design. I had one that was split so badly between three and four that I used it as a telephone stand in my den as a reminder of my frustration with that time period.

"But things went on, the energy crisis abated, and we began to build some experimental blocks, although primarily for NASCAR. There was a place called the Casper Foundry in Elyria, Ohio, and they did some experimental blocks for us. My job one summer was to go back and forth from Detroit to watch the progress on all of that. We got maybe 20 or so good blocks out of that deal."

By that time, things in the drag racing program had changed quite dramatically, but the Casper-cast blocks would end up marking a high note to a dark hour in Chrysler's history before the decade was over.

Racing 1974: Part 1

While the *Mopar Missile* was not campaigned in 1974, there were still a handful of NHRA-focused Chrysler Pro Stock racers. For them, relief came in the form of a rules change after the Gatornationals were over. The weight number moved from 7.00 to 6.90, and Bobby Yowell in Mr. Stepp's Demon actually posted a record-setting effort at an NHRA World Championship Series (WCS) event that May with an 8.89 at a big 154.63 mph (the NHRA record had been reset to an 8.90 minimum following the rules adjustment).

Soon after this, Roy Hill showed that he was also competitive when he posted a final-round finish at the always-humid 1974 Springnationals in Columbus in the former *California Flash* Duster, falling to Glidden's Ford on a red light. Meanwhile, Bill Bagshaw had picked the winning baton from Landy and was posting event-winning efforts at AHRA races during its West Coast–series races with three consecutive wins in his Dart Sport. With Reid Whisnant's Duster winning the IHRA Springnationals in Bristol, boycotts or not, Pro Stock Hemi cars still ran.

However, the "name" Hemi Super Stock warriors were also out in force, with Herb McCandless in a 1971 Hemi 'Cuda convertible for "Brooklyn Heavy," Ronnie Sox in an SS/A 1968 'Cuda, and Dick Landy in a 1970

While the test program went on week in and week out at Milan, Don traveled to locations within a reasonable distance from the shop in the summer of 1974. Running in either B/Gas or B/Altered with Pro Stock–level Hemi power, Don posted a Top Qualifier and win at Sanair and went to the class final at Indy. (Photo Courtesy Bob McClurg)

Meanwhile, Butch Leal was upholding the Hemi honors in Super Stock. Seen here at the NHRA Springnationals racing Dick Landy's Challenger, the reborn SS/B car that looked like Leal's old 1965 S/S car was built by Ron Butler and took headlines and the event title at the Summernationals in Englishtown. (Photo Courtesy Bob McClurg)

SS/D Hemi Challenger. There were new challengers to that effort as well, notably a handful of very hard-running Corvettes creeping up into the SS/C/D/E territory. This resulted in major changes to Super Stock suspension legality, as the OEM Corvette's independent rear suspension (IRS) layout was not able to withstand traction-related problems. Butch Leal, in a very trick new 1965 Plymouth Belvedere that Ron Butler built in the offseason, took victory on the West Coast, as well as class titles, before finally winning it all at the NHRA Summernationals.

The new Sportsnationals in Bowling Green, Kentucky, were a big hit in the late spring of 1974, and new records were set by Landy in SS/D, and 1973 US Nationals winner Terry Earwood in SS/AA. Melvin Yow, running Stepp's 1972 Demon in B/Gas at the event, and Bob Riffle, driving the Rod Shop's ex-Pro Stock Dart Sport in C/Altered trim, did likewise in those classes. While the *Missile* name on a factory race car would not return in 1974

or thereafter, cars lettered for Don Carlton himself would find the winner's circle in this form of racing.

Using a match-race Dart Sport that Clyde Hodges built and a deal signed for a sponsorship with MPC models to campaign it in B/Altered, Carlton raced as a Sportsman entry in 1974. Indeed, only one record of Don racing in Pro Stock, either in sanctioned or match-race trim, is known from this season. This was at the National Challenge race out on Long Island in late August. The replacement for the former Tulsa-based event and no longer under AHRA direction, this event was controversial due to a number of misunderstandings between management and the newly formed PRO organization led by Don Garlits. Pro Stock was run on a flat 6.75 weight for everyone, and Don went to the semifinals in what the media humorous entitled the "Hodges Dodges," before falling to Grumpy Jenkins's Vega. Jenkins, for his part, took his third consecutive crown over a Mopar at the yearly meet, this time beating none other than Mike

On the Road with Dick and Joe

Lock up your daughters? No, Dick and Joe are just hamming it up at a Happy Days (50s-themed) party at one of the team's homes. (Photo Courtesy Dick Oldfield Family)

Though the team did not tour for the racing schedule this year, the times that Dick Oldfield and Joe Pappas drove cross-country were always memorable. While many tales are told of what happened on the racetrack, this between-race road time was as much a part of the process as any. Here are a few of the recollections they brought out during the 2012 roundtable when asked by moderator Gene Yetter.

"One trip, we switched driving about every five minutes!" exclaimed Dick.

"Yeah. We had been up for about three days and we left Detroit to go to California," said Joe. "I drove

The Sox & Martin diesel truck that went West for weeks on end with the team in 1973 is shown. It was not missed. (Photo Courtesy Joe Pappas)

to Dick's house in Huntington Woods, which is about 6 miles away. He took over and drove about 20 miles. I took over. Finally, we got sleep. The unfortunate thing was, we had borrowed the old Sox & Martin diesel. That thing was terrible. It had a broken injector line and it was spewing diesel fuel. We stopped twice on the way to California to have the injector line repaired and twice to have the truck washed because it was bathed in diesel fuel. And Dick and I got arrested in New Mexico . . ."

The audience laughs, though it was not so funny at the time.

"It was his fault!" Joe says, pointing at Oldfield. "We decided we would drive straight through nonstop. No sleeper. We looked pretty bad. We had wanted to go up Scandia Peak [New Mexico]. It's got a tramway up to the top. We drove in there, we went up, and enjoyed the view. We took some pictures, like we always did. We came down and went to a truck stop to get fuel.

"The guy says, 'Where's your diesel fuel permit?' We said, 'We don't need any stinkin' diesel fuel permit. This is owned by Chrysler Corporation!'

"So the guy says, 'No, no, you've got to buy a diesel fuel permit. Didn't you get it at the port of entry?' Heck, no. They saw it looked like a circus wagon, so they waved us through. Pretty soon, the deputy shows up: two pearl-handle revolvers, a big Stetson, khaki uniform, aviator sunglasses.

"He says, 'Where are your logbooks?' We looked at each other and said, 'What logbooks?' The wrong thing to say, and he started writing tickets. We got up to about $300 in tickets, which back in that time was pretty steep.

"He asked us, 'Where are you from?'

'Detroit.'

'When did you leave?'

"Stupidly, we told him. Double-teaming it back in those days, you could spend 20 hours in the truck, but you had to get out. We were 30 hours into the trip and we had never gotten out, except for fuel. He said, 'You have a choice. You can give this man five whole dollars for the permit, pay for your fuel, and I'll escort you to this motel [or you can pay the tickets].' So we went to the motel where he waits for us outside.

"We asked the proprietor if we could stay there a few minutes and talk to him. Soon the deputy left. We waited another 20 minutes, got in the truck, and drove to the Grand Canyon. We wanted to see the Grand Canyon!"

One afternoon at Indy, something important was left at the track.

"Yeah, we were at Indianapolis," recalled Dick. "We both took our sons to the race with us," he said, referring to young Richard Oldfield and young Donnie Carlton. "The instruction was [that] we were going to make a pass, and if the car's running good, we were going to load up, get the hell out, and go back to the motel. 'So every time the car goes out on the track, you kids make sure you come back to the truck. Make sure we were going to stay or leave.' Well, they didn't come back to the truck and we left.

"So we went back, got something to eat, and went to the room to get some sleep. All of the sudden, the Sox & Martin truck pulls up out front and drops the kids off. Of course, they're hungry. We said, 'We already ate. You'll have breakfast in the morning.'

"Donnie and I were walking around the pits going, 'Who's going back to the hotel?'" said Richard.

"How old were you, Richard?" Joe asked.

"Oh, heck. We had to be what, 12?"

"He's still mad at me too," Joe laughed.

With tight quarters in the cab, the boys learned the ropes whether they wanted to or not.

"When the kids rode with us, they had to do the same thing," said Dick. "If you're driving, they had to be up front; it was four on and four off. So, if you have to get up at two o'clock in the morning, they had to get out of the sleeper and sit up front. They didn't care for that either."

Tom Hoover thought for a moment, then recalled something they didn't do with corporate oversight in the 1970s.

"Well, Coors beer was a big issue too back in the old days," Hoover said. "When the guys would go to Pomona, they'd hide Coors beer everyplace they

The trailers are empty. Where can we put the Coors for the run back east? (Photo Courtesy Joe Pappas)

Well, stuff happens. A beautiful morning on a cross-country jaunt, and a tire and subsequent wheel bearing have decided to take the day off. (Photo Courtesy Dick Oldfield Family)

could think of in the truck. And getting through New Mexico was a challenge. I never had that experience personally."

Oldfield had. "We had all the beer in the race car, and the car got a flat tire. There was beer running out the back door."

"The New Mexico cops in those days could tell what a race truck was," noted Tom. "It was so obvious. They would give the guys a hard time."

"Dick Oldfield and I bought about 50 cases and we went to North Carolina," Joe said. "The old house that we used to use as the shop, before Donnie built the building—we backed up and we unloaded the car first, and then all the beer was stacked in front of the car. The house was just down the street from a little prison camp, and it was not uncommon for the highway patrol to come by. They'd see the truck there and they wanted to see what was going on. Trooper walks in, and there's 50 cases of beer sitting there."

That would not have been a problem normally but could be one in Lenoir.

"It was dry county!" exclaimed Dick.

Joe continued. "I said to the trooper, I'd really like to see your car. He flips me the keys and I opened his trunk and threw in a case of beer. He was our best friend!"

"I'm not sure that would have worked with those New Mexico state cops," Mr. Hoover commented.

"No, we used T-shirts there!" laughed Dick. "We were hauling all that liquor, and he said, 'You can't do this across country.' So we took him inside the trailer and we had some T-shirts and stuff. He needed one for his kid, one for his uncle, and so on. He walks out with a pile of T-shirts and he was happy!"

Joe searched his memory again. "Mr. Hoover actually rode with us one time to Englishtown. And I think Tommy [Coddington], you were in the truck too."

"Yeah, we picked him up in Dubois," said Coddington.

"I was driving . . . must have been through Pennsylvania or New York," Joe recalled. "It was kind of foggy out. Tom was asleep in the sleeper. Coming down a long mountain way too fast, I see this little light in the middle of the road. I thought, 'We're going to be good Samaritans and pull over.' It was a state trooper. I stopped and got out, and he said 'You were doing like 90 mph coming down this mountain.' I think the speed limit at the time was 55 or 65. Pennsylvania was screwy.

Still pals, Joe and Dick at Henderson, 2014. (Photo Courtesy Ted Spehar)

"Mr. Hoover was in the sleeper and we didn't want him to know that I was getting stopped for a ticket. He woke up and wanted to know what was going on. Dick said, 'Joe is checking the tires.' Got back in and went a little slower for a while until I got out of Pennsylvania at least. You never knew that—did you, Tom?"

Mr. Hoover, godfather of the 426 Hemi engine, philosophically responded without hesitation. "No, there are a lot of things I don't need to know."

Fons in the just-painted new *Motown Missile* Duster for a $15,000 payday. The Fons car was formerly raced by Irv Beringhaus and had been part of the winning machines built by Dick Landy and Kent Fuller for the 1973 season.

Carlton had won at least one NHRA or IHRA national event title in 1971, 1972, and 1973, something no other Chrysler Pro Stock driver could claim. Now, revved up and actually clocking times in the 8.70s, the Hodge-built Dart Sport in its B/A configuration first showed up at Columbus, where Don went out in round one. The following month at Englishtown, it was the same result, but this time the car was repainted, qualified second in the program, and reset the national record. That left a trip to Canada for the Molson Grandnationals at Sanair, and

there the Don Carlton–lettered machine let it all hang out, qualifying number one, running under the set index while marching through the Competition Eliminator field, and resetting the record to 8.78 (lower than Pro Stock) to post his first 1974 race win. While it was a Sportsman class, it kept the yearly victory streak intact and proved that, while testing was taking up a majority of their time, the team could still make it happen on race day.

One final thing making news in 1974 was the Sox & Martin team splitting with the factory. Actually more a formality, the rules issues had done immense damage to the firm's ability to make a profit building either Chrysler race cars or engines. While the current rumor was that the duo was switching over to a Pinto, in the end, only

Billy "The Kid" Stepp now had fellow Dayton resident Bobby Yowell driving for him. They built a Hemi Colt that made its debut at the 1974 US Nationals in B/Altered trim. (Photo Courtesy Bob McClurg)

Ronnie Sox burns out in the evening light at Minnesota Dragways. Still billed as a USRT event, this race was a match race that pitted big-name drivers in Pro Stock against each other. This Colt was soon after part of the DeChamps/Pomeroy team that owned the 1973 Mopar Missile. (Photo Courtesy Dan Williams)

The Lyles Colt, which Ronnie Lyles raced with co-owner Eugene Coard and future NASCAR wrench Randy Dorton, gives an idea of just how small these cars were. The Hemi seems almost like a caricature by Ed "Big Daddy" Roth! (Photo Courtesy Dan Williams)

Ronnie Lyles, billed as drag racing's first black superstar, also had a Colt built by Sox & Martin's shop at this USRT race. He is seen here inside the car at the hotel where the racers stayed for the event. (Photo Courtesy Dan Williams)

A simple examination of the wire car coming together gives an idea of how light it would be. The front engine support, formed of magnesium, would support both the engine and the front end. The rear support between the engine and transmission was also magnesium. (Photo Courtesy Joe Pappas)

Here is the interior and the basic chassis when the body was first hung on it. There would not be a conventional floor in the car. This substructure would support custom-bent sheets for the driver's footbox and seat support, rising to meet a fabricated interior "box" almost at window level. (Photo Courtesy Joe Pappas)

Ronnie Sox continued on in racing, while Buddy Martin moved on to pursue other businesses. A fire at the race shop put the final nail into what was perhaps the most famed Chrysler team in all of drag racing.

Final Frontier: The Wire Car

Back in Knapp's little shop, while the A-motor was getting flogged in the yellow Dart Sport, the latest *Missile* chassis was brought to life.

"During this era, our big boss, Bob Cahill, certainly began deliberating on whether we were going to keep putting up with this business of NHRA factoring," Al Adam noted during the 2014 discussion. "While he's deliberating, Tom Hoover came to me one day and said, 'Al, we're going to try this one more time. Go design and build a 2,000-pound ready-to-race A-Body.' And I went, 'Gulp!'"

A former member of the Ramchargers operation, Adam had been a primary member of the racing group for much of the past decade, and he would now be given what was a truly heroic undertaking. To get a much smaller Vega or Pinto down to a single ton was nearly impossible. He attempted this but with a Duster.

"I said, 'Okay, boss. I'll get right on it.' I knew I was going to need some help and advice in the chassis and roll-cage construction area. So I summoned two colleagues

Rather than a conventional cage, the car had a cross-braced interior tubing structure, and its rigidity was verified by a computer. The chassis design itself was done by Chrysler Engineering under the direction of Al Adam, using the latest concepts of measuring finite analysis to eliminate all unrequired weight. Here, the team has mocked up the shape of the future inside panels with cardstock. (Photo Courtesy Joe Pappas)

and friends of mine, Bill Surber and John Riesbeck.

"Bill worked directly for Larry Rathgeb in the NAS-CAR side of Chrysler's racing division. He was Larry's right-hand man in building the Chrysler kit car, which was a circuit race car that Chrysler offered; it could be purchased either ready to race or in a kit form. And the

The bracing inside is shown. The "tin work" was actually sheets of magnesium that allowed for support of the body but added minimal additional weight. It was both very innovative and very expensive. (Photo Courtesy Joe Pappas)

buyer would assemble it himself. So Bill was well-learned on how to build race cars.

"John Riesbeck did not work in the race group," Adam said. "He worked in the mainstream of Chrysler, in the advanced area. He was responsible for finite element analysis for the corporation. He did a lot of work on the earlier *Missile* cars in the finite element analysis of the roll-cage construction.

"I got Bill and John together and I asked them, 'Can we build a 2,000-pound car that's ready to race, and that's going to be safe and have the torsion and rigidity that it needs?' Bill said, 'Yes, I think we can. It's going to take some innovation, but we can.'

"I was impressed by Bill's confidence. Here's a guy who comes from the NASCAR side of the fence, where they build Sherman tanks. They're the safest cars in the world! He understood what we needed in drag racing, and he said it could be done. These cars had a four-link rear suspension, so Bill says, 'The back end of the car doesn't do anything but hold up the taillights when it's going down the track, so we don't need any major structure going back there. We'll hold it up with two cables, put turnbuckles in it, attach the two corners of the car up to the roll cage in the C-post area, crisscross the cables, and that's going to hold up the back of the car.'

"And we thought, 'Oh boy! Wait until NHRA sees this one!' But we proceeded," Adam continued. "We had some other innovations. Like the two frame rails that it

has. They started out as just flat stock steel laying on the floor. Dan Knapp, who used to work in the Ramcharger group on the Fuel cars, was an excellent fabricator and welder. He did the frame rails. He rolled them into a rectangular form, welding them full length. The tubes that held up the sills went straight through the frame rails and out the other side, welded on both sides of the frame rails. No butt welding; the tubes go right through the frame rails. So those were some of the main innovations in the structural department.

"In addition, there were a lot of exotic materials in the car: magnesium, aluminum, and titanium. John Riesbeck suggested we do finite element analysis on the roll-cage design. If any of you have seen finite element analysis, it results in a color mat. The pieces that are overstressed show in red, the ones that are okay are green, and the ones that don't do anything are blue. So whenever I'd find a blue tube in there, I got them to make it smaller! We went through four or five iterations of the analysis."

In the end, this car would have been the most advanced, purpose-built chassis in the history of drag racing. Moreover, though it was expensive due to the material required, Al got the car where they wanted it and set up with a motor plate that would use the A-engine design. Once the chassis had been built, actual car construction went to the Troy shop, where Dick and Joe applied their talents to putting the whole thing together in the middle part of the year.

"We built the car and the weight came in on spec," said Adam. "I think Joe can attest to that. In fact, I think it weighs less than 2,000 pounds."

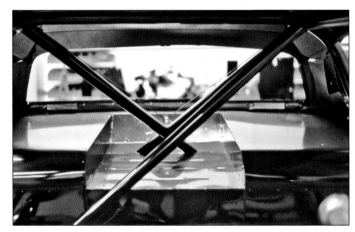

A final view shows the interior (looking back from the driver's area). Since the magnesium interior sheet panels do not form easily without snapping, only minimal curving of the wheel tubs was possible. (Photo Courtesy Joe Pappas)

Changes to the wheel well configuration are shown in the front. Note the space between the front bumper and wheel opening, and the position of the wheel itself. Pro Stock by late 1974 was not "stock" in many regards, but the wire car was far beyond the competitors' ideas. (Photo Courtesy Joe Pappas)

With a mock engine in place, the team fabricated the nose design to be removable as a single section, which had also been done on the yellow car. The hood was separate, but the grille and fenders were constructed to be removed as a single unit. (Photo Courtesy Joe Pappas)

In Don's Troy shop, the wire car was almost competed, showing the one-piece nose design tilted on end. The old "Pro 223" rear quarter windows were the ones taken from the former Stuart McDade ride that became the yellow test car. (Photo Courtesy Joe Pappas)

"Yes. It weighs about 1,850 pounds ready to run," Pappas noted. "But it wasn't to be."

"Right about then, the big boss put the hammer down, and said, 'That's it. We're out of racing,'" Adam remembered. "To my knowledge we never ran or tested that car. So the team broke up—all of us going in different directions in Chrysler. I went back into the mainstream in the company, in the transmission area. I lost track of where the car even went at that point.

"We hauled it to North Carolina and parked it at Don's shop, in front of the building," Joe replied. "And it sat there. We had painted the inside, the underside. The car was, I believe, plumbed, wired. If it had a motor in it, you could run it. It was not painted on the outside. At some point, Don finished the car, painted it with the *Missile* colors. I saw a picture of it with his name on it. But it was subsequently sold to Betty Sigmon."

"The *Missile* Pro Stock program had come to an end," Joe would later recount for the 2015 Mopar Collectors Guide Hall of Fame audience. "I can't say for sure what drove the decision. Rumors were that NHRA had heard about what we were doing and did a swift rule change that would have made the Duster wire car noncompetitive. It also may have been that the A-engine was not quite ready for its debut into the world of Pro Stock racing. And lastly, maybe it was just too good, and Chrysler didn't want to tilt the scales like the Hemi had done. Whatever the reason—it was over."

Racing 1974: Part 2

According to research by expert Bob Frey, Don Carlton made his final 1974 NHRA race appearance at the US Nationals. The car was running Pro Stock–level Hemi power and ended up losing in the class final, which precluded a spot in the eliminator itself.

Larry Huff was the 1974 Mopar torch bearer in the Pro Stock category. In a car Dick Landy built, powered, and tuned, Huff ended up being the AHRA World Champion at season's end due to consistency and race wins. Bill Bagshaw had been his closest Mopar competitor, but a horrific accident at the AHRA Grand American race near St. Louis that summer had put the end to his pursuit. Though the Butler-built car was heavily damaged and there were associated fatalities when the car left the racing surface, Bagshaw himself was grateful to be alive. In an era where safety was being challenged by vehicle speeds and the conditions of the track's own protective

As the year wound down, Don moved the car to B/Gas trim, but it would not race that way in NHRA during the 1974 season. It is seen here at Bradenton. (Photo Courtesy Joe Pappas)

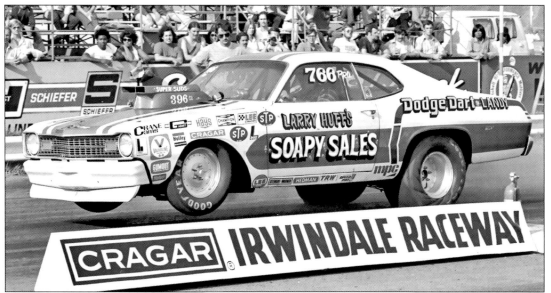

Larry Huff's Dick Landy–tuned Dart is in action at Irwindale, California, in 1974, as Huff moved toward his Pro Stock Championship on the AHRA season. This was a highlight in an otherwise dim year for Mopars in the division. (Photo Courtesy Steve Reyes)

Bill Bagshaw, seen here early in 1974 at Steve Reyes's former home track, Fremont Raceway, was also in the thick of AHRA action until his accident in St. Louis at midseason. Though injured, Bagshaw's life was saved by the Butler-built car's design, and he retired following that incident. (Photo Courtesy Steve Reyes)

Here is Mike Fons in the latest of his Motown Missiles, *which was formerly Irv Beringhaus's Landy/Fuller Dart Sport. This was at the National Challenge race on Long Island, which was also the only Pro Stock appearance of Don Carlton during the 1974 season, though his car was unlettered. (Photo Courtesy Bob McClurg)*

equipment, the accident was frankly devastating to Bagshaw. He retired from driving as a result, thus closing yet another career chapter for a dedicated, well-known Chrysler campaigner.

Meanwhile, as the season went on, the match-race scene became part of Colt history. Normal Plymouth stalwart Ronnie Sox drove one of them late in the season for Ronnie Lyles after selling an earlier version that Don Hardy had built for the Sox & Martin team to test with. The Hardy Sox car went to Nelson DeChamps and Stewart Pomeroy, supplementing their 1973 *Missile* Duster. Bob Riffle and the Rod Shop guys now had one they were committed to racing in Competition Eliminator, as did Billy Stepp and driver Bobby Yowell; so for NHRA fans, these Sportsman-level cars became the Hemi Colts in actual racing.

In the End, the End

At another rules meeting at Indy with the NHRA, Chrysler's pleas for parity again fell on deaf ears. It was at this point that brutal reality met practicality. Chrysler was done with Pro Stock.

"I'll never forget this," Tom Hoover stated during the roundtable. "We were walking out of Indy at the end of the 1974 Nationals. We just said, 'This is not worth doing anymore (Pro Stock).' That was the end. Pow! And I mean it was the end for us. Why pour the company's money in there just to be fodder? Hey, the factoring pencil can beat everybody, baby! I got bullet holes in me all over the place with that factoring pencil!"

Of course, it felt personal, and frankly it was. Wally Parks had alluded in an interview published in *Super Stock* magazine earlier in the season that he had no amicus against Chrysler, but the actual rules after 1971 never played out that way. A moment after the above statement, Tom Coddington reminded Mr. Hoover that Parks did finally make an apology, albeit decades later.

"When the Gen III 5.7-liter Hemi came out, Chrysler put together a reception at the Walter P. Chrysler Museum in Auburn Hills," Hoover noted. "Bob Lutz called me. I was retired back in Pennsylvania at the time. I went to the event and Wally Parks was there. He took me aside that evening in the museum. He was smooth and laid back. He fundamentally apologized for having made us uncompetitive to the point that, essentially, we had to quit in 1974. He realized that was a mistake.

"To Wally, in the final analysis, we were one of his show providers. That is to say, he made the sport, and he made his living, and what have you. We put on the show! Anyway, the man apologized. He wished he hadn't done that, or perhaps done it in a more moderate way—not the big hammer approach."

Nonetheless, the damage was done. Some of the former racers who sat out the 1974 season would come back and run Pro Stock on their own in 1975, and now it was a question of what to do in the aftermath of the late-season decision. As noted, the W2 Pro Stock program work ended without the exotic wire car ever making a lap, even in testing. It was decided to let Donnie have all the exotic stuff and go his own way.

Although the exact details are lost to time, this was an immense undertaking as the Troy shop ultimately closed. Don had already planned for a large new building to house a racing operation on his property in North Carolina, and he would soon be back in the hills of home. Joe remembers spending Thanksgiving week of 1974 driving truckload after truckload of cars and parts down to the new Carlton shop in North Carolina, at one point almost getting stuck in a freak snowstorm. Even the D5 Colt and wire car were sent down, plus a large amount of trick lightweight parts and materials that had been acquired over the previous two years. For his part, Joe's era of being a drag racing roustabout were ending as well.

"I was involved with it from January 1973 to the end of the 1974. I went back to college in January 1975. I needed to get my degree, which I did, in 1976—a Bachelor of Science degree. I decided to go back to college rather than move with Carlton to North Carolina, and Oldfield ended up working at Chrysler Corp., eventually retiring from there. I was in the Chrysler Pro Stock program for two years."

While there was someone to answer the phone in Detroit if Don called a friend, the racing development on a corporate level was over. During the 2014 *Drag Times* roundtable, the last gathering when Mr. Hoover and Dick "Barney" Oldfield were still alive, the team recalled some of what had made that half-decade so unique.

"Back then, like it is now, if you race, you have a passion for it because you are not doing it to get rich," opined Ted Spehar "The amount of time you put in . . . you just can't count the time. With us, if we tested, we would test, and then if we knew we had to go to a race, you had to bring the car back to the shop and switch over what was necessary. If it had a motor that had parts in it that were evaluated and you had to switch engines, by the time all this gets done, it's 10 o'clock at night. You got to get in the truck and go because you got to be at the track the next morning. So, everybody took turns driving." He then wistfully added, "Thank God you race when you're young—not when you're old!"

"I'd like to add something to that," Ron Killen noted. "When we were at the track, especially for a race, we were usually there mid-week. It wasn't unusual for workdays to run 18 to 20 hours, right up until Sunday afternoon. We could be anywhere—California, Florida, wherever—most of us having come from Michigan. I can't remember too many tests when Tom Hoover didn't get us together for dinner, usually on Sunday evening. We'd go over what had happened. Then Tom would say, 'Well, I'll see you guys Wednesday morning back at work.' That usually meant, take a day, stay here. You're still on an expense report. Chill out. There was some recognition that everybody gave all they could give. Take some time and relax. Not just, 'Thanks. Let's get back to work.' The whole team was treated that way."

"We didn't realize at the time," said Tom Hoover in the end, regarding how the factory and team segued their efforts, "but folks eventually become aware of the fact that the Japanese penetrated, revolutionized, and changed the whole automobile industry. That was actually helped by an American military officer, W. Edwards Deming. We didn't know it, but in our Pro Stock team project, we were applying the fundamental principles that he taught the Japanese. It took Detroit a while to

It's over. The equipment is seen in North Carolina, with the yellow test car and the untested wire car turned over to Don when the factory formally ended its Pro Stock program. (Photo Courtesy Joe Pappas)

realize we were in big trouble with Japanese competition. They had to learn how to manage things in a way not unlike the race and *Missile* programs: horizontally. We were doing some things right and didn't realize it."

In light of drag racing history, that is frankly an understatement. The racing era of the *Motown* and *Mopar Missile* programs was extremely evolutionary and competitive, and Pro Stock was often considered the most popular class by the fans at the time. Perhaps to the outsider who counted only race victories, the *Missile* effort might have never seemed fruitful. However, Ronnie Sox won back-to-back NHRA World titles thanks in part to the research done by the factory, and Don Carlton fought against the best drivers on the IHRA to win three straight World Championships in the heyday of that racing organization's history. His occasional-but-annual NHRA event win record was one that not even Sox, Nicholson, or Jenkins could match. Dandy Dick Landy was also privy to the research effort the *Missile* team spearheaded, taking back-to-back AHRA titles in 1973 himself and in 1974 with Larry Huff. In the end, the factory team of Chrysler, SVI, and Carlton Enterprises did a lot of things right.

By year's end, things had changed in other ways. Chrysler as a company was struggling with simple economics in an unsettled and unfriendly marketing, sales, and regulatory environment. Though a rudimentary development program remained in place for some of the Sportsman-level involvement through Direct Connection, the company was working on street models that no longer bore the stylings of performance. Nonetheless, drag racing as a sport continued, and Don Carlton was heard from again before Chrysler's 1970s drag racing involvement concluded.

Ted Spehar on Engines: Part II: 1973 and Up

Ted Spehar continued his work on engines for the factory throughout the 1970s and worked on the small-block LA-series Pro Stock program during the final year of *Missile* development in 1974. Meanwhile, he also continued building Hemi engines as needed, both for testing and for Don Carlton's independent racing program. Here again in Ted's own words are the results of that effort.

"As the racing became more refined, real big horsepower gains didn't show up like they had in the earlier time period; it was much harder to find. When you go back and look, we weren't terribly successful in the beginning. Beyond that, we took a different approach

to the program, more from an engineering side rather than from a purely racing point of view. If we were developing a new piece, it was more about what would go out to the other racers. It had to be good quality, and we focused on that more than simply power output. The pieces that worked would then go through Performance Parts, or later Direct Connection, and it would take a little while before they got out there to everybody.

"The first of the small-blocks was done for 1973. The series was engines number 47 through 50, which show up in many tests later on. Those first blocks were the regular 340-ci A-engine passenger castings, not

Ted works on the Hemi in the B/Altered car in 1975. (Photo Courtesy Tom Hoover Family)

created for racing and cast with thin-bore walls. Eventually, the factory cast up some special versions and stress-relieved them, but not at first.

"The engine's oiling system was a problem right away, especially for high-speed use. I modified some blocks where we eventually went to an external oil pump on the outside and then just fed the oil into the front of the block. In the beginning, these engines used a wet sump for quite a while. We actually tried an external oil pump with a distributor mounted on the back of it, which was a pretty cool idea. But every time Donnie let the clutch out, it had enough endplay that it would break the rotor and shut itself off.

"I think we played with that thing for a day or so trying to make it work and never did; it went on the shelf, and that was the end of it.

"You've got to put yourself back in that time. We were always thinking, just kept moving; what we know now is . . . well, back then, we just weren't that smart, I guess! [laughs] So we went back with the distributor in the factory rear location working with the crank trigger, and that worked fine.

"I built the first small-block with a set of ported J-series Trans-Am heads, which were iron, and Bob Mullen did the work on them. With those heads, Mullen did a lot of work on the exhaust side (changing the port design, increasing the intake valve size), but he did not have a way to normalize them after the brazing work was done, and they would still crack. The truth was, when you did this much work to the OEM head, it was weakened since it was a casting; head durability was a real problem. Now, once they cast the W2s, that was taken into consideration and it was a much better head. That was it; there were no other aftermarket small-block heads available.

"Remember, by 1973, we're racing a 1960s head design against the Ford Cleveland; the Ford was designed for flow right from the start and could be modified. Later, with the W2 head release, that was more [factory engineer and former Ramcharger] John Wehrly, as he was dealing with the NASCAR guys. The W2 configuration was more for that, but the drag racing program, as always, benefited from what was being developed. By then, the NASCAR racers really needed a head that was better than the old Trans-Am version.

"So my early ones basically used a ported T/A head, an Edelbrock tunnel ram, Diamond or Forged True pistons, and different roller cam designs. With the LA small-blocks, we used a roller cam right away. They came from General Kinetics, Cam Dynamics, and Crane; between those three, we always had something to choose from. We eventually began machining the combustion chambers out and using a higher piston to try and get more compression out of the engine, but the durability issue was not fixable. Our suppliers had no CNC machines; you would get the custom piston close to what you wanted, and then you had to hand-fit everything.

"We did work on carbs, between the dual 660 CFMs and some other carbs. A lot of that was Coddington and Bauman, and we would do a lot of launches to see what combination might be better. Eventually, we did get that sorted out as well. You always have to figure out the best way to get the first 60 feet on the clock. After some of that was done, the plenum size and runner length were fairly optimized; we did not make a lot of added changes there. We were still chasing bigger horsepower gains, not small stuff.

"Adopting an A-engine into the Colt was easily possible, but for guys who had to make a living racing, you could put a Hemi into the Colt with a lot less effort for horsepower. To match race, it was the biggest engine in the smallest body, and away you went. Donnie had all the cars by then, and he had to keep the test cars separate from what he and Clyde Hodges built for racing. I provided the engines for the tests, A-engine and Hemis both.

"So, some of the Pro Stock Hemi work applied to the Super Stocks as well. You could use the same R296 Crane cam, just degree it in differently. The heavier cars, such as an SS/B model, liked a 286 Heffington cam over the 296 Crane; we did testing to figure that out. On some of the later motors, we went to a higher rocker ratio on the intake, but oiling was still a problem. We hand-built those, too, until they started making Hemi aluminum rockers later in the 1970s. There was no way back then that we could get 1.000 lift like they do now. The exhaust side wasn't that important, but you mess with the intake port, you can slow down really fast!

"Pushrods were another area that was being worked on; that thing was the weak link. You want to

The small-block program never paid major dividends in terms of competitive horsepower, but it certainly was not for a lack of trying. When asked why so few engine images exist, Ted shrugs. "They were just test engines; nobody thought about it." (Photo Courtesy Joe Pappas)

get it as straight as possible. We used a company called D&D, and it was a tapered pushrod; it worked well for that time period. You look at today's Fuel motors and they have 'telephone poles' in those things. Again, the pushrods had to be exactly right to make power, not flex, and still get oil. A company named Trend figuring all that out was a real breakthrough for all of us, but that was not until the late 1980s.

"We stopped on the small-block Pro Stock project once the factory decided they were out of Pro Stock. A few years later, Koffel made the deal with Glidden, and we gave them everything we had learned, including all of my parts and some of my own paperwork that is no longer in my books. By then, the factory was still supporting some of the Sportsman stuff, focusing on success there, but I was done with small-block development in Pro Stock.

"So when the plug was pulled, Donnie was back home, and sometimes I think he was happier having Clyde and some of his boys down South doing some of those projects. They ended up with the Colts, and the big-engine/small-car deal was the way match racing was going because that's how he was making his living. I still provided some engines for him. Now, on any test days with the factory, I still provided engines."

The Engines

"Engine 34 was for something else, but engine 35 was for the *Missile*, a 366-ci package, and that was done to be able to lower the overall weight in the car. That was using a 426-ci block and shorter stroke. That one was not encouraging, so I rebuilt it as a 396-inch short-rod motor with a 6.96 rod, and in early 1973, it ran 153 mph in the A-Body, and 8.90s.

"Engine 36 was just a 426-ci test motor, nothing spectacular, but my notes say that it gave us 150 cycles [or runs] on it, so it was a really good service motor. Next, I see engine 39, a 396-ci using a 7.06 rod length, which went to Carlton for his Demon and was an IHRA match-race motor that Stu McDade used when he was driving for Donnie. It came back here to be rebuilt, but I don't have a record where it went after that; probably back to Donnie. If they were not being used for testing, I did not keep a lot of records on them; hey, those other ones only came back here when they were broke!

"So engine 40 was the first of the small-blocks we ran in the car, which was a 340 block, General Kinetics cam, Edelbrock intake, and we used it for the early tests. After I disassembled it, we sent the block off to Universal Oil Products (UOP) Shadow Racing in Chicago for a Formula 5000–class open-wheel program they were working with.

"Numbers 41 and 42, I think, were engines for press cars, so the next one is engine 43. That one was a 396-ci, and that one also used the D5 block, which had more room for the pushrods with D4 heads. The pushrods were laid over more and the block required a lot less grinding; you can tell the difference because, on the D5, the pushrod holes were all in-line, while on a production block, the intakes are up higher. The D5 was more robust as a race block, with thicker main webbing and thicker bores to get away from the cracking problem. They were not great castings, but I was the first guy to look at them at Direct Connection back then and got to pick out the ones I thought were best. So number 43 ran at Indy and then it was turned into engine 60. Number 44 was another 396-ci D5 Hemi, and it went to Carlton.

"Engine 46 was another Hemi (400-ci) that ran at Tulsa in 1973 and had an ignition failure and blew out a spark plug. We upped the compression ratio from 12.5 and used it for testing for about a month, raced it at Bristol, and then it spun a bearing at a Milan test. I rebuilt it in November 1973, and it went back to Don. With these engines, we might do a cam change, but it was usually the same heads, same rod lengths, all of that. Number 46 is not noted here as a D5, so that one probably used the standard Hemi block. Of course, all of these blocks were lightened as well.

"Now, paperwork on motors 47 to 50 is missing, so that was the small-block stuff we tested in 1973 and 1974, and I probably gave all that to Glidden when Koffel asked me to. From the 340 Demon test paperwork, I know number 50 was a W2 configuration, number 47 used a W3 head, and then number 50 got the big intake-valve T/A heads; we flogged it with all sorts of intake and carb stuff and, no matter what, it did not change it even a tenth of a second. MPH was always 148, 149.

"Engines 51 to 54 were press motors, so number 55 is next. It was a 360 Super Stock engine, and we got 400 runs out of it. Great engine. We were really not at a power level that required a better crankshaft yet, so those small-blocks were all production cranks as far as I recall. We may have gotten something from the circle-track guys; they had all the money, but I have no record of it.

"We're into 1975 now, and number 56 was another 426, but it did not run very long before it failed a rod bearing and cracked the block at the number-4 main. That engine was for the Altered class Don was running in, and it spun the rotor on the input shaft of the oil pump. No oil, right. Result was a cracked block.

"Now we get to number 60, which had been number 43, which was a D5 block with D4 heads, and we increased it to 400 ci by overboring it by 0.060. We had 12.8 compression and it was used in testing through 1977. It used a 7.174 rod at first, then we went back to the 6.96 rod, which was created for the 396-ci package and was a more robust Street Hemi rod. We then added to that by moving the pin bore up in the piston. It was rebuilt once after it broke a cam; it went back to Don in June of 1977 and that was the engine that was in the test car when Donnie crashed. I rebuilt it again in 1978, and it went back to the Carlton shop at that time, and then it disappears from there.

"Number 61 was a 396-ci built for Carlton in 1976; number 64 was a Hemi stroker motor I built in the summer of 1976. It came out at 454-ci and it was obviously a match-race motor, and it went to Carlton too.

"The next real project was number 65. That was a 383 Hemi. We used a low-deck B-engine block and did everything to it—took all the skirting off the block, shaved it all up, and it required a lot of extra work for putting an oil pan on it. It had to be furnace brazed and normalized; a lot of effort. We used aluminum rods and titanium exhaust valves, and we built it up in April of 1977. It ran well, Donnie was always smiling with it in the car, and it performed admirably.

"The hope was to get higher RPM out of the Hemi head. It was kind of at the end of the whole thing. We got it running, and I'm thinking maybe if we did a custom crank we could make it into something. Then the program was over; that block might have gone out to Landy. I don't know.

"It kind of stopped after that. We weren't really racing anything. I did some engines for Sox & Martin that the factory asked me for, and I've got test engines recorded up through number 85, which was in about 1978, but the experimenting for the factory was over."

This gold-toned model was the first of the successful Colts that Don Carlton and Clyde Hodges raced together. Following a half-season with the Dart Sport in 1976, this car showed up at Indy and ran 8.30s to dominate both the B/Altered category and the class itself, making Carlton the only back-to-back winner in 1975 and 1976. Dan Williams took this picture of the car from the stands during that weekend. (Photo Courtesy Dan Williams)

Chapter Seven

1975-1980:
Retrospective on a Decade

By 1975, Don Carlton, professional driver, was an independent racer and again back in his home state of North Carolina. He continued his active racing efforts with Chrysler-based Pro and Sportsman car entries. (Photo Courtesy Dick Oldfield Family Archives)

For fans of Chrysler drag racing, the back half of the 1970s was set against the greater realities affecting everyday life. Even among the youth, a big cultural rift throughout America erupted during the final years of the decade, as pop music split between the dance soundtrack of *Saturday Night Fever* and Donna Summer and the rising metal popularity of Van Halen, Aerosmith, and Boston.

The resignation of Richard Nixon and the subsequent election of farmer-turned-globalist-promotor Jimmy Carter was part and parcel of that same moment. The resultant economic struggles, and yet another crisis-led gasoline shortage, would ultimately lead to a bitter near-finale for Chrysler as a business, though not as a brand.

Was the factory's 1974 decision to no longer compete in Pro Stock racing the end for Chrysler fans? According to one magazine, Dick Maxwell—the former Ramcharger who was now the manager in charge of all Chrysler racing involvement—was adamant the company would not return to that class as long as the current rules structure continued. For 1975, a number of competitors remained

Returning to Pro Stock as independent drivers, Donnie and Clyde now had a number of cars to run across several divisions. This was the vehicle of choice for the 1975 West Coast swing, seen at the AHRA race at Beeline Dragway. (Photo Courtesy Bob McClurg)

racing with Hemi powerplants, and several, such as Landy, returned unshackled from the factory boycott edicts.

As noted earlier, however, that larger-dimension engine platform itself was proving to be less than competitive in the growing RPM environment that made Pro Stock ever more technical. Independently, Ted Spehar would continue to build and supply some Hemi race engines to Don Carlton at his shop based in Lenoir, North Carolina, but any funding for extended research and development was gone for the moment. Ironically, Landy actually did some of the research and development himself for West Coast customers during the final years of the decade. Dick Landy Industries also began manufacturing select engine components for both Hemi and Wedge applications, but Dick himself would step away from driving, in part due to a serious racing accident in late 1976.

For the gentlemen of the factory racing program, the turn of events would lead some of them back into more standard disciplines within the company. Ted Spehar's SVI business continued to do prototype develop-

ment and managed some of the Sportsman racing parts testing through Direct Connection. Chrysler itself had found there was still a healthy market for the DC line of factory-created and factory-approved aftermarket pieces distributed through wholesalers and dealership parts departments. In this regard, even Hemi Super Stock projects occasionally received attention from SVI. Nonetheless, when the economy soured again at the turn of the decade to push Chrysler's corporate viability toward questionable ends, a number of the more serious minds from the engineering brain trust would seek new employment opportunities. Mr. Hoover took on railroad locomotive development for General Electric, and Tom Coddington eventually became a partner with Mike Koran at SVI when Ted sold his portion of the business.

Southern Nights: Don Carlton and the Post-Factory Era

The change to the way Don Carlton lived and raced was likely dramatic without the amount of factory testing that his employment formerly required. After he and Joe

The IHRA, where Don likely had a contract for 1975, was not spectacular in terms of performance. He is seen here launching the Dart Sport during a summer stop at Great Lakes Dragway in southern Wisconsin. (Photo Courtesy Dan Williams)

Pappas brought the team's cars and related equipment from Michigan down to the Tarheel State in late 1974, Don had at his disposal some of the most exotic parts and raw materials ever created in the Pro Stock category. Mr. Hoover had always made sure that Don had enough in the budget to buy the best before things had shut down, and the company also "sold" Carlton whatever remained in its possession from that testing and development process, including the Butler-modified Colt that had been shelved at one of the warehouses and the unfinished wire car, which Don technically owned anyhow.

Going into 1975, Carlton also wanted to be back in Pro Stock. Clyde Hodges remained his right-hand man, and they began by getting the car that Don had run a couple of match races with during the latter part of 1974 ready for NHRA competition. In the end, Don made three NHRA Pro Stock starts with this car, which were Pomona, Gainesville, and Columbus. Like many of the other Chrysler racers, the combination of A-Body weight/ Hemi engine design put them at a disadvantage against the dominant Cleveland Ford, AMC inline wedge (with its weight advantage), small-block Chevrolet, and even resurgent big-block Chevy combinations. For Don, it was DNQ efforts at the Winternationals in Pomona and the Springnationals in Columbus, where he had won during the final year of the *Missile's* active racing schedule. He was able to get into the Gatornationals in the 16th spot at 9.06, but fell in round one to Ron Hutter.

The only NHRA race where Don made the final eliminator program in Pro Stock that year was here at Gainesville's Gatornationals. This is the same car seen previously, with some additional sponsor decals and Don's 302 competition number. He fell to Ron Hutter (near lane) in this first round-race. (Photo Courtesy Bob McClurg)

The going in IHRA for 1975 was not much better. According to research by Bob Frey, Don's 1975 IHRA Pro Stock events included Amarillo, Texas; Union Grove, Wisconsin (Great Lakes Dragway); Dragway 42 in West Salem, Ohio; Rockingham, North Carolina; and Bristol, Tennessee, running these events with the Dart Sport under the more liberal IHRA-legal weight breaks. However, those rules had pushed the Fords up to the top here as well. At Rockingham's Pro Am event that spring, Don and Clyde both raced near-identical cars lettered as "Don Carlton." They met in round one, with Clyde winning (both at off-par times: 9.41 to 9.43), and Hodges then lost to a blistering 8.88 by Bob Glidden in the following frame. It does not appear they raced as a two-car team at another national event. Stuart McDade would also run one of the team's cars on a regional basis: the former yellow test car set up for a Hemi engine. Don's best IHRA Pro Stock outing for 1975 was at their race at Dragway 42 in Ohio, where he was the number-one qualifier at 8.92 but fell out in round one to Nicholson's Ford, 9.04 to 9.05.

Nonetheless, despite the year-long hiatus from Pro Stock, Carlton remained both well-known and popular among the fans. In the March 1975 issue of *Super Stock*, a profile story with many quotes talked about the move back to Lenoir and the hopes to make a good showing in Pro Stock early in the 1975 season. However, with the NHRA continuing to handicap the engine combination, coupled with crazy long-wheelbase 1970 Mustangs and four-door Mavericks getting even better weight breaks, it was frustrating for Carlton and others.

There were but a handful of event finals for Mopars in 1975, primarily with Roy Hill posting runner-up finishes in both NHRA and IHRA. Indeed, Hill's appearance against Bill Jenkins in the ex-Leal Duster at the Springnationals in Columbus was considered the high point of the NHRA season for Chrysler competitors, so Maxwell's sentiment about not returning to the foray with factory assistance was well-decided.

By midyear, Don had decided to salvage what he could of the season by switching back over to the Sportsman classes, reworking the Dart Sport for Competition Eliminator back into legal B/Altered trim (which offered a flat 5.4-pound weight break per cubic inch, making it quicker than any legal NHRA Pro Stock contender). This car showed up at the *Popular Hot Rodding* event in Michigan in mid-August, and Carlton promptly drove it right to a victory. Though an independent racing event, he joined the likes of Don Prudhomme and Don Nicholson in the winner's circle.

Then came the Big Go at Indy. Even today, the US Nationals remain the most important event on the season's race schedule, and the new car was dialed in so well that Don easily took it to the B/Altered class final against Gene Dunlop in the Nationwise Rod Shop Hemi Colt. When Carlton's Dart broke a couple of valve springs during its top-end charge, Dunlop won the day's most

Dick Landy lines up with Bob Glidden at the NHRA Nationals over Labor Day weekend in 1975. Like many factory drivers who been part of the boycott effort in 1974, Dandy Dick was glad to be back in Pro Stock but had been required to remove "Dodge" from the car. Glidden won this match. (Photo Courtesy Ray Mann Archive, quartermilestones.com)

Kenny Hahn, driving the ex-1973 Missile now in fresh paint following an accident in Florida, lines up against Landy's teammate, Larry Huff, in Indy action as well. Huff would be a serious competitor in the AHRA in 1975 but did not follow up his 1974 AHRA World Championship. (Photo Courtesy Ray Mann Archive, quartermilestones.com)

important match and, frankly, Don should have been towing back home by Monday.

Alas, due to a short field and the need for 16 cars in round one, the NHRA agreed to reinstate the two closest class losers for Monday's eliminator, and so the Carlton Dart was back in. That was all he needed; Carlton beat Danny Townsend and Joe Williamson to go to the semifinal where he again raced Gene Dunlop. This time there

Don (far lane) is seen lining up with Gene Dunlop in the Rod Shop's Hemi Colt. Though Dunlop won the B/A class titles, Don was reinstated to ensure a full program for eliminations. This is Monday's semifinals, which Don won, and he would go on to win the coveted Indy race crown in the final. (Photo Courtesy Ray Mann Archive, quartermilestones .com)

were no problems, and a heads-up 8.64 to 8.76 win sent Carlton on into the finals against the supercharged BB/ Altered of Anthony Terenzio. Thanks to a large handicap between the two combinations (0.7 seconds), Carlton's consistent 8.62 was enough to beat the 8.01 in the other lane. His record of NHRA yearly wins continued.

Meanwhile, more re-motored Mitsubushi/Dodges like Dunlop's were now racing both in IHRA Pro Stock and in the upper NHRA Sportsman ranks. In match-race action, Ronnie Sox took out Jenkins's Vega (Larry Lombardo driving) with consistent 8.60 times at the Super Stock Nationals. To that end, the wild Colts would play an ever larger role in the Carlton saga starting in 1976.

The Spirit of 1976

With America's bicentennial year celebrations underway in the election year of 1976, change was in the offing, and for Don Carlton, it came in the form of a new association with one of the few remaining teams that had some form of factory involvement. Through the Rod Shop's performance business out of Columbus, Ohio, Gil Kirk and Dodge had created one of the most visible racing teams of the 1970s and 1980s. Now, coupling this retail speed parts business with distributor Nationwise had allowed both firms to move into the realm of

greater name recognition, best noted by a trademarked ribbon graphic on the cars. In 1976, they backed Tommy Ivo's new Dodge Funny Car, had multiple cars racing in Sportsman classes, from Super Stock to A/Street Roadster (no Pro Stock, however), and sponsored Don Carlton to begin running under their banner. It is unknown today how much of this effort was still being funded in any way by the Chrysler Corporation, but they certainly were stalwarts in their commitment to running Mopar products. The parts testing at Milan for Direct Connection continued on a minor level, sometimes using Rod Shop–based competitors and vehicles. Carlton joined Dunlop and Bob Riffle in the Comp and Modified ranks using Pro Stock-level technology in current-year bodystyles.

The 1976 season began with Don driving a Rod Shop–painted Dodge Dart Sport in B/A, again as a player in Competition Eliminator. In addition to points races, he would run six national events on the NHRA schedule as a Rod Shop Sportsman entry, winning two of them. This season, the NHRA sanctioned the AHRA's former major winter stop, Beeline Dragway near Phoenix, Arizona. This fresh relationship began with hosting a pre-season NHRA event entitled the Winter Classic. Don qualified (in what appears to be one of his own "Hodges Dodges" A-Bodies that was wearing the Shop's banner-waving graphic paint scheme) and proceeded to race

The wire car is shown at the North Carolina shop. Eventually, a motor would be placed in it, but it is not known if Don did any more than test it briefly before it was sold. (Photo Courtesy Dick Oldfield Family Archive)

This is another look at the wire car from behind. It is amazing that after a number of years being bracket raced and crashed, the car survives to this day. (Photo Courtesy Dick Oldfield Family Archive)

Butch Leal was getting his Arrow ready for action in 1975, and while he match raced it in Pro Stock, the NHRA first moved the little car into the Altered and Gas categories before a Pro Stock rules change regarding wheelbase. (Photo Courtesy Steve Reyes)

Here is the Carlton compound near Lenoir with Don's shop still being completed. Once it was finished, Don and Clyde Hodges built a lot of cars here. (Photo Courtesy Joe Pappas)

four open-wheel dragsters on Sunday to win the event title for Comp Eliminator.

Next came the NHRA Winternationals on the Pomona Fairgrounds, but success did not follow Don to California. He was racing the Hemi Colt of Roger Denney in a heads-up B/A round-two match, and Denney surprised everybody, including himself, when he trailered Carlton on a massive holeshot: 8.74 to a much quicker 8.63. By this time, the Colt design was on the verge of being replaced in some quarters by a new model called the Plymouth Arrow. Indeed, Butch Leal was having an

Arrow built by Ron Butler to run in A/Gas. Though the NHRA had adjusted the rules on short-wheelbase/big-inch engine combinations in Pro Stock following the 1976 Gatornationals, the 93-inch Arrow still did not meet that organization's 94-inch minimum wheelbase.

At that race in Gainesville held in March, Don again appeared in the Dart and qualified number-one with a 0.22-under 8.52 using a 3-speed Lenco. On a Sunday morning test shot, he installed a new clutchless Doug Nash 5-speed in the car, then propelled it to an 8.47 (almost 0.4 faster than legal Pro Stocks were running).

This series of rare color prints show the construction of one of the Colts taken by the late Steward Pomeroy. This is the basic chassis built on jackstands. (Photo Courtesy Dan Williams)

An image from behind shows the mounting of the differential and shock layout. The cage construction appears to rely on a rigid but minimalist idea. (Photo Courtesy Dan Williams)

The rear half of a stock Colt body has been mounted. If this construction was authorized by Chrysler, it is possible the body was acid-dipped at their direction, but based on the need for rear weight with an iron-block Hemi up front, it would have been a minimal benefit. (Photo Courtesy Dan Williams)

Finally, the nose is grafted to the car. Interestingly, it appears that the entire grille structure was being blocked off with tin, though it is possible that this was later trimmed out to allow air to the radiator. This was the latest grille for the Colt model in 1976. (Photo Courtesy Dan Williams)

While Ted supplied engines for factory testing and still occasionally built one for Don's racing effort, here is one in the Lenoir engine room built by Clyde likely for the Colt seen under construction. (Photo Courtesy Dan Williams)

Immediately afterward, the NHRA reportedly outlawed these trick parts with Nash's product joining the 4-speed Lenco models on the "no-no" list for Comp racers in an effort to try to keep costs down. At any rate, with the 3-speed back in the car for the first round early that afternoon, performance fell off into the 8.60s, and the Dart was out in round one.

So it would not be until the Englishtown, New Jersey–hosted Summernationals in July that the Carlton/Rod Shop program began showing benefits at an NHRA-level national event. He was again Top Qualifier, at an 8.42, but this time he marched through the 16-car program on Sunday to keep his yearly NHRA win streak intact. Interestingly, he had some Pro-class contemporaries in the B/A class this weekend: Leal and the new Arrow debuting at 8.46, teammate Riffle's Dart Sport also in at 8.46, the former Gapp & Roush four-door Maverick running in C/A with a Boss 351 engine, and no less than Dyno Don Nicholson, also in B/A trim, using his Pro Stock Mustang II. When it came time for the Sunday afternoon final round, Carlton and "Dyno" were lined up for a heads-up B/A run, and the Carlton Dodge won a close one, 8.55 to Dyno's 8.58.

The final-round streak continued into Canada for the Molson Grandnational, where Don was runner-up to yet

Joe Pappas came to Indy to see Don's new Colt in action, grabbing this image of the car being worked on in the pits. It would be in the winner's circle by Monday night, making Carlton the only driver to go back-to-back at Indy in the 1975–1976 season. (Photo Courtesy Joe Pappas)

another Pro Stock–origin Mustang II, this time driven by the "New York Kid" Scott Shafiroff, which was trimmed to run in C/Altered. The margin of victory was a lot closer on the track than on paper, as Shafiroff won with 9.03 on the C/A 9.15 index to Carlton's 8.50 on the recently reset B/A 8.60 index.

Against the Wind: Colts in the Tunnel

Among the vast images in the Dick Oldfield film library was a series of photos from a wind tunnel event using the gold Colt that had won the 1976 US Nationals title. The idea of testing the Colt in this environment has rarely been noted previously, and unfortunately, these images are not dated. Joe Pappas noted that this was at a facility up in Ottawa, Canada. They most likely date from the latter part of 1976 (before the stretched car for 1977 was built) and may have even had a bearing on that modification. These images also serve as an unquestioned reference that Chrysler was again working seriously on *Missile*-type aerodynamic efforts. Perhaps the lack of any known released data after the fact may have been to "protect the guilty" in Chrysler Engineering from possible trouble with upper management.

The gold Colt, following its victory at Indy, was put into the wind tunnel for development work. (Photo Courtesy Dick Oldfield Family Archive)

Don points at the car as it is lowered into the tunnel. It doesn't matter how cold it is outside, the jackets will be needed as the wind speed crosses over the 150-mph threshold during the test. (Photo Courtesy Dick Oldfield Family Archive)

Now you are looking at tufts on the experimental deck spoiler. The cost of testing in the tunnel was not cheap, and the data recorded would also be compared when Butch Leal's new Arrow also found its way down into the hole. Meanwhile, part of this effort was to see why the Colts were prone to lift in the rear at speed. Note the Car Craft All-Star decal in the rear window. (Photo Courtesy Dick Oldfield Family Archive)

Another area of interest was the hood scoop, which was noted on the A-Body earlier. Here is the original scoop that was on the car at Indianapolis. A white string attached to a pole is being used to show what the moving air is doing from the nose to the scoop. (Photo Courtesy Dick Oldfield Family Archive)

A taller design is installed here, and testing continues. (Photo Courtesy Dick Oldfield Family Archive)

The string was not simply used to see how air flowed into the scoop but also around its base. Though the Missile was now history as a name, science continued to be used for testing at this time, still chasing what could be done to win again. (Photo Courtesy Dick Oldfield Family Archive)

Now it was off to the NHRA's Big Go (Indy 1976) and once again, Don came loaded for hunting bear. However, he was not in the Dart Sport this time. Instead, he was in a new gold-toned Dodge Colt that he and Clyde had just completed. This car dominated, running not one but *five* 8.30s in a row to take Monday's title. So it was 8.35, 8.35, 8.34, and 8.34 to meet none other than Shafiroff in the Labor Day afternoon final. At the green, the man they had termed the cyborg did it again, 8.34 at a big 163.07 mph, while the Mustang fell to a 15-second time due to transmission problems. Don Carlton was the only repeat winner at Indy that year.

This time, the accolades were outstanding. In fact, as the soft-spoken underdog who won quietly and effec-tively, Carlton had so captured the hearts of the serious fans by then that *Car Craft* magazine's readership had just voted him as the Comp Driver of the Year to the *Car Craft* Magazine All-Star team, a prestigious honor that few could claim.

Also racing in Comp with Colts at Indy were Roy Hill, who also had his Duster in Pro Stock (alas, with no success), and Ronnie Sox, whose early-season Sox & Martin lettering now read Billy "The Kid." Billy Stepp had basically bought the Sox Colt outright and hired its name driver after Bobby Yowell had flipped Stepp's Colt at the spring IHRA race at Bristol. Fortunately for Stepp, Gil Kirk had already bought that car just before it was crashed. This was because, only hours earlier, Gene

Seen here wheels-up at the IHRA race in Darlington, South Carolina, in early 1977, Roy Hill was one of the top Chrysler Pro Stock racers of the late 1970s. Hill's Arrow was scheduled to get a W2 small-block combination, but here it is believed to still be Hemi-powered with the IHRA's new "run whatcha brung" engine rule. Note the Petty decal on the scoop. (Photo Courtesy Steve Reyes)

Dunlop had *himself* flipped the Rod Shop's Hemi Colt at Bristol and totaled it! At 160 mph, the cars were dancing on the edge of possible disaster, but Yowell crashed due to a wheelie-bar issue. To end the season, Bob Riffle drove the Rod Shop's *other* Colt (the ex-Roger Denney entry that Don had lost against at Pomona) to an unreal 8.20 clocking at Orange County. This was in a match race against Leal's hot Arrow, reportedly with a little help from a nitrous bottle. It really was the 1970s!

The First Half: 1977

The rule book got a firm look after the dominance of the ex-Pro Stockers in Comp during the 1976 season. The result was a return to a term dear to the hearts of long-time fans: Factory Experimental. A/FX, B/FX, and C/FX would return, using weight breaks of 5.5, 7.5, and 9.5 pounds per cubic inch, respectively, for 1977. Meanwhile, the IHRA decided to toss away all the measured cubic inches in Pro Stock for the new season, in essence saying, "Bring out your 2,400 pounds of race car and whatever engine you want, and *let's go!*" The NHRA still had the Hemi engine at 7.00 (under 105-inch wheelbase) and 6.80 (over 105 inches), but a year of testing by Herb

McCandless and Ted Flack in the new 4-barrel Super/Mod category using the recently released W2-series cylinder head had begun showing real promise that the small-block LA-series Mopar was finally coming into its own.

Speaking of that engine, according to many sources, Don Carlton never got the wire car to the point where it did what it was designed for. Eventually, there was another small-block LA-series engine installed in it, and while minor testing at Hudson Dragway or Wilkesboro might have happened, Donnie Carlton Jr.'s recollection was that his dad only did a few burnouts on the shop's concrete pad outside before it was sold to a local racer named Betty Sigmon. Later, she would have an accident in it which damaged the trick machine and retired it from active competition for a while.

Therefore, the trickest of the *Missiles*, the wire car, would never play a major role in the Carlton saga, and some of the other ex-Carlton cars came to ill ends as well. One of the former Pro Stock Dart Sports from the 1975 effort ended up with female driver Shay Nichols, who ran it as an IHRA Pro Stock entry but had the misfortune of completely destroying it in a single car top-end crash during the IHRA's national event at Amarillo, Texas, in late 1976. Even the trick, big-event-winning 1973 Duster

Ted Spehar is filing videotape of the just-finished lengthened Colt prior to the 1977 Winternationals. The old Charger "whale," seen behind him, is now black. As can be seen, the windshield on the Colt is missing. (Photo Courtesy Dick Oldfield Family Archive)

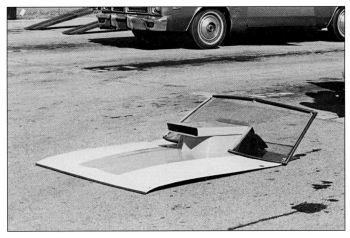

The windshield was now part of the hood and scoop assembly. With the NHRA creating a new version of A/FX for 1977, Don showed up with a car that was unquestionably reconstructed as an Altered, not simply a reclassified Pro Stock refugee. (Photo Courtesy Dick Oldfield Family Archive)

purchased by Stewart Pomeroy had an accident after leaving the Carlton shop, though it was repaired to race again with Kenny Hahn driving.

The reason the small-block car was let go was that, for now, the Carlton race focus would stick with the Hemi engine design and, with backing from Gil Kirk's business, Don also stayed solely in the Sportsman ranks. Though the FX classes offered possibilities, Clyde and Don decided to stay in B/Altered, and subsequently took advantage of a 20-percent engine setback rule by lengthening the wheelbase on the Colt for the new season.

Although they suffered from frustrations with this new combination at both the NHRA Winternationals and Gatornationals as they struggled to find traction with the car's much-shortened rear overhang, the package began responding due to testing and some less-radical wheelbase adjustments. At this time, Don was also doing testing work in a second Colt he and Clyde had pieced together, but the Rod Shop red, white, and blue machine was the car that was visible at the big events.

The refreshened effort started to bear fruit at the unique Sportsnationals, a special event with no Pro class cars, held at Beech Bend Raceway in Kentucky just before Memorial Day weekend. Don was the Low Qualifier at 8.45 on the 8.65 B/A index and proceeded to again go to the final round with a string of 8.45 times to meet the ex-*Grumpy's Toy* 1970 Camaro. Now owned and driven by Dennis Ferrara, this B/EA Chevy was coming off a stout victory at the

Gatornationals. Ferrara was a tough competitor regardless, but when the transmission in the Colt went away at mid-track, the final was already over for Don.

The next big NHRA event took place in June. By now, with Sportsman prize money from the recently created W. R. Grace Cup as the possible reward, Don was focused solely on the NHRA effort with the Rod Shop Colt, and Ted was building engines, which they tested in the other Colt. That car was a bit lighter than the one being raced, and it may have never been formally teched for a racing event. Images from the shop in Dan Williams's archive show that Clyde could probably easily have changed out the back half of a Colt chassis if need be.

The NHRA tour rolled into Columbus for the Springnationals in front of the Rod Shop's home crew on June 9 through 12. Don made it into the tough field in the fifth spot at 8.52 but got better once Sunday continued. The biggest battle came in the second round, again against Ferrara, who had qualified number one. This time, the insides of the transmission stayed there, and Don put an 8.48 on the timers. Ferrara faltered slightly to lose pace, and the Rod Shop Colt would go on to beat two dragster-type competitors to win the entire event. The result gave Carlton an almost unparalleled record of six annual NHRA event crowns starting at Gainesville in 1972, and a challenging new position in the Grace Cup points chase, whose combined "winner take all" prizes included all Sportsman class racers from Pro Comp to Stock.

July 5

The day was hot and humid. The factory was conducting a tire and parts test session at Milan Dragway, recording run after run as Carlton went through his paces driving the test Colt. The Hemi engine, while not under direct development in an official capacity by Chrysler, had been getting refined by a number of aftermarket companies, such as Mullen. As a result, Ted Spehar was on hand that day, working on engine 60 between the front frame rails. Following a cam change late in the afternoon, the unthinkable happened.

"I was standing behind watching, and Donnie came up through the gears like always and the car just started drifting," Spehar recalled. "I mean, it wasn't like it went sideways; it just drifted off the track under power . . ."

There has never been any understanding about just what happened inside the cockpit that hot afternoon the day after Independence Day 1977. Carlton had been doing his normal routine of testing equipment. At 36 years old, he would not have even been considered one of the "old guys" in a class of cars that still saw the likes of 50-year-old Dyno Don Nicholson.

"Well, it dug into the dirt and started flipping," said Spehar. "It wasn't super violent; the parts weren't flying off of it, and after a couple of those twists, it landed on all four wheels. Of course, we started down immediately and my first thought was, 'S——, there's something that didn't get tightened up and there's oil or water on the track.' When we got down there, it was dry, so it wasn't that. Since he had not climbed out, we figured Donnie was probably unconscious. I had seen some bad crashes, and this one just didn't look that bad."

Meanwhile, the ambulance hired to be on hand in case something like this happened was already getting to the wreck. There was no sign of fire, but they obviously wanted to get Carlton out of the car as quickly as possible. Don's wife, Jonnie, and daughter, Robin, were at the track that day as well and had witnessed the accident.

"We got the door off, and Donnie was laying in there and not making any sound. There was no blood, no gore, but at that point, everything got real serious. I remember his glasses were off and laying on the floor, unbroken."

Ted's feeling is that Donnie may have become dehydrated and momentarily passed out due to the regiment of the day's work, possibly coming to once the situation got out of hand. He is more adamant that the construction of the car was in part to blame.

"Whoever had done the seat mountings had used 3/8-inch bolts. That seat got loose when the car began tumbling and Don was moving around in there, and he submarined under the belts. I'm not blaming one person or another, but because people wanted to save weight however they could, that was a bad choice. Especially when you needed to make sure the driver stayed inside the car if there was a problem. We'll never know."

There was no pulse, and no movement. The men quickly helped put him into the ambulance. Upon arrival at the University of Michigan Hospital in nearby Ann Arbor, the admitting physician did a final check and signed off on the pronouncement paperwork. Don Carlton was dead. The cause was noted as internal injuries, likely from breaking his neck during the car's barrel rolls.

For the surviving members of the Chrysler Engineering team and the race crew, this remains the worst day ever in their racing involvement. Many witnesses to this accident would never publicly recount the exact details to outsiders; it was a heartbreaking end, not just to an era but to treasured friendships. It added to the sense of unfairness that every penciled rule change had caused; and for these guys, the world changed forever that afternoon. Obviously, the Carlton family would now deal in even more personal ways with the horrific impact of a loving husband and father taken from them.

The Billboard Top 10 song for the week of July 2, 1977, was "Gonna Fly Now" by Bill Conti. Most people remember it better as the instrumental theme from the movie *Rocky*. During the following decades, the IHRA named an annual sportsmanship award in Carlton's honor, and he has been posthumously entered into a number of motorsports halls of fame. His name is enshrined on the current Bristol Dragway grandstands as well. Most who knew him still admit that there was never anybody like the soft-spoken racer from North Carolina who knew how to make the machine speak.

RIP Don Maynard Carlton: August 4, 1940–July 5, 1977.

A Final Requiem: The Last NHRA World Championship of the 1970s

Don Carlton's fatal accident was news in papers regionally in Michigan and North Carolina but warranted only minor mention in the nation's car magazines. An unfortunate trend of the time period was a basic unwillingness by the racing press to state that such

The lengthened Colt in action at Pomona during the Winternationals was captured on film by Steve Reyes. This racing effort did not have much success due to a lack of possible traction, and the car was eventually converted back into a standard-wheelbase design but kept in B/A for the remainder of Don's 1977 racing effort. (Photo Courtesy Steve Reyes)

occurrences had even happened. The wrecked car was brought back to North Carolina and, in Southern racing fashion, was buried in a landfill less than 5 miles from the shop, above the confines of the old Hudson Dragway where Carlton had been so well known prior to his rise in the drag racing world. His accident was overshadowed two months later, on September 9, when Funny Car racer "Jungle Jim" Liberman, one of the few drivers who actually equaled Carlton's appeal to the fans, died in a vehicular street accident in Pennsylvania.

Clyde Hodges would continue managing work at Carlton Racing Enterprises but frankly did not have the same level of business acumen that Don possessed. Nonetheless, he did not disappear from the scene—not by a long shot.

Ronnie Sox had taken Carlton's death quite seriously. After running Colts and Arrows for Billy Stepp the past 12 months, this was good enough reason to get out of the driver's seat, and Bobby Yowell was back in Stepp's employment for the remainder of 1977. However, Clyde Hodges called Ronnie in August and asked if he was will-

ing to drive the parked Rod Shop B/Altered Colt at the NHRA Nationals in Don's memory. Sox agreed, and they arrived on Saturday morning to take a shot in the very tough Indy field. An 8.57 off the trailer was a start, but the car and Ronnie's jockey-like physical stature found them 12 pounds light at the weigh scales. A Sunday-morning 8.64 attempt ended their weekend, but it was well-received by all. The duo would follow up this effort by rebodying this car as the very first 1978 Dodge Challenger for the A/FX class going into the new season, where Buddy Martin was also part of the program.

Though surpassed by the full-season competitors, Don's points efforts in what was then the W. R. Grace Cup (now the Lucas Oil Sportsman Series) resulted in an announced honor during the formal awards presentation during the annual SEMA show toward the end of 1977, with Jonnie on hand getting both a standing ovation and a donation to a memorial fund established in Don's name.

In the meantime, a focus of the factory program again returned to the Pro Stock class. By 1978, Stepp/ Yowell, Butch Leal, and Roy Hill were all running Arrows,

Following Don's death, the recently retired Ronnie Sox agreed to drive the reworked car at Indy. Don had been killed in a test vehicle, and the gold car from 1976 had already gone to Hahn/Zorian's effort right before the tragedy. Behind the car from left to right are Hodges, Killen, and Oldfield. Unfortunately, the car made only a couple of passes and did not qualify for the tough field that weekend. (Photo Courtesy Dan Williams)

and the rules were finally adjusted to make them legal for NHRA Pro Stock. It was in the middle of this year that Dave Koffel approached Ford racer Bob Glidden regarding a possible Pro Stock development program for the W2-head small-block.

The Glidden family was a notable focus for the NHRA, often held up by the organization as the representation of how "everyone in the family" could be involved. With two young sons in tow, Bob and his wife, Etta, worked tirelessly to find legal ways to beat everyone, and they had proven to be quite successful at it. With Don Nicholson recently crowned the 1977 NHRA Pro Stock World Champion, thanks in part to his young crew chief Jon Kaase, Koffel wondered if Glidden might be amenable to getting weaned off of FoMoCo blue to run a W2 Arrow with factory help.

"It was looking like we might get the bosses to relent and let us go drag racing again," Koffel noted later. "They [Chrysler management] were really fed up with the whole thing, and the rift between Chrysler and the NHRA wasn't going away, but it looked like something might happen. I had a conversational relationship with Bob Glidden at the time; we could sit on the tailgate of the tow vehicle and talk together at the races.

"We were at Milan Dragway for the IHRA Northern Nationals, and I sat down with Glidden and asked him out of the blue, 'How would you like to race a Chrysler?' Well, he looked at me like I was from outer space or something. I asked him, 'What is Ford doing for you?' He replied, 'Ford's never given me a gasket!' So I said, 'I'll give you money to race, a new Chaparrel rig, engine parts, whatever it takes.'

"He told me he needed to think about it. The next big race was in Seattle. I mean, nobody knew about this, not even at Chrysler. Only Dick Maxwell, my immediate boss, knew this was happening. Well, we got to Seattle, got adjoining rooms at a motel there, and worked out this deal without anyone suspecting a thing. By the time we left, we had a deal for him to race in 1979.

"Next, he called [Texas chassis builder] Don Hardy, swore Hardy to secrecy, and told him to start building him a Pro Stock Arrow. The target date to get the car done was by December of 1978. We gave Spehar one of the Caspar blocks to build an engine for the car, and also gave Glidden enough parts to put together two others, which he himself did in his shop.

"So between September and December of that year, we got a pickup and Chaparrel trailer together, got two motors done, and the car was finished," Koffel continued. "I drove the truck and trailer to Whiteland [Indiana, Glidden's then-current hometown] and we loaded the stuff up and went to Orange County International in California to test in the second week of December. The stuff was just thrown together; the truck was so underpowered that we had to drive it out there in third gear most of the way.

"The deal in Orange County was a tire test for Goodyear. We made a couple of shakedown runs and then began testing tires. We must have put 60 runs on the car that week, and we got it dialed in. Well, once we did that, the word was out; but no times were announced, so nobody but us knew how good the car was. The week before Pomona, there was a big test-and-tune at Orange County. We show up with Bob and the car. We didn't run the first time trial, but everybody was watching when we came up for the second one. There must have been 300 people on the starting line watching this car; it was like the 1965 Super Stock Nationals at York.

"I don't recall what the best time of the event had been to that point—I think an 8.61. Bob cleaned the tires, launched, and ran an 8.49. That was pretty much how that year went. We marched through them like Sherman marched through Georgia, and it was wonderful."

Indeed, Bob Glidden and his Arrow would have the sort of race season that most drivers only dreamed of—one like Sox had in 1971, or Jenkins in 1972, or Don Carlton in 1973 in IHRA. He won 7 of 10 events and was in every single final round but one. After dominating the first half of the season undefeated, he had two red-light starts and one actual loss on a holeshot to Frank Iaconio late in the year. It was an unbelievable and, to that time, unequaled string of victories in the sport. But things were not well in Detroit, and the year ended on a low note.

"The second energy crunch hit, and they took away all of our money," Koffel would recall grimly. "We were all back in the bread line. I had to call Bob and tell him, 'The show is over, the money's gone, and I'm unemployed.' It was a shame, because I think that deal could have kept right on winning." And indeed, Glidden did, dominating the class throughout the 1980s, but back in Ford equipment.

For the company, which was trying to revamp its model line, the latest malaise was going to hurt. From a policy perspective, the nation's economy had been mismanaged, and the Iran hostage crisis had again affected gasoline prices. Unfortunately, Chrysler was not going to recover on its own. That eventually took a Herculean effort from Congress and an agreement by President Ronald Reagan to loan Chrysler a lot of money, upward of $100 million, to stay afloat. Ford boss Lee Iacocca, noted as the father of the Mustang, would take over the corporate reins and successfully used his own reputation and the company's legendary innovation to revive the Chrysler Corporation for a new era with the K-car and the minivan.

In turn, that recovery effort allowed Direct Connection to survive as Mopar Performance down to the present era. It also led to the rebirth of Chrysler performance in Pro Stock, with Koffel himself leaving the corporate world and starting his own engine building

Clyde would rebody the car after this event to become a 1978 Dodge Challenger, which ran in A/FX the following two seasons. This particular body design was short-lived in the category once Glidden's Arrow had been successful and the slant-nosed Omni was introduced. (Photo Courtesy Bryan Flack Archive, quartermilestones .com)

Bob Glidden is wheels-up at Indy on his way to another win during his dominant 1979 season. The one-year effort bore huge fruit for Chrysler in terms of racing, but economies of the moment would abruptly end it. (Photo Courtesy Steve Reyes)

Don Carlton is at the end of the track. The man, the machine, and the motors will forever remain part of the 1970s epochal decade of Pro Stock racing. (Photo Courtesy Joe Pappas)

service. After developing a big-block wedge engine combination using a special cylinder head he called the B1 for the now-standard NHRA 500-ci limit on all Pro Stock, Koffel would help return Chrysler to the Pro Stock wars in the 1990s, with Dodge and Mopar again present as sponsors. After the company's sale to Daimler during this same time, Chrysler products made an eventually successful, though temporary, return to the NASCAR ranks through the Dodge brand, and today's FCA-based Dodge Charger and Challenger

street cars remain bellwether examples of the brand's ongoing commitment to automotive performance and excitement.

But that happened decades later. Before all that occurred, the 1980s ignited new political, industrial, and social changes. To that end, the *Motown Missile*, Don Carlton, and the 426 Hemi as a dominant gas-powered race engine (as well as its W2 follow-up effort with Mr. Glidden in 1979) will forever remain part of the legend that is the first decade of Pro Stock.

Ben Donhoff shows the way up at the 2016 Mopar Nationals in the Bulter-built Duster.

Chapter Eight

50 Years Later:
The *Missiles* and Don Carlton Race Cars Today

T he history of drag racing is rife with superstars, both in terms of personality and technology. As collector items, the *Motown* and *Mopar Missiles* were some of the best remembered vehicles of the 1970s. Nonetheless, like most race cars of that time, scant thought was given to preservation when performance advances required new chassis or body stylings, so it has been frankly remarkable that a majority of the *Missiles* have remained not only existent but are now restored to their most noteworthy appearances. To conclude this volume, here is a look at the cars and present owners.

1970–1971 Dodge Challenger: Spehar/ Oldfield/Koran/Chrysler Engineering

The car that started it all was one of the first notable examples of the early Pro Stock era to enter the car hobby. This car won AHRA and IHRA event titles while being driven by Don Carlton, as well as match-race crowns

The 1971 Challenger is pictured after a transmission explosion during an exhibition pass at the Mopar Nationals in 1988. (Photo Courtesy Dan Gallo Jr.)

The 1971 car appears as it does today.

with first driver Dick Oldfield. After being sold in 1972, it raced as *Tennessee Thunder* by the team of Lee Crowder and John Livingston.

Once it was removed from active competition, a collector bought it in the early 1980s and actually did a rudimentary rebuilding. Though its accuracy was not exacting, there was also a brief attempt to race the car in exhibitions prior to 1990. After a period of Mopar car show event displays, this first *Missile* was acquired by Arnie Klann of Irvine, California, who gave it to a California shop named Picture Car Warehouse to restore. Once Klann met Dick Oldfield and Joe Pappas, he further allowed original constructor Oldfield to be involved in the car's final and period-correct restoration.

The 1971 car has been shown at a number of major events, including the two *Missile* Reunions at Henderson, and presently appears as it did during the 1971 season when Don Carlton was its driver.

1972 Plymouth Barracuda: Spehar/Oldfield/ Koran/Chrysler Engineering

The car that won the 1972 Gatornationals and the final Pro-level car built during Ted Spehar's team ownership, the 1972 *Motown Missile* 'Cuda was parked by the team toward the end of that season when the new Ron Butler Duster arrived. The 'Cuda was later purchased by racer Mike Fons after he was let go by the Rod Shop operation, and Fons raced it under the *Motown Missile* moniker because neither Ted Spehar nor the factory were using that title. However, he had no direct assistance or association with Chrysler Engineering during that time and, in fact, did not rent nor license the name either.

When this car was reportedly damaged in an on-track accident, Fons quickly acquired a Landy/

Ted Spehar (in Super Stock shirt) and 1971 NHRA Nationals SS winner Greg Charney look at the 1972 'Cuda while it is on display at the Henderson, North Carolina, event in 2012 prior to restoration.

The Missile 'Cuda that was restored in 2019 is shown. (Photo Courtesy Paul's Body Shop)

Fuller-built Duster that had been originally raced by the late Irv Beringhaus, which he also painted as a *Motown Missile*, again without direct factory association. The 'Cuda was next sold to a race team in Toronto named Beatty & Woods, who repaired it and then ran it regionally. They in turn sold it a year later to bracket racer Jim Stevens, also of Canada, who had a 440 installed in it for his race program. In 1983, the car in running condition was subsequently purchased by enthusiast Mark Williamson of Ottawa, who decided he would store it instead of race it.

In 2011, Williamson entered an agreement with the late Ebbie Merritt to have the car restored, which was done by George Paul's Body Shop in Mississippi. An amazing process ensued to restore the car, which included locating a number of the car's one-off titanium parts from a prior associate of the car, as well as the original rare Fenton wheels. Most recently, an engine was installed in this car to return it to running condition, and it remains in the United States at this time.

1973 Plymouth Duster: Butler/Oldfield/ Chrysler Engineering

The Ron Butler–built Duster represented a true state-of-the-art chassis configuration, which was designed by Tom Coddington and his associated engineering staff and constructed with Dick Oldfield's direct assistance at Butler's shop. Owned by Don Carlton, this car was originally configured as a 1972 model and ran its initial 1973 events in that form; it was converted via parts exchange in the spring of 1973 by Oldfield and new crew member Joe Pappas. This was the winningest of the *Missile* cars, with Carlton going to every final round in IHRA competition and winning five of eight events and the 1973 World Championship.

Following the decision to focus on small-block development, this car was sold to Stewart Pomeroy of Florida, who raced it under the guise of Nelson DeChamps and driver Seymour Guntz (who was actually Pomeroy, attempting to avoid family conflicts as a racing driver; Ken Hahn was also a driver at this time). Pomeroy ended up buying a Colt from the Sox & Martin operation and sold the Duster outright to Hahn and John Zorian. Hahn crashed it at Bradenton in 1975 during a match race, but it was rebuilt; a picture of it from 1976 is shown in chapter 7. A second, more serious accident resulted in enough front-end destruction that it was reconfigured

Ben Donhoff and Larry Mayes stand next to the "world's fastest" Missile.

with a stock-design fiberglass front quarter-panel design and standard wheelbase after racer Ben Donhoff bought it in damaged condition. Currently, it is still owned by Donhoff, also of Florida, who used a nitrous-aided motor to make it the fastest-ever *Missile*, running a 7.83 in Orlando in 2009.

After several years of display at Don Garlits's Museum of Drag Racing, Donhoff has since teamed up with Larry Mayes and has occasionally driven the car in exhibition runs. This car is also the final Don Carlton–associated race car to bear a *Missile* title.

1972 Demon/1974 340 Yellow Test Car: Hodges/Oldfield/Pappas/Chrysler Engineering

As noted, the 1972 match-race Demon built in North Carolina by Clyde Hodges, which Don drove at match races and on the USRT circuit in 1972, first went to local friend Stuart McDade in 1973. It was extensively rebuilt into a 1974 Dart Sport and used for factory testing of the 340 Pro Stock engine package at Carlton's Michigan shop by Pappas and Oldfield.

When that program was ended by Chrysler in late 1974, the body returned with Don to North Carolina and McDade match raced it locally, again with a Hemi engine configuration in partnership with Eddie Ratliff. Later, still under Ratliff's ownership, the car was subsequently destroyed in a racing accident and parted out.

Following the restoration by Gary Henson, Joe Pappas, and Dick Oldfield, the restored wire car was given an honorary Mopar Missile paint scheme even though the car was never actually raced or even tested during Chrysler Engineering's intense 1974 development program.

A Chrysler 340-design small-block engine is now in the wire car, fitted with circa-1970s-era pieces and looking much like it would have during the test days with the yellow car. The engine package proved its worth at the end of the decade under the tutelage of the late Bob Glidden.

1974 Plymouth Duster Wire Car: Knapp/Adam/Pappas/Oldfield

The most technologically advanced vehicle built for Pro Stock under factory direction, the wire car never raced prior to the end of the factory program and was also among the equipment brought to North Carolina in late 1974. The rear quarter window with McDade's former 223 number was installed for transport and is seen on this car throughout its time with Carlton. Never designed for a Hemi, it is believed that Don did install a running Chrysler small-block engine at least once prior to selling it, and it may have been raced, as a Carlton trim and lettered paint scheme is seen on this car around the time it was sold. At any rate, after being acquired by Ray and Betty Sigmon in

1977, the car was bracket raced through the mid-1980s, then purchased and raced by Glen Hicks; these were both racers in the Lenoir area.

In 1992, the wire car was bought from Hicks by Jeff Johnson, who promoted a Mopar event series called the Chrysler Classic. Johnson would use Don Carlton's name on the car at first, but it was later repainted as a *Missile* and made an occasional track lap, notably at the All-Hemi Reunion in Ohio.

Arnie Klann acquired it from Johnson and then enlisted both Oldfield and Pappas to oversee its proper restoration, which was done at the shop of California fabricator Gary Hansen and detailed in the Michigan home shop of Pappas, who has since maintained both of Klann's restored racers as well. Had the racing program continued into 1975, this car would have been the next of the *Mopar Missiles*, so the decision was made to use that name, the 1974 color scheme, and Carlton's 302 NHRA Pro Competition number on the restored car.

1972 Colt: Knapp/Butler/Pappas/ Oldfield/Hodges

The stillborn Hemi Colt initially built by Dan Knapp in Detroit was shown in one period magazine image, reworked by Ron Butler, and then placed into storage by Chrysler Engineering. Any 340/Colt engine work in 1974 was performed in the Rod Shop's entry. When the factory dropped out of Pro Stock, this unused car was sold or given to Don Carlton. It is believed that some testing may have been done with this vehicle, but it likely did not fit into the program of cars that were being created in-house by Carlton and Hodges. As a result, it was sold in 1977.

"The back story is that that car was specifically built for the D5 Hemi," noted Joe Pappas. "Two things happened. One, [the] NHRA said it would not allow Colts to run Hemi engines in Pro Stock; and two, the D5 program was essentially scrapped within the corporation, as it was not showing the results they thought it might. The 340 program had nothing to do with this car. This car was taken to North Carolia and later sold to Mike Belcher and driven by Lynnwood Craft."

It became best known for being raced by Lynnwood Craft, who would campaign it for many seasons in IHRA competition in the Sportsman ranks. As of this writing, this unique vehicle is still in the possession of the Belcher family and has been occasionally on display in Jeff Belcher's Roanoke-based vehicle showroom. Tom Hoover and Dick Oldfield examined and personally verified this is the car.

The "Hodges Dodges" Pro Stocks and More

The A-Body Dusters and Darts constructed by Clyde Hodges are difficult to track. They would include the unlettered Duster that Don raced at the 1974 National Challenge race, the B/Altered car that he raced during 1974's boycott, the two Don Carlton–lettered IHRA cars seen at Rockingham in 1975, the NHRA Pro Stock car of that same time period, the B/Altered he used to win at Indy, the Rod Shop cars from early 1976, etc. Which ones were which (one and the same) remains undetermined,

Mr. Hoover and Dick Oldfield with the D5 Colt at Jeff Belcher's shop in 2010. (Photo Courtesy Joe Pappas)

as the cars were in a regular state of change. To the North Carolina–built group in the post-*Missile* era would belong the Colts, one of which we know was buried after the accident, and at least one other that was rebodied as something else (the 1978 Sox & Martin Challenger). The gold car reportedly went to Hahn/Zorian just before the 1977 accident.

As for the A-Body models, Shay Nichols destroyed one of the above cars at Amarillo in 1976. The Don Carlton–lettered/driven Pro car of early 1975 ran as an IHRA entry late into the 1975 season and was probably the same car used for the NHRA Sportsman effort as well. It is not known if the second car driven by Clyde at Rockingham in 1975 remained part of the Sportsman program or may have been the car sold to Nichols. Gary French presently owns one of the Hodges-built Dart Sports that was believed to be campaigned as a B/Altered. Equipped with a Hemi, it remains unrestored to the Carlton era as he gathers additional information on its origins.

The "Hodges Dodges" B/Altered car now owned by Gary French is shown.

The modern Missile base is shown in the early 21st century. Two late-model Pro Stocks take the stage along with the car that started it all. (Photo Courtesy Arnie Klann)

Chapter Nine

Today's Motown Missle: That Was Then, This Is Now

By Arnie Klann

Note: Technologist and entrepreneur Arnie Klann took ownership of the 1970/1971 Challenger and 1974 wire car to a more serious end when he decided to go ahead and put not just the name but the scientific prowess behind a new Motown Missile Racing Team almost 20 years ago. Today, that effort continues.

When I acquired the old 1970/1971 *Motown Missile* Challenger as a collector car, I also got the desire to go racing again. How hard could it be to get back in? I saw that Billy "The Kid" Stepp had his two Jerry Haas–built Avengers and transporter for sale, buying one of them in early 1998. This was a state-of-the-art lightweight car with titanium and magnesium, everything needed in my vision to recreate the dynamics of the original cars and team. I desired an engine builder, crew chief, and crew

that might duplicate the energy, determination, and technology leadership that is synonymous with the Tom Hoover–directed, Ted Spehar–led team of the 1970s.

With help from Lou Patane, then head of Mopar Motorsports, Dale Eicke came onboard to supply engines. These were the same engines that Scott Geoffrion and Darrell Alderman, the factory "Dodge Boys," were using. Ex-NBA star Larry Nance, and Roy and Allen Johnson's team were also using Eicke's engines at the time. I bought the old Wayne County 53-foot Champion trailer from Eicke as well, while Dave Butner, Mark Pawuk's former crew chief, also joined the team.

It became very apparent that Pro Stock racing at the end of the century was very different than racing in the early 1970s, and we found a steep learning curve that took cubic dollars to master. We hired Mike Bell as the car's driver to learn what we needed to know, and we also acquired a second Jerry Bickle–built Avenger (an ex-Geoffrion car that Eicke owned) to discover which car was the better car and, more importantly, why.

During the first year and a half, we made adjustments to the team with John Geyer becoming the driver of the car. In those early days, we attended around 10 races a season, all of the NHRA's western races and special events, such as Gainesville, Houston, Dallas, and Indy.

However, horsepower and other issues plagued the effort. At this point, I developed and built a data acquisition system that could record what I wanted to understand with design and analysis capability generating new

Then There Was One More . . .

Sportsman racer Mike Wagner is also continuing the Missile's legacy in the modern era with his
9-second-capable 2015 Challenger Drag Pak using a Gen III Hemi engine and running on the
FSS/D index in Super Stock. Chassis man Mike Roth put his touches on the car and it has been a
solid racer, winning class at the 2019 NHRA US Nationals and going rounds during eliminations
when it races, wearing the traditional black with gold lettering. A student of racing history, Mike
often has two cars at the track—this one and a similar Drag Pak for Stock Eliminator lettered up in
the Ramchargers team colors.

Dick Oldfield lends a hand during an NHRA race with the latest 500-ci Nickens-style Hemi Pro Stock engine. (Photo Courtesy Arnie Klann)

performance parameters. Meanwhile, Patrick Hale joined the team as a specific Data Acquisition and Analysis engineer with a background in both data mining and artificial intelligence–based predictive programs. That knowledge was a huge help in getting the cars to perform not only simply better but also optimally. From my viewpoint, Pat was like the Chrysler Engineering team of yore, highly intelligent and disciplined.

With the advent of the new Mopar 99 Hemi Pro Stock engine package developed by David Nickens and others, David became our engine supplier with the blessings of Mopar. A new 2001 Dodge Neon was acquired from Rick Jones, and new sponsors started to appear. For the team, 2001 was going to be a good year.

Then, tragedy struck when John Geyer was diagnosed with brain cancer in 2002, so our racing was suspended until an outcome for John was known; John had been a great driver and a true man of God. His family was a joy to be with. For us, it was a terribly sad day when he passed a few years later.

Mike Corvo joined the team as driver, and we continued to scientifically ascertain what could move the *Missile* toward its optimum technology and performance. Mike complemented that and was a perfect replacement to step into John's shoes, being a great driver and a man of integrity and honor but with a sometimes fierce sense of humor. Many races when we were frustrated, he had everyone in stitches while trying to get the car to go down the track, and there were very few places on tour we wouldn't shut down being the entertainment of the night!

I still felt something was missing—the original spirit of the old team and its members. While racing at Indy in 2002, Joe Pappas and Dick Oldfield walked into the pits and into this story. I had been unsuccessful reaching out previously, having only talked to Ted Spehar early on to get the rights to use the *Motown Missile* name. So on a rain-soaked Saturday, we caught up on 30 years of history, while sitting in the team's trailer.

This T-shirt design for the modern **Missile** *was produced.* (Photo Courtesy Arnie Klann)

From left to right are Joe Pappas, Arnie Klann, and Tom "The Ghost" Coddington with the restored 1971 Missile *during a special Pro Stock car show display. (Photo Courtesy Joe Pappas)*

From that chance meeting, Dick Oldfield became a part of the team. He was an immediate help with his years of racing experience and brought a fine knowledge of scotch as well. He still had determination and taught us all a lot about both racing and having fun after the race. If you knew them, Corvo and Dick together was like having Abbott and Costello in the pits: never a dull moment. One highlight for me in 2003 was talking with Bill "Grumpy" Jenkins, reminiscing of the good old days of Pro Stock at Dallas.

The cars and team were based out of our Irvine, California, shop, so Dick would come out and work on the Neon as well as everything else. Since he had actually built and raced it, Dick headed up the accurate restoration of the original *Motown* Challenger at Ted Moser's Picture Car Warehouse in Reseda, California. Later, when I was able to buy the legendary wire car, it was restored with Joe Pappas helping Oldfield. With his vast knowledge and impeccable memory, Joe was irreplaceable in that, since the wire car required a lot of rare and custom parts to be done correctly. As the owner, it was great seeing that dynamic duo working on the old cars as well as our new car—talk about the odd couple.

Unfortunately, money was drying up to continue racing in the NHRA. Tesoro Refining was one of our

sponsors, and it was hard to convince them and others regarding the financial return on their sponsorship when compared to the value in other venues of advertising. We were not the only ones dealing with this.

The Stratus became the car of choice by Mopar, who was helping our team with parts and bodies, so a new car was ordered from Rick Jones. Chasing the tour wasn't meant to be, however. With the yearly budget approaching $750,000, it was time to find a more reasonable way to compete. The car was parked in 2005.

A different strategy emerged. My son, Richard Klann, became the driver of the car and Dick Oldfield and Joe Lepone Jr. became his instructors. Instead of attending NHRA events, the team only raced in places associated with our sponsor's demographics. I became the crew chief, with Mark Henry and his son, Mark Jr., rounding out the crew with Dick and Pat. The success began to show when Richard posted a runner-up to Mike Murillo at the Street Car Super Nationals Finals in 2012 at Las Vegas Motor Speedway. Today's *Motown* team runs two to three races a year in the Premier Street Car Association (PSCA) and other events around the country.

Still, we are looking with an eye towards 2020 and the 50th year of Pro Stock as this book goes to press, so stay tuned.

Additional books that may interest you...

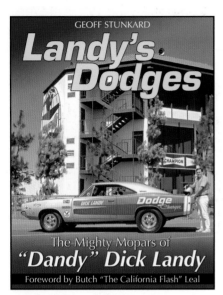

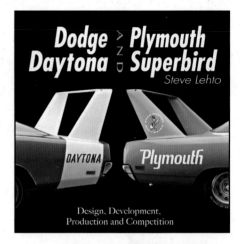